BALKAN GHOSTS

▓ ▓ ROBERT D. KAPLAN

ST. MARTIN'S PRESS   NEW YORK

BALKAN
GHOSTS

A Journey Through History

Grateful acknowledgment is made by the publisher for permission to reprint lines from the following poems: "In Church" by C. P. Cavafy, in *The Greek Poems of C. P. Cavafy. Volume I: The Canon,* translated by Memas Kolaitis. Published by Aristide D. Caratzas, 1989.
"The House Near the Sea" by George Seferis, in *George Seferis: Collected Poems (1924–1955),* translated by Edmund Keeley and Philip Sherrard. Published by Princeton University Press, 1967.

Design by Fritz Metsch

Library of Congress Cataloging-in-Publication Data

Kaplan, Robert D.
    Balkan Ghosts : a journey through history /
  Robert D. Kaplan.
        p. cm.
      ISBN 0-312-08701-2
      "A Thomas Dunne book."
      1. Balkan Peninsula—Description and travel.
      2. Balkan Peninsula—History. 3. Kaplan, Robert
      D.—Journeys—Balkan Peninsula.
  I. Title.
  DR16.K36 1993
  914.9604—dc20   92-43300
                                    CIP

First Edition: March 1993

10 9 8 7 6 5 4 3 2 1

FOR
STEPHEN AND LINDA KAPLAN

✸✸CONTENTS

✽✽PREFACE

In a world rapidly becoming homogenized through the proliferation of luxury hotels, mass tourism, and satellite communications, fewer and fewer unsimulated adventures remain. But the information overflow means that events are now being forgotten at a faster and faster rate. Adventure may invite one, therefore, to use landscape as a vehicle to reveal the past and the historical process.

In *Abroad: British Literary Traveling Between the Wars,* the American scholar Paul Fussell writes that "the secret of the travel book" is "to make essayistic points seem to emerge empirically from material data intimately experienced." In other words, at its very best, travel writing should be a technique to explore history, art, and politics in the liveliest fashion possible. Mary McCarthy's *The Stones of Florence* and Dame Rebecca West's *Black Lamb and Grey Falcon* are the best examples of this that I can think of. I have tried, however clumsily, to aim my star in their direction.

Balkan Ghosts is not a typical survey book. It progresses vertically, in idiosyncratic fashion, from the most specific to the most general: from an essay about the war guilt (or innocence) of one Croatian cleric to a speculation about the fall of empires. My experience in each country was different. In Romania I traveled extensively, meeting all kinds of people, while in Bulgaria I experienced the country through a personal friendship with one individual. In Greece, I didn't so much travel as live in the country, in the Athens area for seven straight years. I hope that the varying styles of the book reflect the variety of my experiences throughout the Balkans.

Regions such as Montenegro in Yugoslavia and Maramures in northwest Romania are not discussed, and Bosnia and Albania are given much less attention than they undoubtedly deserve. Notwithstanding the atrocities committed against the Muslim population there, the ethnic conflict in Bosnia is most effectively explained as an extension of the Serb-Croat dispute. I have therefore discussed Bosnia in the chapter about Croatia. My coverage of Albania is folded into the chapter on "Old Serbia" because I have chosen to explain the Serbs mainly through their historical conflict with Muslim Albanians. Although the world's attention may now be focused on Yugoslavia, my particular Balkan odyssey centered on Romania and Greece, and the book reflects this. The Balkans are a peninsula of which Bosnia is only a part. And while today the headlines may be about Bosnia, tomorrow they may be about a different area of the Balkans, for the whole peninsula has entered a cataclysmic period that will last for many years. Nevertheless, nothing I write should be taken as a justification, however mild, for the war crimes committed by ethnic Serb troops in Bosnia, which I heartily condemn.

Throughout the 1980s, I tried—usually to no avail—to interest editors and the general public in the Balkans and the brewing troubles there. It is sadly ironic that my worst fears have proved correct. One of the victims of the fighting was a journalist with the same name as myself, David Kaplan of ABC News. (My middle initial stands for "David.") I hope that this book may help explain a region that another Kaplan, whom I never knew, lost his life covering.

▓ ▓ ACKNOWLEDGMENTS

As with my earlier books on Ethiopia and Afghanistan, Cullen Murphy and William Whitworth of *The Atlantic* provided encouragement and a willingness to publish a significant portion of the manuscript in the magazine. An excerpt also appeared in *The New York Times Sophisticated Traveler*, through the support of Nancy Newhouse. Other helpful editors included Nancy Sharkey, Janet Piorko, and Agnes Greenhall at *The New York Times*; Dorothy Wickenden at *The New Republic*; Owen Harries at *The National Interest*; and Seth Lipsky, Amity Shlaes, and Peter Keresztes at *The Wall Street Journal* in Brussels. My agent, Carl D. Brandt, kept the faith through troubled waters. My editor, David Sobel, helped make a roughhewn product more presentable, without compromising it.

Grants arranged through the Madison Center for Educational Affairs gave me the wherewithal to turn an idea into reality. For this I must thank Peter Frumkin, Charles Horner, Les Lenkowsky, Patty Pyott, and Tom Skladony.

My interest in the Balkans grew out of reporting trips made in the early 1980s. I thank Joe Geshwiler and Randal Ashly at *The Atlanta Journal-Constitution*, Mark Richards at "ABC Radio News," and Marilyn Dawson at *The Toronto Globe and Mail*, for their indulgence of my Balkan passion.

Ernest Latham, Kiki Munshi, and Phillip E. Wright are Foreign Service officers of whom the United States should be proud, bubbling with scholarly knowledge about the countries in which they served. Their enthusiasm was catching: a precious gift for which I am ever grateful.

Nicholas X. Rizopoulos of the Council on Foreign Relations was an exacting critic. Richard Carpenter kept invaluable archives on the Greek press and on public events in Greece. Alan Luxenberg and Daniel Pipes at the Foreign Policy Research Institute in Philadelphia arranged lectures for me to deliver, which further clarified my ideas. Elinor Appel and Amy Meeker at *The Atlantic*, and Suzanne MacNeille at *The New York Times*, fact-checked parts of the manuscript, thereby making it a better one.

Other help and sage advice came from Paul Anastasi, Renzo Cianfanelli, Bill Edwards, Elizabeth Herring, Mattyas Jevnisek, George Konrad, Barry Levin, Samuel and Kay Longmire, Mircea Milcu, Fritz Molden, P. D. Montzouranis, Alberto Nar, Corneliu Nicolescu, John D. Panitza, Carol Reed, Norman Rosendahl, Tony Smith, Sergiu Stanciu, Nicholas Stavroulakis, Ivan Stefanovic, Gabor Tarnai, Mircea Tanase, Ruxandra Todiras, Admantios Vassilakis, Agayn Ventzislav, and Teddie Weyr.

Thank you all.

Map of the Balkans

AUSTRIA

VIENNA

Danube R.

BUDAPEST

HUNGARY

Klagenfurt

SLOVENIA

Ljubljana

Zagreb

CROATIA

Vukovar

Timisoara

Belgrade

BANAT

SERBIA

Sarajevo

BOSNIA-
HERCEGOVINA

Mostar

MONTENEGRO

Dubrovnik

KOSOVO

Peć

Priština

ADRIATIC SEA

Drin R.

ALBANIA

Durrës

Tirana

Shkumben R.

MACEDONIA

Ohrid

Kruševo

Bitola

Strumitsa R.

Vardar R.

GREECE

Corfu

Pindus Mts.

BUCOVINA

Putna

Moldovita

Suceava

Jassy

Bistrita

MOLDAVIA

Cluj

Tirgu Mures

TRANSYLVANIA

Alba Iulia

Sibiu

ROMANIA

Transylvanian Alps

DANUBE
DELTA

Sfîntu
Gheorghe

Tulcea

MUNTENIA

BUCHAREST

WALLACHIA

Giurgiu

Danube R.

Ruse

Constanţa

Iskar R.

Sofia

Batak

Rila
Monastery

Balkan Mts.

BULGARIA

Rhodope Mts.

Varna

BLACK SEA

Edirne

ISTANBUL

Pirin Mts.

Karié

THRACE

Kilkís

Kaválla

Alexandroúpolis

SEA OF MARMARA

Salonika

Mt. Áthos

TURKEY

AEGEAN SEA

Athens

Hydra

MEDITERRANEAN SEA

The Balkans, which in Turkish means "mountains," run roughly from the Danube to the Dardanelles, from Istria to Istanbul, and is a term for the little lands of Hungary, Rumania, Jugoslavia, Albania, Bulgaria, Greece and part of Turkey, although neither Hungarian nor Greek welcomes inclusion in the label. It is, or was, a gay peninsula filled with sprightly people who ate peppered foods, drank strong liquors, wore flamboyant clothes, loved and murdered easily and had a splendid talent for starting wars. Less imaginative westerners looked down on them with secret envy, sniffing at their royalty, scoffing at their pretensions, and fearing their savage terrorists. Karl Marx called them "ethnic trash." I, as a footloose youngster in my twenties, adored them.
—C. L. SULZBERGER, A Long Row of Candles

I hate the corpses of empires, they stink as nothing else.
—REBECCA WEST, Black Lamb and Grey Falcon

❊ ❊ PROLOGUE:
SAINTS, TERRORISTS, BLOOD, AND HOLY WATER

I shivered and groped. I deliberately chose this awful, predawn hour to visit the monastery of Pec in "Old Serbia." In the Eastern Orthodox Church, spiritual instruction exacts toil and rewards it with a revelation of hell and redemption that is equally physical. If the intruder from the West is not willing to feel with his whole being, he cannot hope to understand.

Inside the Church of the Apostles, painted in A.D. 1250, my eyes needed time. The minutes were long and, like the unbroken centuries, full of defeat. I carried neither a flashlight nor a candle. Nothing focuses the will like blindness.

The "blind man is not hindered by eyes; he keeps . . . steady on the same road, like a drunk man holding onto the fence," wrote Petar Petrovic Njegos in *The Mountain Wreath*, the greatest poem of the Serbian language. In it the mass murder of Islamic converts is justified as a means to sustain a local battle against the

Muslim Turks.[1] Fleetingly, just as the darkness began to recede, I grasped what real struggle, desperation, and hatred are all about.

The workings of my eyes taught me the first canon of national survival: that an entire world can be created out of very little light. It took only another minute or so for the faces to emerge out of the gloom—haunted and hunger-ravaged faces from a preconscious, Serb past, evincing a spirituality and primitivism that the West knows best through the characters of Dostoyevsky. I felt as though I were inside a skull into which the collective memories of a people had been burned.

Dreams took shape, hallucinations: St. Nicholas, with his purple robe and black, reminding eyes at the back of my head; St. Sava, Serbia's patron saint and founder of this very church, who descended through the watery void to proffer gifts of mercy and inspiration; the Ascended Christ, a dehumanized peasant-god beyond the last stage of physical suffering, more fearful than any conqueror or earthly ideology.

Apostles and saints intermingled with medieval Serbian kings and archbishops. They all appeared through a faith's distorting mirror: with elongated bodies and monstrous hands and heads. Many of the saints' eyes had been scratched out. According to a peasant belief, the plaster and dye used to depict a saint's eyes can cure blindness.

Superstition, idolatry? That would be a Western mind talking. A mind that, in Joseph Conrad's words, did "not have an hereditary and personal knowledge of the means by which an historical autocracy represses ideas, guards its power, and defends its existence. It would never occur" to a citizen of the West, writes Conrad in *Under Western Eyes*, "that he could be beaten with whips as a practical measure either of investigation or of punishment."

This church posted a warning: the deeper the darkness grows, the less rational and more terrifying becomes the resistance.

"In Bulgaria and in Greece, in Yugoslavia, in all the countries of Europe which have lived under Turkish rule it is the same," lamented the incarcerated Madame Deltchev, the victim of a Stalinist purge in Eric Ambler's *Judgement on Deltchev*. "Then, our

1. Njegos was a nineteenth-century bishop of Montenegro, a mountainous area adjacent to Serbia. The mass murder he wrote about took place near the end of the seventeenth century.

people lived behind their walls in small worlds of illusion . . . they painted the walls with scenes of national life. . . . Now that we are again inside our walls, the habits of our parents and our childhood return."

The distance these monumental forms had to travel while my eyes adjusted to the dark was infinite: through Ottoman centuries, the most evil wars, and communist rule. Here, in this sanctum of dogma, mysticism, and savage beauty, national life was lived. Only from here could it ever emerge.

"You don't know what it is to kill with a hammer, with nails, clubs, do you?"

Ismail shouted above the music, his face flashing purple from blinking, Day-Glo lights. I was still in Pec, in Old Serbia, in a disco frequented by Muslim Albanians, not far from the Serbian monastery.

"Do you know why I don't like to drink plum brandy, why I drink beer always? Because the Chetniks [World War II Serbian partisans] used to do their killing after drinking plum brandy. Do you know what it is to throw a child in the air and catch it on a knife in front of its mother? To be tied to a burning log? To have your ass split with an axe so that you beg the Serbs, beg them, to shoot you in the head and they don't?

"And they go to their church after. They go to their goddamn church. I have no words. . . ."

Ismail shuddered. "There are things that are beyond evil, that you just can't speak about."

He went on shouting. Ismail was only twenty-six; he had no personal knowledge of the events he described. Rats infest his house, he told me. The Serbs were to blame.

It was 10:30 A.M., November 30, 1940. Snow was beginning to fall in Bucharest. Inside the Church of Ilie Gorgani, built in the seventeenth century to honor a Romanian general who fought the Turks, hundreds of candles illumined the red-robed Christ in the dome. Coffins, draped in green flags with gold embroidery, lined the sides of the nave. Altar boys carried in trays of *coliva* (colored sugar bread) for the dead. Fourteen members of the Legion of the Archangel Michael—the fascist "Iron Guard"—

including the organization's leader, Corneliu Zelea Codreanu, were about to be buried and canonized as "national saints" by priests of the Romanian Orthodox Church, who had been chanting and swinging censers all night.

Two years earlier, in 1938, King Carol II's police had strangled the fourteen men, stripped the bodies naked, and doused them with sulfuric acid in a common ditch to hasten their decomposition. But in late 1940, Carol fled and Romania fell under an Iron Guard regime. The victims' remains, little more than heaps of earth, were dug up and placed in fourteen coffins for reburial. At the end of the funeral service, the worshipers heard a voice recording of the dead Legionnaire leader, Codreanu. "You must await the day to avenge our martyrs," he shrieked.

A few weeks later, revenge was taken. On the night of January 22, 1941, the Legionnaires of the Archangel Michael—after singing Orthodox hymns, putting packets of Romanian soil around their necks, drinking each other's blood, and anointing themselves with holy water—abducted 200 men, women, and children from their homes. The Legionnaires packed the victims into trucks and drove them to the municipal slaughterhouse, a group of red brick buildings in the southern part of Bucharest near the Dimbovitsa River. They made the victims, all Jews, strip naked in the freezing dark and get down on all fours on the conveyor ramp. Whining in terror, the Jews were driven through all the automated stages of slaughter. Blood gushing from decapitated and limbless torsos, the Legionnaires thrust each on a hook and stamped it: "fit for human consumption." The trunk of a five-year-old girl they hung upside down, "smeared with blood . . . like a calf," according to an eyewitness the next morning.

It was 10 P.M., December 17, 1989. At the monastery of Moldovitsa in Moldavia,[2] it was too dark to see the frescos, but Mother Tatulici Georgeta Benedicta imagined the scene of the Last Judgment: wild animals disgorging all the people they have eaten; a few good deeds outweighing all the bad deeds on the Scales of

2. In the early 1990s, after the breakup of the Soviet Union, the region on both sides of the Romanian-Soviet border reverted to its Romanian name, Moldova. Because the travel writers I quote from, as well as the people I interviewed in the course of my visits, always spoke of "Moldavia," I have kept the old term for the sake of narrative consistency.

Justice; angels, painted in glowing sulfur dye, wrapping up the signs of the zodiac to announce that time itself has come to an end.

Mother Benedicta prayed for her customary eight hours. Unlike in Bucharest, there were no informers here, no microphones in the confession box. In the beech forests of Romania's far north, the regime—like those of the Turks long before—"has fewer eyes." The weather had been unusually warm. Mother Benedicta saw a rainbow the other day, although there was no rain. On this day, she heard rumors about a massacre of children. For the first time in her life, she remained all night in the church and prayed.

Joined by other sisters, she spent the next three nights in the church, praying.

"Then God performs his miracle. He puts an idea into the Drac's [Devil's] head to call a televised meeting, at which the people, no longer afraid, humiliate the Drac. And thus he who was like Herod, who killed the children of Timisoara just as Herod killed the children of Palestine, is executed on the same day that our Lord was born."

"In Romania, the Bible lives," declared Mother Benedicta to me. "The Christmas story has been reenacted. Now, the people have the duty to pray and consider all their sins through history."

In the late eighteenth century, at the blackest hour of the long night of Turkish occupation, a Bulgarian monk named Rafail spent twelve years inside the Rila Monastery carving a wooden crucifix. It depicted 600 human figures, each no larger than a grain of rice.

"How much is such a cross worth?" cried Father Bonifacius, a tiny hunchback with flowing, iron-gray hair, a beard, and a baby's soft skin, who had been living within the monastery's walls for twenty-seven years. Answering his own question, he cried again: "What is the price of a man's life? Rafail went blind carving this crucifix!"

Time after time, Rila was plundered and razed by the Turks. Each time it was rebuilt: the striped archways, the tooled wooden balconies, the bell tower, the complex of churches housing frescoes where color takes on a new glory set against the mountain snow. During the Turkish occupation, 300 monks inhabited Rila. Under the rule of Bulgaria's communists, the number went down to twelve. Twelve souls in these massive mice-ridden passageways to preserve the heritage of an entire nation! There are bolted rooms here that have not been walked in for centuries.

Now they were being unlocked.

I returned to the Rila Monastery in 1990, nine years after my previous visit. Father Bonifacius was dead. The church, once dark and eerie, was filled with worshipers and a crackling forest of candles. In a corner was a photograph of King Boris III, buried at the monastery in 1943, whose grave the Communists removed in 1946 after they came to power. Boris's image was surrounded by candles, wildflowers, and Eucharist cakes. People leaned over to kiss it. "Jesus Christ has returned to Bulgaria," my guide matter-of-factly told me. "We must make the Communists tell us where Boris is buried. Now there are many secrets to be uncovered in Bulgaria."

"Blood will flow in Northern Epirus," announced the roadside graffiti near Greece's northwestern frontier with Albania. "Northern Epirus"—southern Albania, that is—is historically part of Greece: the birthplace of Alexander the Great's mother, Olympias, and of King Pyrrhus, whose difficult military fortunes are commemorated in the term "pyrrhic victory."

But on account of a "shameful" 1913 Protocol that incorporated "Northern Epirus" into "the hitherto non-existent petty state of Albania," Greece today is a "dismembered" nation, explained Sevastianos, the Metropolitan Archbishop in this border region.[3] On his map, Northern Epirus, home to nearly half a million Greeks, encompasses 50 percent of all Albania's territory. Sevastianos, called "Greece's Khomeini" by some, was once rumored to be infiltrating armed guerrillas into southern Albania to prepare for its union with Greece in the post-Communist era.

My bus descended into a labyrinthine complex of limestone canyons, bony and deforested, upon crossing the international border into Albania. Oxcarts, driven by soldiers with shaven heads, clogged the cratered roads. Gangs of women, wearing white

3. During World War I, and again during World War II, the Greek army held Northern Epirus, withdrawing for the last time in 1944. An official "state of war" with Albania remained in force until 1988.

smocks and kerchiefs, with scythes and shovels over their shoulders, silently plodded back from grain and tobacco fields. Apartment houses built of corrugated metal and badly mortared brick stood in empty lots, surrounded by barbed wire and concrete bunkers. Every man-made object—the rough cakes of soap, the water taps, the door handles—manifested a primitive, just-invented quality. Lignite and lead fumes clouded the landscape, giving it the grainy and yellowy aura of an old photograph. Under sodium lamps, I examined the faces of these ethnic Greek Albanians. The expressions in their eyes seemed far away. They were like shadows almost. In one home, in the town of Serande ("Aghios Saranda" in Greek), five members of a family crowded around an old black-and-white Russian television set to watch "Dynasty" and CNN on a Greek frequency. "How is life here?" I asked. "It's fine. We have everything we need," the father told me. The children remained silent.

The oldest son accompanied me back to my hotel. "I was secretly baptized," he confided in the dark. "I am a Greek. What else can I be? I believe in God. . . . All of us here are *foukarades* [poor, miserable bastards]." Four days later, in a nearby village, two Greeks were shot trying to cross the border into Greece. Their bodies were hung upside down in the public square.

This was a time-capsule world: a dim stage upon which people raged, spilled blood, experienced visions and ecstasies. Yet their expressions remained fixed and distant, like dusty statuary. "Here, we are completely submerged under our own histories," Luben Gotzev, Bulgaria's former Foreign Minister, told me.

Thus, I developed an obsession with medieval churches and monasteries, with old books and old photographs. On the road, when I met people, I asked them always about the past. Only in this way could the present become comprehensible.

These lands require a love for the obscure. For months I ransacked rare-book shops and dealers. I knew that the books that best explained the violence of Romania's December 1989 revolution had been out of print for decades, in some cases for half a century or more.

From April through October 1915, the American journalist and political radical John Reed, accompanied by sketch artist

Boardman Robinson, traveled through Serbia, Macedonia, Romania, Bulgaria, Greece, and Turkey. Reed published the account of their journey, *The War in Eastern Europe*, in 1916, the year before he traveled to Russia and wrote *Ten Days That Shook the World*. Of all Reed's books, *The War in Eastern Europe* is his least known. I had to pay $389.11 for a first edition inscribed by the author. Wax sheets protected some of the pencil drawings. Reed writes:

"In the excitement of sudden invasion, desperate resistance, capture and destruction of cities, men seem to lose their distinctive personal or racial flavor, and become alike in the mad democracy of battle." Reed preferred to observe them after "they had settled down to war as a business, had begun to adjust themselves to this new way of life and to talk and think of other things."

I wanted to do likewise: to see Europe's forgotten rear door not in the midst of revolutions or epochal elections, but in the immediate aftermath, when the various peoples *had begun to adjust themselves to this new way of life.*

Among the old photographs I looked at was one of the Habsburg Archduke, Franz Ferdinand, on military maneuvers outside Sarajevo, June 27, 1914, the day before he was assassinated—the crime that ignited World War I. Horses' hooves kicked up the dust. Franz Ferdinand rode erect, his visible foot deep in the stirrup, a saber at his side. His bearded face expressed a certainty belonging to a more innocent and easily shocked age, a world still vaguely ascribable to Metternich's restoration and unknowing (though only by days and weeks) of the technological evils of modern war and totalitarianism.

Another photo was of Franz Ferdinand's assassin, Gavrilo Princip, a Bosnian Serb from near Sarajevo. Princip was still in his teens and looked deceptively fragile: a sprig of tendons and sinews. His eyes full of animal activity, different from the dead eyes of modern-day terrorists, who murder from a distance with automatic rifles and bombs activated by midair gyroscopes.

The most intensive seventy-five years in world history had elapsed, all in fine focus, since those pictures were snapped. But when set against the people I met and the voices I heard now on the road, those pictures did not seem so old.

Belgrade, Bucharest, Sofia, Athens, Adrianople. These were once the datelines of choice for ambitious journalists—the Saigon,

Beirut, and Managua of a younger world. Ernest Hemingway filed his most famous dispatch from Adrianople (now Edirne, in Turkish Thrace) in 1922, describing Greek refugees "walking blindly along in the rain," with all their possessions piled on oxcarts beside them.

The Balkans were the original Third World, long before the Western media coined the term. In this mountainous peninsula bordering the Middle East, newspaper correspondents filed the first twentieth-century accounts of mud-streaked refugee marches and produced the first books of gonzo journalism and travel writing, in an age when Asia and Africa were still a bit too far afield.

Whatever has happened in Beirut or elsewhere happened first, long ago, in the Balkans.

The Balkans produced the century's first terrorists. IMRO (the Internal Macedonian Revolutionary Organization) was the Palestine Liberation Organization of the 1920s and 1930s, with Bulgarian paymasters, dedicated to recovering the parts of Macedonia taken by Greece and Yugoslavia after the Second Balkan War. Like the present-day Shiites of Beirut's southern suburbs, the IMRO's killers, who swore allegiance over a gun and an Orthodox Bible, came from the rootless, peasant proletariat of the Skopje, Belgrade, and Sofia slums. Hostage taking and the wholesale slaughter of innocents were common. Even the fanaticism of the Iranian clergy has a Balkan precedent. During the Balkan Wars of 1912 and 1913, a Greek bishop in Macedonia ordered the assassination of a Bulgarian politician and then had the severed head brought back to the church to be photographed.

Twentieth-century history came from the Balkans. Here men have been isolated by poverty and ethnic rivalry, dooming them to hate. Here politics has been reduced to a level of near anarchy that from time to time in history has flowed up the Danube into Central Europe.

Nazism, for instance, can claim Balkan origins. Among the flophouses of Vienna, a breeding ground of ethnic resentments close to the southern Slavic world, Hitler learned how to hate so infectiously.

What does the earth look like in the places where people commit atrocities? Is there a bad smell, a genius loci, something about the landscape that might incriminate?

I began my journey in Central Europe, in Nuremberg and Dachau, but there I felt almost nothing. These places were museums; they no longer lived and breathed fire. The retaining wall of the stadium where the Nazis held mass rallies was now a squash court for German yuppies.

In Vienna, I first caught a whiff of something. In Vienna, Wolfgang Amadeus Mozart rates only a statue, an alley, and a square. Dr. Karl Lueger gets a bigger monument, a bigger square, and the most august section of the Ringstrasse, the Dr. Karl Lueger Ring: site of the neoclassical Parliament, the Renaissance University building, the baroque Burgtheater, the Gothic Town Hall, and the Volksgarten.

Lueger, Vienna's turn-of-the-century mayor, was, along with Georg von Schonerer, another Austrian politician of the same era, the father of political anti-Semitism. Adolf Hitler writes in *Mein Kampf*: "I regard this man as the greatest German mayor of all times . . . . If Dr. Karl Lueger had lived in Germany, he would have ranked among the great minds of our people." Hitler writes that his own ideas come directly from Lueger. On May 29, 1895, the very night that Theodor Herzl heard the news of Lueger's victory in the Vienna City Council elections, Herzl went to his desk to sketch a plan for a Jewish exodus from Europe.

I stared at the Lueger monument, on Dr. Karl Lueger Square (not to be confused with the Dr. Karl Lueger Ring). Hand on heart, in sartorial splendor, *der schone Karl* ("beautiful Karl") looked forward into the future, his eyes brimming with determination; muscular, naked-to-the-waist workers armed with shovels and pickaxes surrounded him on the plinth.

In today's Germany, such a monument would cause a scandal. But in Austria there was no apology. "Karl Lueger was Vienna's greatest mayor," a local Austrian journalist said, shrugging. "He was not really an anti-Semite. He used anti-Semitism only as a political technique."

I traveled on. Metternich said the Balkans begin at the Rennweg, the road leading east and south out of Vienna.

The closer one gets to either the eastern or the southern fringe of the German-speaking world—the closer one gets, in other words, to the threatening and more numerous Slavs—the more insecure and dangerous German nationalism becomes. On the

German world's eastern frontier, Pomeranian and Silesian Germans question the legitimacy of the Polish border. To the south, in Austria, where blood from the Slavic world actually flows in "German" veins, denial of this elemental fact takes the form of unreconstructed, pan-Germanic paranoia.

I came to Klagenfurt, the capital of Austria's southernmost province of Carinthia, known as "an El Dorado for former Nazis." In proportion to its size, Carinthia produced more death-camp guards than any other region of Germany or Austria. In Klagenfurt, in the 1980s, there was a movement for segregated schools: God forbid that German children should learn alongside Slovenes, who are ethnic Slavs. I went to the offices of the right-wing Freedom Party and the Carinthian Heimatdienst—a militialike organization founded after World War I and resurrected, with a neo-Nazi orientation, in the 1950s. I tried to provoke a party spokesman. I was disappointed.

QUESTION: "Simon Wiesenthal told me that any political party in a democratic country like Austria that uses the word 'freedom' in its name is either Nazi or Communist. How do you respond?"

ANSWER: "Herr Wiesenthal is a very respected man. He is entitled to his views. However, may I suggest why we differ. . . ."

The idea of a Greater Germany including Austria is dead, I was told. The Austrian right wing was interested only in preserving the integrity of the German language in a linguistic frontier region.

Insipid modern art, not banners or old regimental photos, decorated the Freedom Party's walls. Then a further disappointment: instead of a nasty, brown-shirted provincialism on Klagenfurt's streets, I encountered Thorstein Veblen's leisure class.

Preppy-looking teens glided by on rainbow-striped mountain bikes. I saw a man in a purple suede blazer and Giorgio Armani optics, and women done up by Jil Sander or Guerlain, wearing silk scarves of the most subtle autumn tones. Except for the chrome-tinted office windows, the pseudo-baroque buildings were like finely cut slices of Black Forest cherry cake. Hobby trains, Samsonite, Lego space stations, and *schmuck* (jewelry) from Tiffany's filled glass display cases in the middle of the sidewalk. A few doors from Mothercare, a shop sold women's undergarments from Paris that were as expensive as they were naughty. The perfume worn by the blonde shop girl had a sweaty, animal scent. The offspring of the SS have become expensively groomed, performing tigers, safely tucked away in middle-class box houses.

Everyone here motored along in their daily grooves. The only banners I saw were those of the credit card companies. On the travel agency windows, Israel was just another winter destination for local sun worshippers. The true believers at the Freedom Party and the Heimatdienst were increasingly isolated and forced to maintain a cover of respectability. Instead of anti-Semitism and the other traditional excesses, there was now a wanton consumerism. Carinthians have become a tamed species.

And since 1989, the Freedom Party, in order to increase the number of its parliamentary seats, talks more and more about cooperation with the Slovenes. The old Nazi hunter Wiesenthal gave me the reason: "Without an economic crisis, the Freedom Party can do nothing except adapt." Evil, lectured this *ancient*, in knowing, skeletal repose, required no suffering or repentance to be cured, only the numbing sedation of bourgeois democracy and prosperity for decade after decade after decade, until the pattern becomes so ingrained that not even an economic disaster can affect it.

It was the last decade of the twentieth century. I heeded Wiesenthal, not Metternich: the Balkans no longer begin at the gates of Vienna, or even at those of Klagenfurt.

At Austria's southern border with what used to be Yugoslavia, the heating, even in the first-class compartments of the train, went off. The restaurant car was decoupled. The car that replaced it was only a stand-up zinc counter for beer, plum brandy, and foul cigarettes without filters. As more stops accumulated, men with grimy fingernails crowded the counter to drink and smoke. When not shouting at each other or slugging back alcohol, they worked their way quietly through pornographic magazines. Unlike their working-class counterparts in Austria, they did not have unisex haircuts and obviously did not anticipate winter vacations in Tunisia or Israel. Here, had they been lucky enough to have a poor nativist constituency, the Freedom Party and the Heimatdienst could have discarded their modern art and their deceptively neutered responses to a reporter's questions.

Snow beat upon the window. Black lignite fumes rose from brick and scrap-iron chimneys. The earth here had the harsh, exhausted face of a prostitute, cursing bitterly between coughs. The landscape of atrocities is easy to recognize: Communism had been the Great Preserver.

My time was thus short. Soon, whether in the late 1990s or in the decades following, the entire canvas would go dull, as it already had in Klagenfurt.

❖❖PART I

Yugoslavia: Historical Overtures

I had come to Yugoslavia to see what history meant in flesh and blood.
—REBECCA WEST, Black Lamb and Grey Falcon

CHAPTER ONE

Croatia: "Just So They Could Go to Heaven"

The past in Zagreb was underfoot: a soft, thick carpet of leaves, soggy from rain, that my feet sank in and out of, confusing with the present. Leaving the railway station, I walked through curtains of fog tinted yellow by coal fires, the chemical equivalent of burning memories. The fog moved swiftly and was rent by holes, a fragment of wrought iron or baroque dome appeared momentarily in fine focus. *There*. That too was the past, I realized: a hole in the fog you could see right through.

The capital of the former Yugoslav Republic of Croatia is the last railway city in Europe where a traveler is absolutely expected to arrive by train, since the Esplanade, built in 1925 and still considered among the world's best hotels, is just across the street from the station.

This century's greatest travel book begins at the Zagreb railway station in the rainy spring of 1937.

When Dame Rebecca West's *Black Lamb and Grey Falcon* was first published four years later, in 1941, *The New York Times Book Review* called it the apotheosis of the travel genre. The *New Yorker* said it was comparable only to T. E. Lawrence's *Seven Pillars of Wisdom*. Narrowly defined, the book is the account of a six-week journey through Yugoslavia.[1] By any broader definition, *Black Lamb and Grey Falcon* is, like Yugoslavia, a sprawling world unto itself: a two-volume, half-a-million-word encyclopedic inventory of a country; a dynastic saga of the Habsburgs and the Kara-georgevitches; a scholarly thesis on Byzantine archaeology, pagan folklore, and Christian and Islamic philosophy. The book also offers a breathtaking psychoanalysis of the German mind and of the nineteenth-century origins of fascism and terrorism. It was a warning, of near-perfect clairvoyance, of the danger that totali-tarianism posed to Europe in the 1940s and beyond. Like the Talmud, one can read the book over and over again for different levels of meaning.

"If Rebecca West had been a mediaeval woman, and rich, she would have been a great abbess. If she would have been a sev-enteenth-century woman, and poor, she would have been burnt as a witch," writes Victoria Glendinning, in *Rebecca West: A Life*. Glendinning calls *Black Lamb and Grey Falcon* "the central book" of the author's long life, in which Dame Rebecca—writer of twenty other nonfictional works and novels, young mistress of H. G. Wells, social outcast, and sexual rebel—constructed "her views on religion, ethics, art, myth, and gender."

The very title of the book is an attack on the Christian doctrine of the Crucifixion and atonement, in which our sins are forgiven by God in return for the sacrifice of Jesus on the cross.

The "black lamb" represents an animal Dame Rebecca saw slaughtered in a Muslim fertility rite in Macedonia: "All our West-ern thought is founded on this repulsive pretence that pain is the proper price of any good thing," she writes. The "grey falcon" stands for humanity's tragic response to the sacrifice of the "black lamb." In a Serbian poem, the prophet Elijah, disguised as a fal-con, gives a Serbian general the choice between an earthly or a

1. Although Yugoslavia, as we have known it, no longer exists, the term is still useful as a geographical and cultural definition, since the word means "South (Yugo) Slav." Almost all of the other Slavs in Eurasia live farther north.

heavenly kingdom. The general chooses the latter, erecting a church instead of positioning his army, so that the Turks defeat him. In other words, rages the author, paraphrasing the pacifist's secret desire: "Since it is wrong to be the priest and sacrifice the lamb, I will be the lamb and be sacrificed by the priest."

This conundrum of how good should confront evil, of what constitutes the proper relationship between a priest and his flock, haunts Zagreb today.

After only a few days in the city, Dame Rebecca realized that Zagreb was, tragically, a "shadow-show." So absorbed were its people in their own divisions, of Catholic Croat versus Orthodox Serb, that they had become phantoms even before the Nazis arrived.

The Nazi occupation detonated these tensions. In primitive ferocity—if not in sheer numbers—the massacre in Catholic Croatia and neighboring Bosnia-Hercegovina of Orthodox Serbs was as bad as anything in German-occupied Europe. Forty-five years of systematized poverty under Tito's Communists kept the wounds fresh.

I arrived in Zagreb by train from Klagenfurt. The last decade of the century was upon me. My ears were tuned to smoldering, phantom voices that I knew were about to explode once again.

An ethnic Serb I met on the train told me: "The Croatian fascists did not have gas chambers at Jesenovac. They had only knives and mallets with which to commit mass murder against the Serbs. The slaughter was chaotic, nobody bothered to keep count. So here we are, decades behind Poland. There, Jews and Catholics battle over significance. Here, Croats and Serbs still argue over numbers."

Numbers are all that have ever counted in Zagreb. For instance, if you were to say that the Croatian Ustashe ("Insurrectionists") murdered 700,000 Serbs at Jesenovac, a World War II death camp located sixty-five miles southeast of Zagreb, you would be recognized as a Serbian nationalist who despises Croats as well as Albanians, who judges the late Croatian cardinal and Zagreb archbishop, Alojzije Stepinac, "a Nazi war criminal," and who supports Slobodan Milosevic, the rabble-rousing nationalist leader of Serbia. But if you were to say that the Ustashe fascists murdered only

60,000 Serbs, you would be pegged as a Croat nationalist who considers Cardinal Stepinac "a beloved saint" and who despises Serbs and their leader, Milosevic.

Cardinal Stepinac, a Croatian figure of the late 1930s and 1940s, is a weapon against Milosevic, a Serbian figure of the 1990s—and vice versa. Because history has not moved in Zagreb, the late 1930s and 1940s still seem like the present. Nowhere in Europe is the legacy of Nazi war crimes so unresolved as in Croatia.

Zagreb is an urban landscape of volume and space arrangement, where color is secondary. The city requires no sunshine to show it off. Clouds are better, and a chilling drizzle is better still. I walked a hundred yards in the rain from the railway station to the Esplanade Hotel: a massive, sea-green edifice that might easily be mistaken for a government ministry, manifesting the luxurious decadence—the delicious gloom—of Edwardian England or fin-de-siècle Vienna. I entered a ribbed, black-and-white marble lobby adorned with gold-framed mirrors, drawn velvet curtains and valences, and purple carpets. The furniture was jet black, and the lamp shades were golden yellow. The lobby and dining hall resembled a cluttered art gallery whose pictures recalled the universe of Sigmund Freud, Gustav Klimt, and Oskar Kokoschka: modernist iconography that indicates social disintegration and the triumph of violence and sexual instinct over the rule of law.

Slavenka Draculic is a Zagreb journalist who writes in Croatian for *Danas* (*Today*), a local magazine, and in English for *The New Republic* and *The Nation*. Wearing designer black glasses and a bright red headband that perfectly matched her red blouse and lipstick, she—and the other women in the hotel bistro—dressed with a panache that complemented the boldness of the hotel's art. The overall message was unmistakable: *despite Communist-inflicted poverty and the damp, badly heated apartments and the sorry displays in the shop windows all around, we Croats are Roman Catholic, and Zagreb is the eastern bastion of the West; you, the visitor, are still in the orbit of Austria-Hungary, of Vienna—where the modern world was practically invented—and don't you forget it!*

Like an expert sketch artist, Slavenka, her fingers flying, outlined the Yugoslav dilemma: "This place is not Hungary, Poland, or Romania. Rather, it is the Soviet Union in miniature. For example, this is happening in Lithuania, but that is happening in

Tajikistan. This is happening in Croatia, but that is happening in Serbia or Macedonia. Each situation is unique. There are no easy themes here. Because of Tito's break with Stalin, the enemy in Yugoslavia was always within, not without. For years we were fooled by what was only an illusion of freedom . . ."

I immediately grasped that the counterrevolution in Eastern Europe included Yugoslavia, too. But because the pressure of discontent was being released horizontally, in the form of one group against another, rather than vertically against the Communist powers in Belgrade, the revolutionary path in Yugoslavia was at first more tortuous and, therefore, more disguised. That was why the outside world did not take notice until 1991, when fighting started.

It took no clairvoyance to see what was coming, however. My visit to Yugoslavia was eerie precisely because everyone I spoke with—locals and foreign diplomats alike—was already resigned to big violence ahead. Yugoslavia did not deteriorate suddenly, but gradually and methodically, step by step, through the 1980s, becoming poorer and meaner and more hate-filled by the year. That's why every conversation I had was so sad. We were all shouting to the outside world about a coming catastrophe, but no one wanted to hear our awful secret. No one was interested. Few were even sure where Croatia (for example) was. On the phone from my room at the Esplanade, when I told people I was in the Balkans, they kept confusing it with the Baltics.

"You need a few weeks in Zagreb at least. There are so many people to see. The strands here are so subtle, so interwoven. It's all so complex . . . " Slavenka's fingers seemed to give up in frustration and fall to the table. Here, she implied, the battle between Communism and capitalism is merely one dimension of a struggle that pits Catholicism against Orthodoxy, Rome against Constantinople, the legacy of Habsburg Austria-Hungary against that of Ottoman Turkey—in other words, West against East, the ultimate historical and cultural conflict.

In the days ahead, Zagreb and the Esplanade Hotel were to contract into a piercing echo chamber: a succession of brilliant monologues, prolonged and made more memorable by rain, in which landscape and architecture faded away and abstract ideas took over.

It was no coincidence that *Black Lamb and Grey Falcon* begins in Zagreb, focuses on Yugoslavia, and is written by a woman: such a book almost had to be all of these things. The fussiness and creativity of an accomplished cook and embroiderer, combined with the earthly sensitivities of a countrywoman and soon-to-be grandmother, were undoubtedly necessary characteristics to enable Dame Rebecca to reel in the thoughts, passions, and national histories of Europe and Asia, and to remake them into a coherent, morally focused tapestry.

On October 9, 1934, only two and a half years before her journey, Dame Rebecca uttered the word *Yugoslavia* for the first time. On that day, bedridden from a recent operation, she heard the news on the radio that agents of the Croatian Ustashe had murdered the head of the Serbian royal house, King Alexander I Karageorgevitch, after he had arrived in Marseille for a state visit. A few days later she saw a newsreel film of the assassination; as the camera moved in on the face of the dying, forty-six-year-old king, the author conceived an obsession for his country. She knew instinctively that this noble, dying visage was one more signpost on the road to a horrific cataclysm, even worse than World War I, that she couldn't as yet describe. So she came to Yugoslavia to investigate the nature of the looming cataclysm, just as I came to investigate the nature of another looming cataclysm. Politics in Yugoslavia perfectly mirrors the process of history and is thus more predictable than most people think.

Black Lamb and Grey Falcon drew me to Yugoslavia. Until the 1990s, travel there spelled neither life-threatening adventure nor an escape into the visually exotic; instead, it offered a collision with the most terrifying and basic issues of the century. Yugoslavia was also a story of ethnic subtlety atop subtlety that resisted condensation on the news pages. As a man who had previously covered wars in Africa and Asia, I felt both intoxicated and inadequate. My guide was a deceased woman whose living thoughts I found more passionate and exacting than any male writer's could ever be. I would rather have lost my passport and money than my heavily thumbed and annotated copy of *Black Lamb and Grey Falcon*. Along with John Reed's *The War in Eastern Europe*, it never remained back in my hotel room. I carried them everywhere in Yugoslavia.

*   *   *

Zagreb means "behind the hill," the hill being the site of the upper town, which dominates a lower one. In the lower town are the railway station, the Esplanade hotel, the turn-of-the-century neo-Renaissance, Art Nouveau, and Secession-style buildings and pavilions, separated by leafy expanses. High on the hill, staring down at the lower town, is the fortified gothic Cathedral of Zagreb, a veritable mini-Kremlin, consecrated in the thirteenth century and restored at the end of the nineteenth. The cathedral is the largest Roman Catholic structure in the Balkans and is the seat of the Zagreb archbishopric. After visiting it on Easter Eve 1937, Dame Rebecca exclaimed, "There was an intensity of feeling that was not only of immense and exhilarating force, but had an honourable origin, proceeding from realist passion, from whole belief."

Until that moment, there was much to recommend that majestic description. For hundreds of years, partly as a reaction to the iniquities of Austro-Hungarian rule, Catholic theologians in Croatia were increasingly drawn toward Christian unity among the South (*"Yugo"*) Slavs. These theologians looked beyond the schism of 1054 between Rome and Constantinople, back to the ninth century apostles, Cyril and Methodius, who had converted the Slavs to Christianity. But after the 1054 schism, most of Cyril and Methodius's converts had become members of the rival Orthodox church, so Croatians were practically alone among the world's Catholics in their passion for the two apostles.

In the nineteenth century, the figures of Cyril and Methodius began to emerge in Croatian church circles as symbols of unity between the Catholic and Orthodox churches. Promoting that goal was the protean figure of Bishop Josip Strossmayer—Croatian patriot, philanthropist, founder of the University of Zagreb, accomplished linguist and gardener, breeder of Lippizaner horses, wine connoisseur, and raconteur. As a Croatian Catholic intellectual, Strossmayer accepted in full the equality and legitimacy of the Serbian Orthodox church. When he sent a letter of congratulations to Orthodox bishops on the millennium of Methodius's birth, he was denounced by his fellow Catholics in Austria-Hungary and the Vatican. The Habsburg Emperor, Franz Joseph, insulted Strossmayer to his face. Strossmayer, in response, warned

the Habsburgs that continued misrule in Bosnia-Hercegovina—
the province south and east of Croatia, where many Croats lived
among Serbs and local Muslims—would lead to the collapse of
their empire, which is exactly what happened. Dame Rebecca
lauded Strossmayer as a "fearless denunciator of Austro-
Hungarian tyranny." She writes that Strossmayer, who battled
both anti-Semitism and anti-Serb racism, was hated by the
nineteenth-century Vatican because, in its eyes, he was "lament-
ably deficient in bigotry."

However, when Dame Rebecca visited Zagreb in the spring of
1937, a new spirit of Christian Slav unity, rather different from
that of Strossmayer's, was gaining force in the minds of Croatia's
Catholics. The change proceeded under the dynamic influence of
the archbishop-coadjutor, Alojzije Stepinac, who before the end
of the year would assume the full title of Archbishop of Zagreb.

Stepinac was born in 1898 into a prosperous peasant family
west of Zagreb, the fifth of eight children. After fighting in World
War I, he studied agronomy and became an active member of a
Catholic student association. In 1924, he broke off his engagement
to a local girl and joined the priesthood, spending the next seven
years at the prestigious, Jesuit-run Gregorian University in Rome,
which his wealthy father was able to pay for. Upon graduation,
Stepinac requested an assignment to a small parish. But (undoubtedly due to Stepinac's academic credentials), Zagreb's
then-archbishop, Antun Bauer, brought the thirty-two-year-old
prodigy to work at the cathedral chancery.

It is hard to think of two Catholic Croatians more different
than Strossmayer and Stepinac. Strossmayer was a South Slav
nationalist struggling against the Austrians and the Vatican, while
Stepinac was a purely Croat nationalist who embraced the Vatican
and the Austrians in a struggle against his fellow South Slavs, the
Serbs. From his early youth, Stepinac was, in Archbishop Bauer's
own words, "excessively pious," unlike Strossmayer, who loved
wine, horses, and the good life.

The young Stepinac had found his companions in the Catholic
student association insufficiently religious. At his engagement ceremony before going into the priesthood, Stepinac refused even
to kiss his beloved, saying "this is not the sacrament." Upon taking
over the post of archbishop-coadjutor in 1934, Stepinac had him-

self mantled with the girdle and scapular of the Franciscans, in order to be publicly identified with the ideal of poverty. He soon organized special masses and processions against swearing and the sins of the flesh. His railings, especially against sunbathing and mixed swimming, lent a Cromwellian air to his leadership. According to Stepinac's own diary, he believed that Catholic ideals of purity should extend to Orthodox Serbia too. "If there were more freedom . . . Serbia would be Catholic in twenty years," wrote Stepinac. His dogmatism caused him to think of the Orthodox as apostates. "The most ideal thing would be for the Serbs to return to the faith of their fathers; that is, to bow the head before Christ's representative, the Holy Father. Then we could at last breathe in this part of Europe, for Byzantinism has played a frightful role . . . in connection with the Turks."

When Stepinac "was later during World War II faced with the fruits in practice of these ideas, he was horrified," observed Stella Alexander, in a detailed and compassionate account of Stepinac's career, *The Triple Myth: A Life of Archbishop Alojzije Stepinac.*

I entered Zagreb Cathedral and noticed a series of posters bearing the picture of Pope John Paul II. The Pope's image has always been a particularly powerful one in Croatia because of a single fact: despite Croatia's being next door to Italy and the Vatican and despite its forming the common border of Western and Eastern Christianity whose reconciliation the Pope has long sought, this Pope, who had traveled to the farthest reaches of Africa and Asia, had through his first dozen years as pontiff still not come to Croatia. This was mainly due to the legacy of Cardinal Stepinac.

Inside the nave, my eyes were drawn to a massive bronze cast of the suffering Jesus, the "Calvary" of the Croatian sculptor Ivan Orlic. Placed to the right of the cathedral entrance in 1978, the sculpture exudes strength and muscularity. A group of nuns in white habits dropped to their knees before it in silent prayer. Gold stars on a painted blue ceiling shone down on them. I advanced up the nave, as far as the left side of the altar, where Stepinac, in stone relief, kneels and receives Jesus' blessing. This is Stepinac's tomb. He was buried in 1960 inside the cathedral wall at this spot. The monument was made by another, more famous Croatian sculptor, Ivan Mestrovic, and paid for by Croatian-Americans. It is deliberately small, understated and naive, composed of the fewest possible knifelike lines. People passed by and dropped to their knees, just as they were doing before the much larger and more impressive statue of Jesus at Calvary. Before this humble monument, Pope John Paul II has also wished to fall to his knees. For this specific wish, the federal authorities in Belgrade—Serbs mainly—long refused him permission to visit Zagreb.

In 1984, when I first visited Stepinac's tomb, an old woman approached me and pleaded, "Write well of him. He was our hero, not a war criminal." But an official of the Communist regime had told me in Belgrade that "the judgment for us is final: Stepinac was a quisling butcher—the priest who baptized with one hand and slaughtered with the other." The official then told me of how Catholic priests, under the direction of Stepinac, officiated at forced mass conversions of Orthodox Serbs minutes before their execution by the Croatian Ustashe, "just so they could go to heaven."

I thought then that I had a good feature story. Afterward, I read *A Long Row of Candles*, the memoirs of C. L. Sulzberger, the former Chief Foreign Correspondent and columnist for *The New York Times*. It turns out that he had done exactly the same story thirty-four years before, in 1950. Sulzberger recalled: "Orthodox Serbs of all political shades came up to me and growled: 'Stepinac should have been hanged. It was he who condoned the murder of thousands of the Orthodox.' . . . When I got back to Zagreb, two men rushed up to me in the street and asked: 'Are you the American journalist? Did you see the Archbishop (who was in a Communist jail at the time)?' 'Ah, he is a fine man, a saint. Tell the American people he is our hero.' "

And when I returned to Zagreb five years later, at the end of 1989, the guilt or innocence of Stepinac was still The Story. Three years earlier, in 1986, the former Interior Minister of the Nazi puppet state of Croatia during World War II, Andrija Artukovic, had been deported from the United States to stand trial for war crimes in Zagreb. Artukovic's presence on his native soil had stirred old memories, and the Communist authorities had responded only with a poorly managed, Stalinist-style show trial that served to inflame passions on the related Stepinac issue. Artukovic, a sick old man, had been found guilty and sentenced to death, but he died in custody before the sentence could be carried out. The site of his grave was not revealed: the Communists in Belgrade, most of whom were Serbs, feared Croats would turn it into a shrine. The treatment of Artukovic was a disgrace.

An observer could see the hatred building, year by year. In the late 1980s, the dimensions of the Stepinac issue grew as the conflicting Serb and Croat positions hardened under the weight of increased poverty, an annual inflation rate of several thousand percent, and the fragmentation of the Yugoslav federation. *Genocide* became a word thrown around a lot.

And during my late 1989 visit to Zagreb, a new factor was added: the publication of selected portions of Stepinac's private diaries in the weekly magazine *Danas*. The diaries were uncovered by a local historian, Ljubo Boban. Boban, a Croat, refused to reveal where or how he obtained them. "It is a secret," he told me. In his office at Zagreb University, he noted that the entries for a very sensitive six-month period in 1942 were "mysteriously missing." He implied that the Church was hiding them. The published diaries, whose authenticity has not been challenged, are not complimentary to Stepinac. They reveal a man who, though the product of a university education in Rome, was influenced by bedrock peasant superstitions and took such notions as Masonic conspiracies quite seriously.

I left the cathedral and walked down the street to the home of Monsignor Duro Koksa, who received me graciously, as he had five years before, even though I had not phoned in advance for an appointment. Next to the current Cardinal of Zagreb, Franjo Kuharic, Msgr. Koksa was the most important figure in the Croatian church in the 1980s and early 1990s. Because Msgr. Koksa had lived abroad for many years and could speak foreign languages, he felt it was his duty to receive all visitors, no matter how hostile, in order to explain to the world the Croatian Church's position on a painful historical episode—one he considered too complicated to judge or to simplify, except by enemies of the Church.

"Stepinac is a great ecclesiastical figure of Europe; we will not let them drag him down. We will defend him. So he hated Masons;

that was the attitude of Christians at the time. What do you expect?"

Msgr. Koksa sat under a crucifix, dressed simply in black with a priest's white collar. Typical Balkan carpets and tablecloths adorned his study. He was an old man with white hair. His eyes appeared to grimace, not only in frustration, but with obvious fatigue. The wrinkles on his forehead were like the scars of old battles.

"It is so unfair. These diaries represent a man's private thoughts. They have been published too soon." (In that heated political climate, fifty years did seem too short an interval.) "Only the Church has the right to give permission for publication of the diaries—not the Communists." Msgr. Koksa insinuated that the historian, Boban, was the agent of Communist Yugoslav (that is, Serbian) officials, who were determined to undermine the Catholic Church and the Croat nation. Ever since Stepinac's martyrdom at the hands of Tito in 1946, the Yugoslav state has lacked legitimacy in the eyes of the Catholic Church here.

"Let the Communists go down on their knees like Brandt— not the Church!" Msgr. Koksa was referring to the famous incident in Warsaw, in the summer of 1970, when the West German Chancellor Willy Brandt dropped to his knees in contrition before a monument to Jewish victims of the Warsaw Ghetto. "War is half-criminal anyway. Why single out Stepinac? We can't deny everything. What happened at Jesenovac was tragic; maybe sixty thousand were killed, maybe a little more, certainly not seven hundred thousand."

The monsignor went on: "Croatia is the martyr of all Yugoslavia. Our nationalism is young, it's not even actualized. But all this is too complicated for you to understand. It is a question of mentality." Msgr. Koksa's whole body appeared to tighten in frustration, like his forehead: he knew that if he continued in that vein it would all come out wrong—that I would think him an unreconstructed, anti-Serb racist and insensitive to Jews as well. His eyes narrowed at me, as if to exclaim: *So you think I am the enemy, young man, but I am not. You have no idea what it was like here during World War II. It is so easy for you to come from America, where nothing bad ever happens, and to judge us. But you are not superior. Beware of your judgments!*

I got up to leave. Msgr. Koksa told me that I would always be welcome and that I could come back to ask him questions about Stepinac as many times as I liked. I thanked him. I knew that even if I wrote terrible things about him or Stepinac, he would always be willing to see me again. Msgr. Koksa was known for seeking out his adversaries. At a reception once, he buttonholed Slavko Goldstajn, one of the leaders of the local Jewish community. The two men drove to the cathedral for a discussion, but the debate became so heated that they never left the car. They sat inside the vehicle, parked in front of the cathedral atop the sleeping city, and argued for hours, throwing wildly disparate numbers at each other. The Croatian Ustashe murdered 20,000 Jews and 30,000 Gypsies at Jesenovac, said Goldstajn. But if both Goldstajn's figures and the Church's total figure of 60,000 victims at Jesenovac were accurate, only 10,000 Serbs could have been killed there. But all parties agree that Orthodox Serbs were, numerically, the Ustashe's principal victims, so Msgr. Koksa disputed Goldstajn's figures about Jews and Gypsies. But whatever the numbers are, Stepinac, Msgr. Koksa said, was innocent. "Come and see me again," the monsignor had implored Goldstajn, and he said the same to me, too. *This is my fate: God has chosen it for me.*

Stepinac's ghost serves as the elemental symbol of the Serb-Croat dispute, around which every other ethnic hatred in this now-fragmented, the largest and most definitive of Balkan nations, is arranged. The greater the volume of blood shed in the Yugoslav civil war of the 1990s, the more relevant the story of Stepinac's story became. One could approach this issue through the psychological theory of nations advanced by the Bulgarian-born Nobel laureate, Elias Canetti, which is based on "crowd symbols."

For example, Canetti said the crowd symbol for the English is the "*sea* . . . The Englishman's disasters have been experienced at sea. . . . His life at home is complementary to life at sea; security and monotony are its essential characteristics. . . ." For the Germans, the crowd symbol is the "*marching forest.*" For the French, it is "their *revolution.*" For the Jews, it is "the Exodus from Egypt. . . . The image of this multitude moving year after year through the desert has become the crowd symbol of the Jews."[2] Canetti, unfortunately, did not discuss the people of the Balkans. The psychologically closed, tribal nature of the Serbs, Croats, and others makes them as suited to crowd symbols as the Jews, and more so than the English and the Germans.

Since Croats are ethnically indistinguishable from Serbs—they come from the same Slavic race, they speak the same language, their names are usually the same—their identity rests on their Roman Catholicism. Therefore, the Croatian crowd symbol might be the *Church* or more specifically, the confused and embattled *legacy of Archbishop Stepinac*.

The facts surrounding his career as a wartime archbishop, more than any other single issue, keep Serbs and Croats—and therefore Yugoslavia—psychologically divided. For that reason, and to be fair to the man himself, some facts require our attention.

On April 10, 1941, on the heels of German and Italian invasion, the fascist Ustashe proclaimed the "Independent State of Croatia." Archbishop Stepinac's reaction was "joyful," since he saw the creation of a "free" Croatia as a God-granted blessing on the thirteenth centenary of Croatia's first ties with the Church of Rome. On April 16, he paid an official visit to the Ustashe leader, Ante Pavelic. On April 28, in a circular to Croatian clergy, he wrote:

> The times are such that it is no longer the tongue which speaks but the blood with its mysterious links with the country, in which we have seen the light of God. . . . Do we need to say that the blood flows more quickly in our veins, that the hearts in our breasts beat faster: . . . no honest person can resent this, for love of one's own people has been written by God's laws. Who can reproach us if we also, as spiritual pastors add our contribution to the pride and rejoicing of the people, . . . it is easy to see God's hand at work here.

Not that Stepinac liked or even trusted the Germans, whose Nazi ideology he viewed as "pagan." But over the years, he had

2. In recent decades, partly owing to the prominence of Jerusalem in Middle East politics, one could argue that the Wailing Wall has supplanted the Exodus as the Jewish crowd symbol.

developed an obsessive fear of Communism; and he, like so many contemporaneous Vatican officials, thought of that ideology in connection with the Orthodox Church in Russia, and by association, with the Orthodox Church in Serbia. Under his influence as archbishop-coadjutor in 1935 and 1936, the semi-official paper of the Croatian Church, *Katolicki List*, had aggressively attacked "Jew-Marxists" in Russia, who were "alien to the people over whom they rule. . . ." But by 1937, Stepinac had seen how the Nazis could transform the traditional anti-Semitism he had grown up with into something far more extreme. And thenceforth anti-Semitic references were absent from *Katolicki List*'s anti-Communist tirades.

Such ambivalence was, tragically, typical of the archbishop. For example, when the Ustashe authorities, one month after they seized power, ordered all Jews in Croatia to wear a special insignia, Stepinac suggested privately to the Interior Minister, Andrija Artukovic (who would later find refuge in the United States), that perhaps the Jews should be required to buy the insignias, in order to repay the state for production costs, without actually having to wear them. Stepinac then requested that all measures against Jews and Serbs, especially children, be carried out in a "humane" fashion.

At that juncture, Stepinac possessed a naïveté so sense-dulling that his awareness bordered on blindness. Thus, when he welcomed the Ustashe regime, he said: "Knowing the men who today guide the destiny of the Croatian people . . . we believe and expect that the church in our resurrected Croatian State will be able in full freedom to proclaim the indisputable principles of eternal truth and justice."

The archbishop evidently didn't realize that Croatia under the Ustashe was nothing but a puppet state divided between Nazi Germany and fascist Italy. In *The Triple Myth*, Stella Alexander notes: "Two things stand out. He feared Communism above all (especially above fascism); and he found it hard to grasp that anything beyond the boundaries of Croatia, always excepting the Holy See, was quite real."

At a time when Ustashe fascist units in neighboring Bosnia were throwing Serbian Orthodox women and children off cliffs and Adolf Hitler's troops were marching across the Soviet Union, building death camps and committing every sort of atrocity, Stepinac was stoutly declaring: "The whole civilized world is fighting against the terrible dangers of Communism which now threatens not only Christianity but all the positive values of humanity."

Alexander writes that the record until early 1942 "is clear." Whatever doubts Stepinac harbored as a result of the increasingly frequent rumors of state-organized brutality against Orthodox Serbs and Jews were eased by Ustashe dictator Pavelic's other actions, such as the prohibition of provocative portraits of women in shop windows and the establishment of short prison terms for those caught swearing in public and working in the fields on Sunday.

From then on, however, as Alexander demonstrates in her book, Stepinac was gradually overwhelmed by reports of mass killings; as a result, he slowly began to see the truth and to find his voice. In a speech to students in March 1942, the archbishop proclaimed that "freedom without complete respect for the fulfillment of God's laws is an empty fiction. . . ." And on an April Sunday of 1942, Stepinac greeted the dictator Pavelic on the steps on Zagreb Cathedral with bread and salt in his hands. Looking into the dictator's eyes, Stepinac intoned, "The Sixth Commandment says, thou shalt not kill." An enraged Pavelic then refused to enter the Cathedral.[3]

By March 1943, when the Ustashe ordered all remaining Jews to register with the police, Stepinac declared in a public sermon:

> Everyone, no matter to what race or nation he belongs . . . bears within himself the stamp of God and has inalienable rights of which no earthly power has the right to deprive him. . . . Last week there were many occasions to see the tears and hear the sighs of men and the cries of defenseless women threatened . . . because their family life does not conform to the theories of racism. As representatives of the church we cannot and dare not be silent. . . .

Six months later, Stepinac spoke more plainly still:

> The Catholic Church knows nothing of races born to rule and races doomed to slavery. The Catholic Church knows races and

3. This story was told to me by Stephen Hanich, a Croatian-American, who was standing only a few feet away from Stepinac and Pavelic.

nations as creatures of God . . . for it the negro of Central Africa is as much a man as a European. . . . The system of shooting hundreds of hostages for a crime [which the Ustashe was constantly doing] is a pagan system which only results in evil.

At last, midway through the Holocaust, the archbishop was publicly confronting the Ustashe. Distrusted by the fascists and hated by the Communists, Stepinac refused every offer to flee to Rome, despite knowing full well that whoever won the wartime struggle would be able to make him a convenient scapegoat. Nor did he break his links completely with the Ustashe regime, although he knew that such an action would have saved his reputation. According to Alexander, Stepinac felt that such a break would have left him "unable to help anybody; the most important thing was to save what could be saved." Increasingly, as the war dragged on, Stepinac gained the trust of Jews, Serbs, and resistance figures, who thought of him as a lone ally in the midst of hell.

On the other hand, until the very last days of the war, he continued to organize processions against swearing and to believe in an "honest" aspect to the Ustashe movement. As late as February 22, 1945, a photo shows Stepinac shaking hands with the dictator Pavelic. While his attitude toward Communism was always quick and uncompromising, irrespective of the risks to himself and others, his attitude toward the Ustashe's crimes against humanity was vitiated by repeated compromises and contradictory actions. During the war, he hid a Jewish rabbi and his family in the cathedral compound. After the war's end, he met with and—albeit unwittingly—helped hide the former Ustashe police chief from the new Communist authorities. Always he exhibited a maddening lack of political acumen and narrowness of perspective; these, more than anything else, separated him from Strossmayer. Stepinac truly believed that "without exaggeration . . . no people during this war has been so cruelly stricken as the unhappy Croatian people." What had occurred throughout the rest of Yugoslavia (and throughout the rest of Europe) to Serbs, Jews, Gypsies, Muslims, and others simply had little reality for him.

In perhaps the kindest assessment offered by a non-Croat specialist about this beclouded figure, Stella Alexander says: "He lived in the midst of apocalyptic events, bearing responsibilities which he had not sought. . . . In the end one is left feeling that he was not quite great enough for his role. Given his limitations he behaved very well, certainly much better than most of his own people, and he grew in spiritual stature during the course of his long ordeal."

"The Catholic Church here has never searched its soul. The young priests are now uneducated. Only when educated young men are attracted to the priesthood can pressure mount from below for the Church to look seriously at its own past and at Stepinac," explained Zarko Puhovski, a Croatian Catholic and liberal politician, over a plum brandy at the Esplanade bar.

The Church, like so much of Zagreb, was for decades a wounded being. Since 1945, the Church's raison d'être, its all-consuming responsibility to its flock, was its own physical survival. Communism had backed the Church against a wall, as the last sovereign remnant of the Croat nation—hunted, oppressed, attracting only the uneducated poor to its clerical ranks. In contrast, the Orthodox churches were accustomed to this kind of oppression. Under the Ottoman Turks, they had learned the art of survival: how to deal with rulers whose malevolence was presumed as an ordinary, uncontrollable force of nature, like wind or sleet, in order to preserve what was most important. But the Croatian Church, with no comparable experience under the Catholic Habsburgs and, furthermore, emboldened by an external protector, the Holy See in Rome, was unwilling to concede an inch of disputed historical ground, defending even what need not and should not have been defended. Msgr. Koksa was correct: he was not the enemy—not of the Jews or even of the Serbs. He was just another victim.

In Zagreb, I learned that the struggle for bare survival leaves little room for renewal or for creation. While Ukrainians and others openly apologized for their actions against Jews during the Holocaust, Croatian groups only issued denials. The statistics on mass murder in Croatia were exaggerated, I was told. Weren't the Serbs also guilty of atrocities in World War II? And weren't the remaining Jews in Croatia being treated well? Undoubtedly, these arguments had a certain validity. What troubled me, however, was the Croats' evident need to hide behind them, as if a simple apology without qualifiers might delegitimate them as a nation. Croatia's tragedy was that its modern nationalism coalesced at a time when fascism was dominant in Europe, forcing its proponents to become entangled with Nazism. A brave and unambiguous appraisal of the past is necessary to untangle these threads.

Why did the Ukrainians act one way and the Croats another? Because the Ukrainians, in 1991 and 1992, were not having their cities bombed and their people brutalized in an unprovoked war of aggression. The war in Yugoslavia—the struggle for survival—has postponed the self-examination of Holocaust history in Croatia. But come it must.

Tito and Communism, not the Catholic Church, made Stepinac into a martyr for the Croats. In 1945, ignoring Stepinac's early statements of support for the Ustashe and the open collaboration of many Catholic priests with the murderers at the Jesenovac concentration camp, Tito met twice with Stepinac. At these meetings he attempted to coerce the archbishop to form a "national Catholic church" independent of the Vatican, which would, like the Orthodox churches in Yugoslavia, be subservient to his Communist regime. Stepinac, painfully aware that Tito possessed evidence linking him to the Ustashe, nevertheless refused to be blackmailed. Not only did he not break with the Vatican, he continued his public denunciations of the Communists. Stepinac's arrest and his staged show trial as a "war criminal" followed in 1946.

The forced conversions of Orthodox believers to Catholicism in Bosnia stirred the blood lust of the Serbs, and also provided the government with the means to destroy the archbishop. Had the archbishop not written about his desire for the schismatic Serbs to return to the true faith? Had Catholic priests (at least nominally under Stepinac's control) not enthusiastically carried out these conversions minutes before the same Serbs were slaughtered en masse?

In fact, Stepinac had absolutely no way to discipline the clergy in Bosnia, where most of the atrocities were taking place. On the map, Bosnia is next door to Croatia, and seen from far away—

especially during the decades when Yugoslavia was one country—
the two regions might have struck a foreigner as indistinguishable.
But Bosnia was always light-years removed from Zagreb. Zagreb
is an urbane, ethnically uniform community on the plain, while
Bosnia is a morass of ethnically mixed villages in the mountains.
Bosnia is rural, isolated, and full of suspicions and hatreds to a
degree that the sophisticated Croats of Zagreb could barely imagine. Bosnia represents an intensification and a complication of the
Serb-Croat dispute. Just as Croats felt their western Catholicism
more intensely than did the Austrians or the Italians, precisely
because of their uneasy proximity to the Eastern Orthodox and
Muslim worlds, so the Croats of Bosnia—because they shared the
same mountains with both Orthodox Serbs and Muslims—felt
their Croatianism much more intensely than did the Croats in
Croatia proper, who enjoyed the psychological luxury of having
only their ethnic compatriots as immediate neighbors. The same,
of course, was true of the Serbs in Bosnia. Complicating matters
in Bosnia was the existence of a large community of Muslims.
These were Slavs, whether originally Croat or Serb, who had been
converted to Islam in the late Middle Ages by the Turkish oc-
cupiers and whose religion gradually became synonymous with
their ethnic identity. Bosnia did have one sophisticated urban
center, however; Sarajevo, where Croats, Serbs, Muslims, and Jews
had traditionally lived together in reasonable harmony. But the
villages all around were full of savage hatreds, leavened by poverty
and alcoholism. The fact that the most horrifying violence—during both World War II and the 1990s—occurred in Bosnia was
no accident. In late 1991, a time when fighting raged in Croatia
while Bosnia remained strangely quiet, Croats and Serbs alike had
no illusion about the tragedy that lay ahead. *Why was there no
fighting in Bosnia?* went the joke. *Because Bosnia has advanced directly
to the finals.*

As soon as Stepinac felt certain that the conversions in Bosnia
were not voluntary, he gave orders in a confidential circular to
allow the swift conversion of Jews and Orthodox Serbs if it would
help "save their lives . . . The role and task of Christians is first
of all to save people. When these sad and savage times have
passed," those who did not convert out of belief "will return to
their own [faiths] when the danger is over."

But Tito's prosecutors were not interested in such minutiae. Tito was merely being honest when he explained, in a September 26, 1946, speech, "We arrested Stepinac and we will arrest everyone who resists the present state of affairs, whether he likes it or not." Milovan Djilas, then a member of Tito's inner circle, subsequently wrote that Stepinac "would certainly not have been brought to trial for his conduct in the war and his collaboration with the Croatian fascist leader Ante Pavelic had he not continued to oppose the new Communist regime."

Stepinac was found guilty on all counts. He served five years in solitary confinement, before being exiled to his native village of Krasic.

In the years following his trial, hundreds of Catholic priests were arrested, and sometimes tortured and murdered. In a 1950 interview with the journalist C. L. Sulzberger, conducted at the Lepoglava prison fifty miles from Zagreb, Stepinac remained defiant: "I am content to suffer for the Catholic Church." Two years later, recognizing his service to a church besieged by Communists, Pope Pius XII made Stepinac a cardinal. Since then, no sign has emerged from the Vatican to indicate it is prepared to see Stepinac in any other role than as a hero against Communism.

There were reckonings aplenty here.

As the flood waters of Communism receded and the land became recognizable again, much that was understandable and easily forgiven through the 1980s, the last decade of the postwar era, ceased to be so. Only against the backdrop of Tito's grim, industrial feudalism and the steel jaws of his secret police could the legacy of Habsburg Austria-Hungary and the Roman Catholic Church—and by extension, of Pope John Paul II—look so benign. Indeed, the aspect of Croatian nationalism that saw itself as culturally superior to the Serbs—the very nationalist tradition that had inspired Stepinac's original desire to see the Serbs converted to Catholicism—could not have come about without the active incitement of the Habsburg court and the Vatican.

Of all the Slav tribes to settle in the western part of the Balkan peninsula in the sixth and seventh centuries A.D., the Croats were the first (in 924) to free themselves from Byzantine rule and establish their own kingdom. Their first free king was Tomislav, whose statue punctuates the main square in front of Zagreb's railway station. The bronze cast is of a warrior on horseback, brandishing a cross.

I stared up at the statue. Horse and rider appeared to merge into one naked batch of muscle: not so much of a man or of a horse, but of a weapon, piercing and heartless, like the Croatian plain, upon which the threat of the Ottoman Turks, who in 1453 replaced the Byzantines at Constantinople, rose and fell. In the sixteenth and seventeenth centuries, the Turks occupied Croatia. When the Turks fell back from the plain, they withdrew only as far as the adjacent territories of Serbia and Bosnia-Hercegovina, where the Sultan's forces remained for another 200 years.[4] The sculptor may have had a purpose in depicting Tomislav this way: for a western Catholic nation to survive in the Balkans—a peninsula dominated first by Orthodox Christians and then by Muslims—it must harden its own heart so that no tender point in its armor remains.

In 1089, Kresmir, the last in the line of kings descended from Tomislav, died without a successor, and Croatia (along with the Adriatic coastal territory of Dalmatia) fell under the domination of King Ladislas I of Hungary. Threatened by Venice, an ally of the hated Byzantines, both Croatia and Dalmatia actually welcomed this Hungarian protection. Nor did they mind interference from the Vatican, which was a useful bulwark against the Byzantines. This psychological pattern was shaped further by the 1278–1282 birth of the Habsburg Alpine domain and the 1526–1527 Habsburg expansion into Hungary and Croatia. Fear of the East, as manifested by Constantinople—whether Byzantine or Turkish—swept the Croats willingly into the arms of Catholic popes, Hungarian kings, and Austrian-Habsburg emperors. The kings and emperors exploited the Croats in the way of all colonial subjects and provided spiritual sustenance for the Croats' hostility toward the Orthodox Serbs, despite the efforts of Catholic theologians like Strossmayer to bring the two groups together.

4. Bosnia and Hercegovina are two neighboring regions that became amalgamated. Strictly speaking, Sarajevo is in Bosnia, as was much of the fighting during World War II and the 1990s that I have already referred to.

To the Catholic powers of Europe, and also to many Croats, it mattered not that Serbs and Croats were fellow Slavs. The Serbs were Eastern Orthodox and, therefore, as much a part of the hated East as the Muslim Turks.

"The Serbs and the Croats were, as regards race and language, originally one people, the two names having merely geographical signification," writes the British expert Nevill Forbes in a classic 1915 study of the Balkans. Were it not originally for religion, there would be little basis for Serb-Croat enmity.

Religion in this case is no mean thing. Because Catholicism arose in the West and Orthodoxy in the East, the difference between them is greater than that between, say, Catholicism and Protestantism, or even Catholicism and Judaism (which, on account of the Diaspora, also developed in the West). While Western religions emphasize ideas and deeds, Eastern religions emphasize beauty and magic. The Eastern church service is almost a physical re-creation of heaven on earth. Even Catholicism, the most baroque of western religions, is, by the standards of Eastern Orthodoxy, austere and intellectual. Catholic monks (Franciscans, Jesuits, and so on) live industriously, participating in such worldly endeavors as teaching, writing, and community work. In contrast, Orthodox monks tend to be contemplatives, for whom work is almost a distraction, since it keeps them from the worship of heavenly beauty.

Such differences, over centuries, engender conflicting approaches to daily life. At a café across the street from the Zagreb Cathedral, a Catholic friend explained: "When I entered the Yugoslav army, I met Serbs for the first time in my life. They told me that a traditional Serbian wedding lasts four days. Four days of prayers and feasting. Who needs that? One day is enough. After that you should go back to work. The Serbs struck me as weird, irrational, like Gypsies. They actually liked the army. How can anyone like the army! I hated the army. The army for Slovenes and Croats is a waste of time; we could be out making money instead. Who wants to go to Belgrade? Belgrade's the Third World. I feel much closer to Vienna."

And Karla Kunz-Cizelj, the Croatian translator of John Steinbeck's novels, told me with deliberate pride: "I feel closer to Vienna than to Belgrade. Zagreb is still Europe. I remember, after the last war, Lawrence Durrell, the British writer—who worked at the British Embassy in Belgrade at the time—would arrive here every weekend after driving several hours in a jeep on a bumpy, dusty road, and exclaim to me: 'Thank God, Karla, I'm in the West again.' "

No matter how exploitative the Habsburg Austrians were, no matter how much the Croats pined for freedom from them, the glitter of Vienna has always been symbolic in Croatia of the West and of Catholicism, and for this reason Croatians have forgiven the Habsburg dynasty for all its sins.

To modern Croats, the Habsburgs represent the last normal and stable epoch in Central European history prior to the horrific detour through Nazism and Communism. But the Croats forget that, before Nazism and Communism, informed individuals had little good to say about the Habsburgs. In the words of Dame Rebecca: "This family, from the unlucky day in 1273 when the College of Electors chose Rudolf of Habsburg to be King of the Romans, on account of his mediocrity, till the abdication of Charles II, in 1918, produced no genius, only two rulers of ability in Charles V and Maria Theresa, countless dullards, and not a few imbeciles and lunatics."

In fact, the wealth of Habsburg Vienna and Budapest was built on the broken backs of their Slav subjects. In response to periodic revolts, unrest was put down by a combination of mass executions and such devious stratagems as giving the Serb minority in Croatia special privileges, in order to incite the Croats against the Serbs. Beginning in the mid-nineteenth century, although modern Croats like to discount it, their forebears were attracted by the prospect of a "South Slav (Yugoslav)" federation with the Serbs, independent of Austria-Hungary. This feeling grew in 1878, when, at the Congress of Berlin, the Habsburgs grabbed the adjacent territory of Bosnia-Hercegovina (which had just freed itself from the Turks) and soon demonstrated that they could rule just as viciously as the Turks. In 1908, the Habsburgs formally annexed Bosnia, whose population consisted of Muslim Slavs and Croats, as well as Serbs.

Gavrilo Princip, the assassin of the Habsburg heir apparent, Archduke Franz Ferdinand, was a Serb from Bosnia. The Catholic

Habsburgs reacted to Franz Ferdinand's death by rounding up hundreds of Orthodox Serb peasants, who knew nothing of the assassination, and executing them. The Habsburgs then declared war on Serbia, setting off World War I. "War, for the Austrian army, began with a series of courts martial," recalled Joseph Roth in *The Radetzky March*, a memoir about the decline of the Habsburg empire. "For days on end traitors, real or supposed, swung from the trees in village churchyards, to inspire the living with fear." The Habsburg empire died exactly as did the much-despised Turkish empire: amid a welter of cruelties directed against a host of small nations, struggling to break free.

By the 1930s, however, the Croats had already forgotten all of this. Centuries of Habsburg rule had helped convince the Croats that they were culturally superior to the Serbs. Thus, when the Serbian royal house of Karageorgevitch was given dominion over the Croats in the newly created state of Yugoslavia after World War I, communal hate took root with a vengeance in Croatia. In 1934 came the crime that first made Dame Rebecca aware of Yugoslavia: the Croatian Ustashe assassination of Serbian King Alexander Karageorgevitch. In the 1980s and early 1990s, a popular revisionist theory credited the Habsburgs with building a peaceful climate of ethnic tolerance, but in Croatia tolerance was definitely not a part of their legacy.

The Vatican also bears its share of guilt. The greatest stimulus to anti-Serb feeling in Croatia always came from the Roman Catholic Church, which much preferred the Catholic Croats to be under the rule of their fellow-Catholic Austrians and Hungarians, than to be outnumbered in a state dominated by the Eastern Orthodox Serbs, who, for historic-religious reasons, were psychologically aligned with the Bolshevist Russians. The Vatican was never happy with Yugoslavia, even before World War II, when the nation was non-Communist. And by refusing to set foot on Yugoslav territory unless he could publicly pray at the controversial and (to many) compromised symbol of Croation devoutness, Stepinac's tomb, Pope John Paul II throughout the 1980s seemed insensitive to the collective memories of Orthodox Serbs— as well as to those of Jews and Gypsies, for whom Stepinac did too little, too late. For decades, the Vatican was judged and rewarded solely on the basis of its anti-Communism, thus postponing discussion of its wider historical role and attitudes in this part of the world. No longer is this the case.

I walked in the rain away from the statue of Tomislav and past the neoclassical Art Pavilion, its facade yellow as a daguerreotype. Hidden in the leaf-strewn park behind the Art Pavilion stood the statue of Bishop Strossmayer.

The sculptor depicted Strossmayer with horns, the way Michelangelo did Moses. A tall, sinewy quality of the work, embodying an inner glow and strength, drew me closer, as if the bronze were real warm flesh. "We left the lovely statue smiling under the heavy rain," recollected Dame Rebecca about her visit to this spot.

The sculptor who had executed the statue of Strossmayer was Ivan Mestrovic—the same Ivan Mestrovic who, many years later, in 1960, carved the tomb of another local patriot, Alojzije Stepinac. There was no contradiction here. Mestrovic was a personal witness to the noble side of Stepinac's character. In 1943, during a brief visit by Stepinac to Rome, Mestrovic begged Stepinac not to go back to Croatia because his life was increasingly at risk there. Stepinac replied that he had already accepted his fate: if the Ustashe didn't kill him, the Communists would. Having started at a point of complete political blindness, the archbishop brutally applied to himself the correct lesson of the "black lamb" and the "grey falcon": he was willing to be the sacrificial lamb, not out of self-righteousness, but in order to fight for others.

History in this gray, intimate city was indeed subject to many interpretations. Pope John Paul II seemed poised to give his.[5] If and when the Pope did come to this outpost of Western Christianity, so near and yet so far from the Vatican, he would have to break with Vatican tradition concerning Yugoslavia and come to heal and to reconcile. I stood respectfully in the chilling rain before the statue of Bishop Strossmayer, lover of Cyril and Methodius, aware that this was the monument in Zagreb, more than the one in the cathedral, that the Pope must bow down before.

5. As of late 1992, there were still no official plans for a Papal visit to Zagreb. But given the geographical closeness of this Catholic city to the Vatican, and the sufferings endured by the Croats in the civil war, it seems highly conceivable that the Pope will pay a visit sometime in this decade.

CHAPTER TWO

Old Serbia and Albania: Balkan "West Bank"

Mother Tatiana lifted her hand out of the darkness to block a beam of sunlight. "There," she said, my eyes now protected from the glare, "witness the heritage of the *Srbski narod* (Serbian people)."

The accusing eyes of John the Baptist imprinted themselves on the wall in the north chapel. I saw John coming out of the Judean desert. His hair and beard were tied in weedy serpents' knots, his body was distorted by hunger and an artistic vision of a sort usually ascribed to El Greco or William Blake. No Western artist—no product of the Italian Renaissance—could approach this obscure fourteenth-century Serbo-Byzantine master's ability to understand, and thus render, the Baptist of St. Mark's Gospel.[1] "*And John was clothed with camel's hair, and with the girdle of a skin*

1. The painter was either Michael Astrapas or a certain Eutychios, both of Salonika.

about his loins; and he did eat locusts and wild honey." John's face, seething with revelation, moved like the point of a flame in the apse: not a man at all, but a disembodied, fire-breathing spirit in human form.

Because John was too preoccupied with ideas to notice his physical suffering, he suffered not. This particularly oriental strength provides a starting point toward understanding why the Serbs have behaved as they have in this century.

Mother Tatiana led me under a steep, ascending wave of cylindrical vaults and archways. I felt the earth give way.

"This is our root, our vertical," she said, a statement both literal and figurative. The central dome was supported by four fifty-foot pillars that, on account of their closeness, created the sensation of dizzying, tapering height. I gazed up through a shroud of incense at hundreds upon hundreds of breathing flames, each as bright as John, robed in the dyes of mulberry and pomegranate, with the tragic golden faces of dying autumn leaves. Imagine the simplicity and monumental grace of classical Greek sculpture superimposed on a luxuriant eastern carpet. If heaven is mirrored anywhere on earth, it is here, inside the Serbian monastery of Grachanitsa.

Such "wealth is past our computation," exclaimed Dame Rebecca, who had stood in this same chapel over half a century ago. "Our cup has not been empty, but it was never full like those in this world, at a spot where Asia met Europe. . . ."

Leaving the seemingly vast black entrails of the church through the outer narthex, I passed into a different silence, intensified by sheep bells tinkling on the lawn and a sparrow chipping at the mortar between rows of wafer-thin brick. Seen from the outside, this church appeared almost tiny. A perfectly synthesized verticality in which four powder-blue domes range closely around the narrow, rising neck of another dome, begot this most attractive of architectural deceptions: what looked deliciously petite from the outside looked limitless from the inside.

Grachanitsa, Pec, and thirty or so other Serbian monasteries distinguish the landscape of southern Yugoslavia. I came here direct from Zagreb in the north. As I had tried to intuit the sensibility of Croatia's national problem through its cathedral, I tried to do the same with respect to Serbia through its monasteries.

The Serbian monasteries are the legacy of the Nemanjic dynasty, founded toward the end of the twelveth century by a tribal chieftain, Stefan Nemanja, who carved out the first Serbian state independent of the Byzantine rulers in Constantinople. From its inception, Serbia was among the most civilized states in Europe. While Stefan could sign his name, the Holy Roman Emperor in Germany, Frederick I Barbarossa, could only manage a thumbprint.

Stefan Nemanja's son, the traveling monk known as Saint Sava, founded and organized the Serbian Orthodox Church. A later descendant of Stefan Nemanja, King Milutin, expanded Serbia into a great Orthodox Christian empire at the beginning of the fourteenth century, richer even than the Byzantine Empire at the time.

Virility seems to drip from Milutin's gold-encrusted sleeves. Like the Tudor King Henry VIII, Milutin lusted after women, marrying and discarding wives according to his sexual proclivities and imperialist ambitions. Each insatiable desire abetted the other, as he grabbed territory to the south and east and co-opted archbishops to divorce and remarry him. His sexual appetite was matched only by his appetite for building and artistic adornment, which he thought would bring him immortality in the same way as the many children he begot. Milutin financed the building of churches and palaces in Constantinople, Salonika, and all over Serbia. He bestowed gold, jewels, and icons on religious institutions as far away as Jerusalem and the Holy Mountain of Athos in northeast Greece. On a wall of Grachanitsa's south chapel, Milutin's words are inscribed: "I saw the ruins of the Church of the Virgin of Grachanitsa, . . . built it from its very foundations and painted and decorated it inside and out."

When Milutin built Grachanitsa he was married to his fourth wife, Simonide, the daughter of the Byzantine Emperor, Andronicus II Palaeologus. To keep Milutin's armies out of Constantinople, Andronicus had given Milutin his six-year-old daughter. Milutin, not waiting for the girl to grow up, immediately consummated the marriage. Still, the Serbian king was more civilized than his English Tudor counterpart in some respects: he only discarded his previous wives, never murdering them.

In the royal portraits on a lower wall at Grachanitsa, Milutin is already a frail old man, and Simonide a grown woman. Their faces showed a deathly pallor, and one of the Milutin's eyes had been rubbed out. They seemed far less real than their crowns, their jeweled robes, and the model of the Grachanitsa church that the king cradled in his arms. The human being, this Serbo-Byzantine artist seemed to be saying, is ephemeral, but its material creations are indestructible.

Grachanitsa, frescoes and all, was finished in 1321, when across the Adriatic Sea, the sun was just rising on the Florentine Renaissance. On Grachanitsa's walls I witnessed a sense of anatomy and bodily sexuality (one lacking in other schools of Byzantine iconography, in which the body is strictly a symbol for the immaterial spirit) that would soon find culmination in the works of Michelangelo and Leonardo da Vinci. But never could any Renaissance artist duplicate the supernatural and spiritual element achieved here by the medieval Serbs. Mother Tatiana did not hint, therefore: "We would have been even greater than the Italians, were it not for the Turks."

That was the refrain you heard throughout the Balkans, in Dame Rebecca's day and in mine. Dame Rebecca writes: "The Turks ruined the Balkans, with a ruin so great that it has not yet been repaired. . . . There is a lot of emotion loose about the Balkans which has lost its legitimate employment now that the Turks have been expelled."

If like the Russian Nobel laureate Joseph Brodsky you view the Communist Empire as the twentieth-century equivalent of the Ottoman Turkish Empire, with the historical compass line of decrepit, Eastern despotism traveling north from Istanbul (formerly Constantinople) to Moscow—from the Sultan's Topkapi Palace to the Kremlin—then Dame Rebecca had already capsulized the situation in Serbia, in the rest of former Yugoslavia, and in the other Balkan states for the 1990s. Now that Communism has fallen and the Soviets have been expelled, *there is a lot of emotion loose about the Balkans which has lost its legitimate employment.*

For decades, prostrate under Tito, Mother Tatiana had other worries, other battles to fight. But with that plague ending, she was back to fighting the Turks, although she now called the problem by another name.

*　　*　　*

Because the Serbs were spread out over wooded and mountainous land that was difficult to subdue, and because they were geographically farther removed from Turkey than either Bulgaria or Greece, the Ottoman yoke was never as complete in Serbia as it was in those countries. Moving pockets of resistance always existed, particularly in the black granite fastnesses of neighboring Montenegro. But Serbia was still not far enough away.

In Serbian legend, the Nemanjic kingdom sacrificed itself to the Turkish hordes in order to gain a new kingdom in heaven; meanwhile, here on earth, Serbia's sacrifice allowed Italy and Central Europe to stay alive and to continue to develop.

"The greatness of Italy and the other nations of Europe was constructed over our bones," said Mother Tatiana bitterly. "Come," she said, beckoning, "I will tell you about our suffering."

I entered a typical Turkish building, with madder roof tiles, yellow stone walls, and overhanging wooden balconies adorned with plants. Mother Tatiana labeled it "typical Serbian" architecture. In Bulgaria, such buildings were considered "typical Bulgarian revivalist" architecture; in Greece, "typical Greek" architecture. The salon was dark. I sat freezing with my coat on, my feet on a Turkish-style rug. Mother Tatiana's black nun's habit appeared in silhouette against white curtains. Another sister poured thick, heavily sugared Turkish coffee from a cylindrical gold metal beaker. Next, the sister poured the monastery's clear, homemade plum brandy into glasses. Mother Tatiana slugged back a brandy. Then her large peasant's hands once more came up out of the darkness:

"I am not the Prophet Samuel, but it would be better to die honestly than to live in shame. . . .

"I am a good Christian, but I'll not turn the other cheek if some Albanian plucks out the eyes of a fellow Serb, or rapes a little girl, or castrates a twelve-year-old Serbian boy." She knifed the air over her thighs with her hand. "You know about that incident, don't you?"

I did not, but I nodded anyway.

Mother Tatiana put her elbows on the table and leaned closer to me. My eyes adjusted to the darkness, and for the first time I got a good look at her face. She had a strong, lusty appearance, with high cheekbones and fiery, maternal eyes. She was a hand-some old woman who clearly was once quite attractive. Her eyes, while fiery, also appeared strangely unfocused, as though blotted out by superstition, like the saints' eyes in the church. Her white fingertips flickered to the rhythm of her words. I recalled what John Reed wrote after a journey through Serbia in 1915: "The rapid, flexible eloquence of the Serbian language struck on our ears like a jet of fresh water."

"Did you know," said Mother Tatiana, "that these young Albanian boys actually dropped their pants in front of the other sisters?"

I nodded again.

"Serbia is being bled dry by these people. It's a lie that they are poor and unemployed. Why, they list their dying grandfathers as out of work. They are all smugglers and they have lots of foreign exchange stashed away. They only dress poor and dirty because that is their habit.

"The Albanians, you know, want to conquer the world by out-breeding us. You know that no hodja [an Albanian Moslem cleric] will come to the house of a family that doesn't have at least five children? And that Azen Vlasi [an Albanian political leader], he is just a lecher who screws with the local whore.

"And what is your nationality?" she asked me suddenly.

"I'm an American," I answered.

"I know that, but all Americans are something else. What are you? You're dark. You don't look like real Americans are sup-posed to look."

"I'm a Jew."

"Hah, ha. I like Jews, but I still want to baptize you." She laughed, her face exuding a protective kindness. "I admire the ladies of Israel who carry guns. If I were only forty again I'd carry a gun. There is no faith in Yugoslavia. Only here in Serbia is there real faith. . . . I know that I am a strong Serbian nationalist. Things will get worse between us and the Albanians—you'll see. There can be no reconciliation."

Mother Tatiana gripped my hand with both of hers and pressed it, as though blessing me.

"I have remained inside these walls for thirty-five years. We have two hectares [five acres] and support ourselves by raising pigs and sheep. In 1539, there was a printing press here. *Out there*," lifting her hand, "it is all dirty and uncared for."

Out there is what Nevill Forbes and John Reed in 1915, what Dame Rebecca in 1937, and what Mother Tatiana now called "Old Serbia": the "Judea and Samaria" of the Serbian national consciousness, the place where it all happened, where the great Nemanjic kingdom was born, grew to greatness, and was destroyed. In recent decades, however, this hallowed ground has been demographically reclaimed, not by the Turks, but by their historical appendants, the Muslim Albanians. Thus this region is no longer referred to as Old Serbia, but as "Kossovo."

Yet it was "the Turk" that Mother Tatiana still meant to hate. Without the cultural and economic limbo of half a millennium of Turkish rule, Communism might not have been established here so easily, and the Albanians might never have been converted to Islam and settled in such large numbers as they were in old Serbia.

And so the Serbs, in Elias Canetti's words, also have their "crowd symbols." The Serbs, in fact, have two of them—two pillars of fire that define their national attitude and historical predicament. Both are legacies of the Nemanjic dynasty.

The first (and shorter) pillar is the *medieval monasteries*, safe-boxes of art and magic, most powerfully symbolized by Grachanitsa, due to its proximity to the other (and taller) pillar: *Kossovo Polje*, the "Field of Black Birds," where the Turks delivered the final defeat to the Serbs on June 28, 1389, leaving their bodies for carrion birds to devour.

While 1989 will be remembered by other peoples as the year when the Cold War ended and the Communist system collapsed, for Mother Tatiana and 8.55 million Serbs, 1989 signified something altogether different: the six hundredth anniversary of their defeat.

King Milutin died in 1321, the year that his master painters completed the frescoes at Grachanitsa. His son, King Stefan Uros, succeeded him; and ten years later, Milutin's grandson, Stefan Dushan, ascended the Serbian throne. In the Serbian language, Dushan is an endearing diminutive of *dusha*, meaning "soul"— the cognomen one would expect for a king under whom Serbia reached its zenith of glory. Dushan sanctioned religious freedom and permitted foreign embassies to be attached to his court. He established a taxation system and a rule of law—the Dushan code—that featured trials by jury. Dushan's empire extended as far as the Croatian border to the north, the Adriatic Sea to the west, the Aegean Sea to the south, and the gates of Constantinople to the east. It comprised Bosnia-Hercegovina, Montenegro, Albania, Macedonia, northern Greece, and Bulgaria. Had Dushan not been interrupted by an invasion of Catholic Hungarians, which forced him to redeploy troops to the northwest, he might have followed up a siege of Salonika with an attack on Constantinople itself.

In 1354, Dushan was again in a position to conquer the Byzantine Empire. Desperate, the rulers in Constantinople allowed the Turkish armies massing in the east to cross Asia Minor into Europe and thus to erect a bridgehead at Gallipoli, in order to stave off Dushan's Serbian troops. Although this maneuver proved unnecessary—Dushan died suddenly the next year, in 1355—it had an unintended consequence: the Turks remained in Gallipoli, using it to invade Bulgaria and Greece, prior to sacking Constantinople and the Byzantine Empire a century later, in 1453.

Dushan's son Uros was the last Nemanjic king. Under his weak rule, Serbian feudal lords increased their power at the expense of the royal court. To meet the Turkish threat after Uros died in 1371, the Serbian lords elected one Knez ("Prince") Lazar as their national leader. In the ensuing years, although the Turks were conquering more and more Balkan territory and the Serbs posed the main Christian obstacle in Europe to the Muslim advance, Lazar got little support from the peoples of Central and Western Europe. Finally, in 1389, came the battle that sealed the fate of Serbia and the whole Balkan peninsula for more than 500 years— until the First Balkan War of 1912.

I rode up and down apple green, dome-shaped hills on my way north from Grachanitsa. The bucolic caress of Serbian folk tunes issued from the driver's cassette—the Balkan equivalent of Stephen Foster melodies. The earth heaved up a flat, uninspiring plain in the distance: Kossovo Polje, the Field of Black Birds.

The Serbian knights had marched onto this plain on that hot June day arrayed in heavy mail, their armor engraved in gold and silver, and magnificent plumes atop their helmets. The lightly clad Turks, mounted on tireless Mongolian ponies, picked the Serbs apart in the way of guerrilla fighters cutting up a modern, conventional force. In a last-ditch attempt to save the day, a Serbian nobleman, Milosh Obilich, deserted to the Turks; brought before Sultan Murad, Obilich pulled out a hidden dagger and killed the Turkish commander. This, however, had no military effect. Command passed immediately to Murad's heir, Bayezit (the "Thunderer"), who finished the Serbs and captured and executed their leader, Lazar. (A few years later, Bayezit would decimate another Orthodox Christian people, the Bulgarians.)

But the legend inscribed in a Serbian poem told a different tale:

> *There flies a grey bird, a falcon,*
> *From Jerusalem the holy,*
> *And in his beak he bears a swallow.*
>
> *That is no falcon, no grey bird,*
> *But it is the Saint Elijah.*
> *He carries no swallow,*
> *But a book from the Mother of God.*
> *He comes to the Tsar [Knez Lazar] at Kossovo,*
> *He lays the book on the Tsar's knees [and asks] . . .*
> *Of what kind will you have your kingdom?*
> *Do you want a heavenly kingdom?*
> *Do you want an earthly kingdom? . . .*
>
> *The Tsar chose a heavenly kingdom,*
> *And not an earthly kingdom,*
> *He built a church on Kossovo . . .*
> *Then he gave his soldiers the Eucharist . . .*
> *Then the Turks overwhelmed Lazar, . . .*
> *And his army was destroyed with him,*
> *Of seven and seventy thousand soldiers.*
>
> *All was holy, all was honorable*
> *And the goodness of God was fulfilled.*

And as the living death of Ottoman Turkish rule began to seep in, with its physical cruelty, economic exploitation, and barren intellectual life, the Serbs perverted this myth of noble sacrifice. They filled their hearts with vengeful sadness and defeat: feelings whose atmospheric effect bore an uncanny resemblance to those that for centuries propelled Iranian Shiites.

Not kings Stefan Nemanja, Milutin, and Stefan Dushan, nor even Saint Sava, elicit the intense emotions among Serbs that Knez Lazar does: a shadowy figure who was not a Nemanja, who fought only one battle (which he lost), and who thus, writes Dame Rebecca, "did not preserve his people, who lay a blackened and much-travelled mummy in the exile of the Frushka Gora [a hill region northwest of Belgrade]."

On June 28, 1988, the year-long countdown to the sixth centenary of Lazar's martyrdom at Kossovo Polje began when his coffin began a tour of every town and village in Serbia, before returning to Ravanica, its original resting place prior to the Frushka Gora exile. The coffin drew huge, black-clad crowds of wailing mourners at every stop.

Lazar's very defeat and martyrdom attracted the Serbs. The throngs of shrieking mourners surrounding his wooden coffin resembled mourners at the bier of the Imam Husain, another shadowy figure of failure (but one holy to Shiites), massacred on a Mesopotamian battlefield in A.D. 680 by the Sunni armies of Yazid. Like the Shiites, unreconstructed Serbs like Mother Tatiana granted no legitimacy to their temporal rulers, whether Ottoman Turks or Yugoslav Communists. In this way, they ignored the physical world. They knew that, one day soon, Knez Lazar in heaven would reclaim what was rightfully his on earth. "Every [Serbian] peasant soldier knows what he is fighting for," noted John Reed, at the front in World War I. "When he was a baby, his mother greeted him, 'Hail, little avenger of Kossovo!' "

To Mother Tatiana and to many other Serbs, Tito's Yugoslavia signified—like the former Turkish Empire—just another anti-Serbian plot. This was because Yugoslav nationalism, as Tito (a half-Croat, half-Slovene) defined it, meant undercutting the power of the numerically dominant Serbs in order to placate other groups, particularly the Croats and the Albanians.

By giving the Albanians their own autonomous province, Kossovo, and by placing this province within the Yugoslav Republic of Serbia, Tito thought he had reconciled the aspirations of both the Albanians and the Serbs. The Serbs thought differently. *Why should these Muslim foreigners, who came only 300 years ago to Old Serbia, the historic heartland of our nation, have autonomy there? Never!*

Communism poured acid in this wound. It dictated that the Serbs must feel ashamed of everything in their collective past that came before the rise of Tito; that such personages as Milutin, Dushan, and Lazar were "imperialists"; that the Serbs killed along with Lazar at Kossovo Polje were guilty of "reactionary nationalism."[2]

On the eve of battle, Knez Lazar warned:

> *Whoever is a Serb and of Serbian birth,*
> *And who does not come to Kossovo Polje*
> *to do battle against the Turks,*
> *Let him have neither a male*
> *nor a female offspring,*
> *Let him have no crop, . . .*

I saw these words were written on a block of grim, blood-colored stone, about 100 feet high, well-socketed on a wind-swept hill overlooking Kossovo Polje. The monument rested on a platform surrounded by bullet-shaped cement towers inscribed with a sword and the numbers "1389–1989." Atop each tower was a fresh laurel wreath.

In 1987, an ambitious Serbian Communist party leader, Slobodan Milosevic, came to this area on the June 28 anniversary of Lazar's defeat. He pointed his finger in the distance—at what Mother Tatiana had labeled *out there*—and, as legend now has it, pledged: "They'll never do this to you again. Never again will anyone defeat you."

At that moment, as the crowd roared, the Serbian revolt against the Yugoslav federation began; it soon spread laterally to the other republics. One by one, Serbs gathered the courage to remove the fearful icon of Tito from their homes and shops, replacing it with

2. See Richard West's "The Agincourt of Yugoslavia" in *The Spectator*, December 19/26, 1987.

a photo of the plump, baby-faced Milosevic. The only Eastern European Communist leader in the late 1980s who managed to save himself and his party from collapse did so by making a direct appeal to racial hatred.

Milosevic himself ordered the building of the melancholy, hill-top monument. When he first pointed his finger at the begrimed and defaced hills of Old Serbia, smelling of exhaust from a nearby factory and crisscrossed with power lines, and promised, "Never again will anyone defeat you," he knew exactly the effect of his words.[3]

In the spring of 1937, when Dame Rebecca had come to these same hills—Milosevic was a little boy at the time—she saw already how "defeat had taken all":

> [S]habby, empty hills which in Milutin's time had been covered with villages . . . receded into distances that were truly vast, for a traveller could penetrate them for many miles before he came on life that was gentle, where the meals were full and delicate. . . . Yet when Grachanitsa was built the people . . . had eaten game and fine fattened meats off gold and silver. . . . But because the Christians had lost the battle of Kossovo all this life had perished. . . . Nothing . . . was left . . . the residue was pitifully thin, thin as a shadow cast by a clouded sun.

Forty years on, "defeat" is more than just a writer's historical metaphor. It is an overpowering reality written in streaks of tar, cinder blocks, and corrugated metal, easily visible from the hill overlooking the famous battle. Defeat even has a name: Prishtina, the Tito-built, Albanian-dominated, slum capital of "autonomous" Kossovo, situated, as though as a deliberate insult, midway between the two Serbian crowd symbols of Grachanitsa and Kossovo Polje. To travel from one to the other, you must pass through Prishtina.

Prishtina was one of several capitals of the moving Nemanjic court. Dame Rebecca described it as a "dull and dusty little village," inhabited by "men in Western clothes more fantastic than any peasant costume could be, because they and their tailors had never

---

3. In actuality, Milosevic's exact words were, "Nobody, either now or in the future, has the right to beat you." But legend has created many variations of what he said.

seen a suit till they were grown men." Today, minus the cubist architecture and smashed-up shopping malls, Prishtina, swelled to a population of 150,000, is the same "dusty little village" filled with men who still look as though they had never seen a Western suit until yesterday.

Not until I traveled to Prishtina did I fully grasp the extent of the crime committed by Tito and the other sultans going all the way back to Murad.

The Albanian men crowding next to me on the back seat of the bus south from Zagreb had eyes glazed over by trachoma. They wore threadbare pants held up by safety pins in places where zippers should have been. They were Muslims, yet their breath reeked of alcohol; even in the most avowedly secular of Islamic countries, this was rare. As everywhere in Yugoslavia, pornographic magazines were ubiquitous, along with loud Western rock-and-roll music blaring from cheap transistors. There was a fight over a seat. Two men began shouting: this I was used to. They began shoving each other and would have come to blows if others had not intervened. This I had never seen in the Muslim world, where almost all violence is political. Suddenly, I did not feel quite safe. Never have I felt that way among Muslims, except in a war zone.

The first warning of Prishtina was a jumble of wooden stalls illuminated by sodium lamps, clapped together against prefabricated apartment blocks that appeared to reel like drunks on cratered hillsides. Coal dust filled my nostrils, along with the odors of garbage and mixed cement. I thought of the liver-hued suburbs of Ankara and Istanbul, dusty with pollution. Prishtina seemed a regurgitation not only of the Turkish past, but of the Turkish present too. As the bus swept around an uphill curve and the lip of a beer bottle dug into my backside from the fellow next to me, another housing project came into view: a messy jigsaw of brown brick, plate glass, and bathroom tiles employed as outdoor facades.

The Grand Hotel Prishtina, the city's tallest skyscraper, had five huge stars atop its roof. The elevator reminded me of a graffiti-scarred toilet stall. The lock on my room was broken. Inside, the room smelled of the previous occupant—unfiltered cigarettes and hair tonic. The bile-green carpet had innumerable stains. Despite the touch-tone receiver, all calls in the hotel went through a central operator who plugged wires into an old wooden box.

The Yugoslav Communist government had equipped the hotel with three dining halls. Each had an orchestra, a seating capacity of several hundred people, and a similar menu. All three were usually empty. The waiters and the members of the three orchestras sat on lounge chairs, smoking, and became annoyed whenever a customer entered. The hotel's few guests knew enough to eat their lunches and dinners elsewhere. When I thought of where Western bank loans to Yugoslavia and the rest of Eastern Europe went in the 1970s, I always thought of the Grand Hotel Prishtina.

Here was the problem: In the late 1960s and 1970s, Tito and the Israelis thought along similar lines. But Tito, being a Marxist-Leninist, operated on a bigger, more madcap scale. Both assumed that, if you built *things* for people, they would stop hating you. On the West Bank, the Israelis built water, electrical, and health-care systems. This improved the quality of life and ignited a mass uprising, fueled by demographic pressure and higher expectations. Of course, I am oversimplifying. There were many differences between the Palestinian and Albanian *intifadas*; but there were also similarities, and knowledge of one helped me get a handle on the other. Having just experienced the Grand Hotel, I spent my first day in Prishtina walking around, observing other *things* Tito and his heirs had built to keep the Albanians from hating the Serbs.

Up the hill from the Grand Hotel was the library of Prishtina University, made of marble blocks of varying colors. It was the kind of daring edifice, evocative of both the desert and the Space Age, that one might expect to find at a world's fair or on a university campus in the American southwest. The library sat in the middle of a dirt field littered with broken glass and garbage and preyed upon by a few goats and Gypsy children. As I walked across the brown dirt away from the begging Gypsies, it occurred to me that green was the one color you never saw in Prishtina.

Just behind the Grand Hotel soared the cathedral-like roof of the soccer stadium and sports complex. Against the sports complex, like some weird dermatological growth, was a prefab apartment building with sagging clotheslines, on which clustered more bazaar stalls. The exit points from the soccer stadium led through a pedestrian shopping mall—a battlefield of refuse mounds and cracked and overturned stone benches. I waited there with a small group of Yugoslav journalists and a unit of federal *milicija*. The troops, drawn mainly from Serbia, wore blue-and-gray uniforms and blue helmets with wired-plastic head visors, and they carried assault rifles. An armored personnel carrier idled with its motor on, and a mobile water cannon had been strategically positioned up the street. The soccer match had just ended. We were all waiting for the crowds of young Albanian men to emerge from the stadium.

What we were waiting for, in fact, was the kind of riot that had been going on for years already in Prishtina. Had the world paid more attention to these desultory riots throughout the 1980s in Kossovo, it would have been less surprised by the greater violence that the Serbs—angry and frustrated over their dilemma with the Albanians—later inflicted upon helpless Croats and Bosnian Muslims.

Edward Gibbon, writing from England in the late eighteenth century, depicted Albania as a land "within the sight of Italy which is less known than the interior of America." Even supposing that the interior of America had remained unexplored, Gibbon's remarks about Albania would still have been true through 1990.

Perched in their mountain fortress on the Adriatic, like the black eagles for which they and their land were named—Shqiperia, the "Land of the Eagle"—the 3.4 million inhabitants of Albania, adjacent to Kossovo, were at the start of the last decade of the twentieth century still an enigma: tyrannized by a Stalinist regime that, true to Albania's lonely past, was ready to take on the entire world.

Albanians descend from ancient Illyrian tribes that by some accounts came to the Balkan Peninsula even before the Greeks did, and more than a thousand years before the Slavs. The Albanian language, Shqip, also derives from that of the Illyrian tribes and bears no similarity to any other known tongue. The cruelty and xenophobia of the Stalinist regime, headed by the World War II guerrilla leader Enver Hoxha, toward the outside world—and toward Yugoslavia in particular—was not without some historical logic.

Although Serbs prefer not to talk about it, Albanians, too, had their national development arrested by the Turks. The only bright flash in their long, dark night of servitude was the career of George Scanderbeg, a fifteenth-century Albanian officer in the Ottoman army, who deserted to lead a successful revolt in his native land. His death twenty-five years later, in 1468, led to a new round of Ottoman subjugation, but his example inspired many brave (if hopeless) Albanian acts of resistance against the Turkish sultanate, as well as a poem by Henry Wadsworth Longfellow and an opera by Antonio Vivaldi.

When Turkish rule in Albania finally began to collapse during the First Balkan War of 1912, the Albanians once again found themselves alone against larger enemies. Serbs, Greeks, and Bulgarians all invaded Albania, claiming to liberate it but in fact intending to carve it up into various spheres of influence. In 1913, Great Power intercession resulted in the creation of an independent Albanian state, minus the Muslim province of Kossovo, which the Serbs grabbed.

A year later, in 1914, Serbian troops again invaded Albania proper; so when the forces of Habsburg Austria-Hungary flooded into Albania in pursuit of the Serbs, the Albanians actually welcomed them. "In their utter helplessness, the luxury of being able to choose one's protectors was not for them; they [the Albanians] would have gone to the devil himself for . . . succour," writes Albanian author Anton Logoreci in *The Albanians: Europe's Forgotten Survivors*.

While the defeat and dissolution of Austria-Hungary at the end of World War I was greeted with joy everywhere else in the Balkans, for the Albanians it meant losing their only friend and being left at the mercy of ravenous neighbors.

World War II was no different for Albania. In April 1939, fascist Italy's invasion of Albania, in Logoreci's words, "caused hardly a ripple on the waters of appeasement. . . ." When Mussolini next invaded Greece, in October 1940, Greek Prime Minister George Metaxas announced that his forces would fight not only to regain parts of Greece, but to conquer Albania as well. The Albanians thus had not only Italian occupation to fight against, but Greek liberation to fear.

In the summer of 1943, the Mussolini regime collapsed and Italian forces were replaced in Albania by the Nazis. Enver Hoxha, an Albanian in his early thirties who had converted to Communism while studying in France, led the Resistance struggle, defeating not only the Nazis but a collection of non-Communist Albanian forces. World War II ended with 7.3 percent of the Albanian population dead or crippled and the rest on the brink of starvation. Every bridge and factory had been destroyed. Hoxha used weapons supplied by the Western Allies more often against his fellow Albanian partisans, who happened to be non-Communist, than against the Nazis. But the West cared too little about Albania to bother about how Hoxha was using the weapons. At a meeting in Moscow between Joseph Stalin and Winston Churchill in October 1944, when the two leaders divided up the Balkans, country by country, Albania wasn't mentioned. At Yalta, in February 1945, Albania alone among war-torn European nations remained off the agenda.

Meanwhile, Tito had placed the neighboring province of Kossovo within the jurisdiction of the Yugoslav Republic of Serbia. Tito's Serbian partisans were murdering large numbers of Kossovo's ethnic Albanians, whom they accused of having collaborated with Mussolini's Italian troops. These massacres disillusioned even the Albanian Communists, who to that point had cooperated with Tito. Unrest among Kossovo's more than 1 million Muslim Albanians simmered for decades afterwards. Tito answered with glass and concrete for a "new Prishtina," which included a university. In March 1981, not long after the city's completion, the new university's students, whose books and education were being paid for by the Communist Yugoslav government, revolted. That's when rioting became a normal feature of life. Six years later, Milosevic rose to power in Serbia and promised to crack down. When he tried to strip Kossovo of its autonomous status, the violence accelerated.

At that point in Albania itself, the clock was only starting to tick. There, in the port city of Durres, the Roman Dyrrachium, once the greatest city on the eastern shore of the Adriatic, I managed to escape for a few hours from my closely guarded tour group in late 1990. I found a Roman amphitheater from the second century A.D. surrounded by heaps of garbage, a wall used as a public toilet, and other forms of desolation. The only shops in abundance were occupied by tailors and cobblers. Albania's was a primitive service economy: little was imported and there were no factories mass producing shoes or clothes. A one-eyed Gypsy youth, semi-naked and with a shaven head, begged me for gum. Even in the poorest Third World countries, children sold gum: here there was none to sell. I saw a crowd of people gather around a kiosk to look at an exhibition of safety razors, the kind I remember my father using when I was a little boy in the 1950s. Hope and wonder registered in their eyes.

Beneath the amphitheater I found the apse of a tenth-century Byzantine church, whose black, white, and yellow mosaic tiles depicted an angel. I admired the loving care of that brickwork. Everything on either side of these few feet of history was of an inferior construction standard: to save water and cement, the mortar between the bricks holding up Albanian apartment houses was usually full of holes.

Walking along the beach that night in Durres, past a line of domed concrete bunkers that had been built in the 1960s to defend Albania against an invasion force of "Anglo-American imperialists" and "Russo-Bulgar revisionists," I heard the music of Deep Purple blaring from somewhere out in the mist, a few hundred feet from shore. I spied a walkway leading out to sea, and I followed it to a ramshackle building where a group of young men were slumped back in chairs, drinking *raki* and smoking cigarettes. The stereo speakers were only a few feet from their ears. One of the men, it turned out, was an engineer who spoke English. To hear each other, we had to scream. But neither of us wanted to turn down the volume; the loud music, I realized, was a form of protest.

"From what country are you?"

"America."

"Do you know of the writer Jack London?"

"Yes," I answered. "He wrote stories about the American Northwest at the beginning of the century."

"Yes, we have been told. We hear that some of his books may soon come to the library."

There was silence, except for the loud music. The shore was half-concealed by the mist.

"Our hearts are pounding. We know what has happened in

Romania and the rest of Eastern Europe. Albania is still alone, and we are not proud of this fact. . . . The example of Yugoslavia inspires us. We need our freedom in order to fight alongside our brothers in Kossovo."

It had occurred to me that in southern Albania you only heard about Greece, where so many ethnic-Greek Albanians had relatives. But here in central Albania, the overwhelming fact was Kossovo and the battle there against the Serbs. For decades, this little land had been able to hide behind its limestone fastnesses. Now, it was as if the mountains were swiftly falling. Greece and Serbia were once more threatening Albania. And the West, which might help, was completely unknown—unknown as far in the past as Jack London.

"Here they come," warned the journalist next to me, a Serb from Belgrade. "Rankovich was right, he knew how to control these people."[4]

Packs of tough-looking young men, their faces riddled with acne, their hands clutching the midsections of empty *piva* (beer) bottles, advanced toward us from the Prishtina soccer stadium. They wore jackets of imitation leather with lots of zippers. Some had no socks, and in place of shoes wore brown plaid slippers over bare feet. I had seen these men everywhere in Prishtina. On Saturdays they walked with their wives, whose faces were half-concealed in dark kerchiefs. On Sundays they went to the soccer game. The rest of the week they went to badly paid, dead-end jobs or were unemployed.

The *milicija* beside me were stone-faced. One soldier half-rolled his eyes. This had been going on for nearly a decade, six years longer than the Palestinian *intifada*.

"*A-zen Vla-si, A-zen Vla-si,*" the Albanian youths began to chant, like a steam train chugging. Azen Vlasi was a local Albanian leader—a "lecher," according to Mother Tatiana—who had just been put on trial, charged by Milosevic's Serbian authorities with treason.

"*Eh-O, Eh-O.*" The new chant referred to Enver Hoxha, the

4. Until his fall from power in 1964, Aleksandar-Leka Rankovich, a Serb, was Tito's feared head of the secret police.

late Stalinist tyrant of Albania. "Those poor bastards," the Serb journalist remarked. "Hoxha's the only hero they have."

A youth lobbed a *piva* bottle in our direction. Then the soldiers fired the water cannon and chased the demonstrators up a hill. In the distance, another pack of young Albanian males began setting a mountain of tires on fire. People leaned over balconies. "Fascists," they shouted down as the mainly Serb soldiers eagerly took out their clubs. Then the real violence began. Below me spread the skyline of "new Prishtina": a vomit of geodesic, concrete shapes built by Tito to erase the divisive, "reactionary" past. In response, the past had risen up in Prishtina and laid these buildings low.

Dusk set in. Gangs of big black crows started croaking in the bare acacia trees that lined Prishtina's main boulevard. It made me think of the black birds devouring the flesh of Lazar's troops. I returned to the Grand Hotel and turned on the BBC World Service.

It was November 8, 1989. Yugoslavia did not yet exist in the world's consciousness. The East German authorities had just announced that they were going to break holes in the Berlin Wall and declare Berlin an open city at midnight. The Cold War and the false division of Europe were over. A different, more historically grounded division of Europe was about to open up, I knew. Instead of democratic Western Europe and a Communist Eastern Europe, there would now be Europe and the Balkans. But who cared? I was definitely not where The Story was. It struck me just how far away from The Story, in both time and space, the Balkans were.

CHAPTER THREE

Macedonia: "A Hand Thirsting Towards the Realm of the Stars"

The landscape here needed to be read, not just looked at. I closed my eyes to reimagine the grainy, smoke-ridden tableaux according to each racial and linguistic claim, and different interpretation of history. The print was small, the sentences long and confused.

My direction was southerly, from Old Serbia into Macedonia. Canted roofs of smelting works ran parallel to slopes grooved with snow, not white but a light charcoal gray shade. I saw fir forests and stately poplars. Here and there the earth was clear of snow. Plaid, velvety shawls of maroon and sienna draped hillsides that folded down upon willow-braided streams. When the veil of soot returned, I closed my eyes. When no longer a reality but a lost ideal, the precious beauty of the land increased: I saw why its poets spoke bitterly and in hyperbole.

In Skopje, the Macedonian capital, Turkish minarets soared

above silver domes and a ramble of bazaar stalls, emphasizing the lonely, horizontal quality of the valley, where no barrier stood up to the wind: an intimation of the chaos of Asia.

The Turkish residue was thick in Skopje. Men in white skullcaps played backgammon and drank rose-hip tea from small hourglass-shaped receptacles. I took off my muddy shoes and warmed my feet on the overlapping carpets in the fifteenth-century Mosque of Mustapha Pasha. My eyes became lost in the arabesque wall designs. The patterns went on and on, indecipherably, in a linear fashion. Like the contours of the desert, Islam is a world of abstraction, mathematical in severity, fearsome and alienating to the most mystical of Eastern Christians.

On these marches, Orthodox Christianity defended itself with sympathetic magic. In the nearby Church of St. Dimitrios, I saw icons behind glass covers that refracted light in such a way that the saints' faces appeared alive and in constant motion. Their bodies lay concealed behind a mass of cheap silver plates, depicting afflictions against which invalids seek cures. I inhaled the perfume of beeswax from a forest of crackling censers. The walls of the church were completely black from candle smoke, like the warm breath of patriots. This was a world inspired by the miraculous darkness of prebirth, a world where the Turks had not yet departed.

I crossed the flagstone bridge over the Vardar River, built on Roman foundations that had withstood major earthquakes in A.D. 518, 1535, and 1963 (the last left a hundred thousand people homeless). The wind pulled at the mud-colored faces passing me, magnifying them in my eyes. They could have been Greek, Turkish, Serbian, or Bulgarian, depending on the particular folk song I was whistling or the last book I had read. On the bridge, a Gypsy boy displayed watches on a cardboard box. The watches held down a mound of 100-dinar notes, keeping them from blowing away. Even by the Gypsy's miserable standards, inflation had made these notes almost worthless.

Ahead of me was "new" Skopje, rising defiantly from the ruins of the 1963 earthquake: massive triangles and spheres of poured concrete that, as in Prishtina, were already cracked and stained from dampness. Graffiti was everywhere—not in Slavic, but in a self-taught, *Clockwork Orange* English:

Hors hav hardons . . . bad end . . . no futur, mucky pup

Gane Todorovski, a poet of the city, understood what all this is about:

> *The Vardar is mute. It swells and passes*
> *carrying something or other day and night for centuries,*
> *rolling filth, illusions, names*
> *of extinct, outlived, rootless*
> *trunk, stumps, destinies, empires, greatnesses,*
> *carrying all, crushing all, rolling all*
> *unstably, ignobly, without dignity.*[1]

Only the Turkish mosque, the smoke-blackened chapel, and the Roman bridge stones appeared to have solid foundations. Macedonia—from which Alexander the Great had set out to conquer the known world, and where Spartacus had begun his slave revolt—was a historical and geographical reactor furnace. Here the ethnic hatreds released by the decline of the Ottoman Empire had first exploded, forming the radials of twentieth-century European and Middle Eastern conflict. Macedonia was like the chaos at the beginning of time, out of which, the poet Todorovski told me, "the smallest light can be created, or the smallest light can be smashed."

"Who but the Devil himself could have fashioned so fair a charnel-house," cried a British scholar, Mercia MacDermott, in *Freedom or Death: The Life of Gotse Delchev*, the story of the man who led the Macedonian guerrilla struggle against the Turks. By MacDermott's lights, Delchev was a Bulgarian and Macedonia is therefore western Bulgaria. Claims on Macedonian blood and soil are legion. The tectonic plates of Africa, Asia, and Europe collide and overlap here, synthesizing the earth's most diverse landscapes and launching the most far-flung of lava flows. The Afridi tribesmen of eastern Afghanistan, for example, boast Macedonian lineage from Alexander's soldiers, who swept as far eastward as India.

I closed my eyes, erasing the visible environmental effects of forty-five years of Yugoslav Communism. At that moment, I saw

1. "By the Old Bridge in Skopje," by Gane Todorovski.

the landscape of northern Greece: the clarity of Aegean light; lakes like dusty mirrors that reinforced the most peaceful of introspections; autumnal foliage that, while less spectacular than in North America, was unrivaled in its subtlety born of grays and reddish-browns. And I saw—when I ignored the howling wind from Central Asia—an Eastern form of mystery and magic, domesticated by the West into something completely wholesome: the background of a fairy tale. "Macedonia is the country I have always seen between sleeping and waking," writes Dame Rebecca, "from childhood, when I was weary of the place where I was, I wished it would turn into a town like Yaitse or . . . Bitolj or Ochrid."

The twentieth century began and could yet end with such towns. I took John Reed's *The War in Eastern Europe* out of my backpack. In 1916 Reed wrote:

> The Macedonian question has been the cause of every great European war for the last fifty years, and until that is settled there will be no more peace either in the Balkans or out of them. Macedonia is the most frightful mix-up of races ever imagined. Turks, Albanians, Serbs, Rumanians, Greeks and Bulgarians live there side by side without mingling—and have so lived since the days of St. Paul.

Macedonia, according to Lord Kinross, taking up Reed's theme, "was a projection in miniature" of the whole Ottoman Empire. It lay smack in the heart of the southern Balkans: the region called "Turkey in Europe" at the turn of the century and known to the Turks themselves as Rumeli—a word applied to them by the Byzantine Greeks, meaning "the Land of the Romans."

"Turkey in Europe" began cracking up early in the nineteenth century, when the Greeks, Serbs, and Montenegrins won bloody struggles for self-rule from the Ottoman Empire. However, the Russian Czar Alexander II's war to liberate Bulgaria from Turkish occupation, begun in April 1877, planted the first, identifiable seed of modern Great Power conflict.

The czar's troops, joined by Romanian units and many Bulgarian guerrilla reinforcements gathered on the march south from Russia, had slugged their way to the top of the Shipka Pass in central Bulgaria. There, despite being outnumbered more than four to one, they defeated a Turkish force in the summer of 1877. In December, the Russians occupied the Bulgarian capital of Sofia. By March, with Russian forces at Adrianople (a day's auto journey from Istanbul), Count Ignatiev, the Russian ambassador to Sultan Abdul Hamid II's court, drove to a dusty Thracian city where he dictated to the defeated Turks the Treaty of San Stefano: the first fuse of the "Balkan Powder Keg."[2]

From the Treaty of San Stefano rose the "Principality of Bulgaria," which, although nominally under Turkish suzerainty, was in fact a bold and independent re-creation of the medieval Bulgarian kingdom. It was to encompass not just present-day Bulgaria but all of geographical Macedonia besides—that is, the Yugoslav Republic of Macedonia, parts of Albania to the west, and a huge chunk of Greek land that virtually surrounded the city of Salonika, providing Bulgaria an outlet on the Aegean Sea.

As fantastic as it may seem, this Russian-midwifed "Greater Bulgaria" fairly closely complied with the Wilsonian standard of national self-determination, decades before Woodrow Wilson began thinking about the map of Europe. For example, the huge bulge of Greek Macedonia awarded to Bulgaria was, at the time, mainly inhabited by Bulgarians, albeit with significant Greek, Turkish, and Jewish minorities. In the rest of Macedonia, although it is now vehemently denied there by almost everyone, Bulgarian nationalism was far more advanced than the nationalisms of the Greeks and the Serbs. John Reed, with a vantage point much closer in time than my own, observed that "the vast majority of the population of Macedonia are Bulgars. . . . They were the first people, when Macedonia was a Turkish province, to found national schools there, and when the Bulgarian church revolted from the Greek Patriarch . . . the Turks allowed them to establish bishoprics, because it was so evident that Macedonia was Bulgarian." Reed went on to explain that the Serbs and Greeks built schools in Macedonia—and infiltrated guerrillas there—only as a reaction to rising Bulgarian nationalism in the region.

Although tolerable on ethnic grounds, the union of Macedonia with Bulgaria created a new and preeminently powerful pro-Russian state in the Balkans that Great Britain, Germany, and (es-

---

2. San Stefano, a town on the Sea of Marmara, on the western outskirts of Istanbul, is now called Yesilkoy.

pecially) Germany's ally, Austria-Hungary—with its own Balkan holdings to defend—could not accept. The Treaty of San Stefano had to be amended. Jolted by this reality, the German Chancellor Prince Otto von Bismarck-Schonhausen convened a meeting in June 1878 to solve this and other Great Power problems; it became known in history as the Congress of Berlin.

Bismarck, a prescient cynic, saw exactly where the Balkans were leading the Great Powers. "The whole of the Balkans," he cautioned, "is not worth the healthy bones of a single Pomeranian musketeer."

The German Chancellor meant such statements as a double warning: first to Great Britain, that it should make greater efforts to contain Russia in the Balkans, because Germany—at least while he was in charge—had no intention of getting involved there; second to Germany's principal ally, Austria-Hungary, that the Habsburg court should not count on German support if it were so foolish as to start a war with Russia over a godforsaken land like Bulgaria. Bismarck would turn out to be wrong about Bulgaria. World war started over a crisis in Serbia, but the roots of this crisis extended back to Bulgaria's claim on Macedonia.

Bismarck's genius, as well as his great flaw, was the same as that of another outstanding nineteenth-century politician of the German-speaking world, Prince Clemens Metternich. Both men were artificers, able to hold off the future by building a fragile present out of pieces of the past. Metternich's Congress of Vienna, which in 1814 attempted to restore the pre-Napoleonic order, was emblematic of this technique. So was Bismarck's 1878 Congress of Berlin.

Bismarck was helped by the British delegate to the Congress, Benjamin Disraeli, who had made it clear to the Russians that going forward with creating a Greater Bulgaria would mean war with Great Britain. Bismarck's Congress was thus able to dismember Greater Bulgaria before it ever came into existence. Most of Bulgaria's northern half, between the Danube River and the Balkan Mountain Range, did get its freedom, as promised by the Treaty of San Stefano.[3] But the southern half of Bulgaria, between the Balkan Mountains and the Greek border, became a Turkish

---

3. Though a section in the northeast by the Black Sea, in what is known as the Dobruja, was awarded to Romania.

province, with local autonomy exercised under a Bulgarian Orthodox Christian governor. Macedonia was abandoned to direct Turkish rule, as if the Russian army had never stormed through Bulgaria in the first place and the Treaty of San Stefano had never existed.

However, the Russians did not leave Berlin unhappy. Bismarck compensated them for the loss of Macedonia with new lands in Bessarabia, taken from the Romanians, and in northeastern Anatolia, taken from the Turks. Moreover, the Treaty of Berlin granted full independence to Russia's Slavic allies, the Serbs. And to compensate Habsburg Austria-Hungary for this new provocation, Bismarck arranged for Bosnia, the province next door to Serbia, with a Serbian population that also wanted independence, to be transferred from Ottoman rule to Habsburg rule—the immediate cause of World War I. Great Britain, for its part, received from the Turks the island of Cyprus.

Rather than finesse the problem of Macedonia, Bismarck's Congress of Berlin invented it: the "Eastern Question" that finally boiled over in 1914 was largely an early packaging of the "Macedonian Question," which in the 1990s still eats away, as only hatred can, at Turkey's former dominions in Europe.

Within Macedonia, the Treaty of Berlin sparked an orgy of violence overnight. The Sultan's forces, rather than having to evacuate the area in accordance with the Treaty of San Stefano, could now act without restraint. In Ochrid, the Turks raped young girls and then tortured them with boiling oil and hot irons. They stole cattle, broke into stores, and buried people in mud inside pigsties for not paying exorbitant taxes. In Skatsintsi, south of Skopje, Turkish soldiers gouged out the eyes and cut off the ears and nose of one Petur Lazov, keeping him in agony for several days before cutting off his head.

In addition, the advance of the Russian army through the newly liberated, northern half of Bulgaria had ignited an exodus of enraged ethnic Turks, who, along with Muslim Bosnians fleeing the Habsburg advance into Bosnia, now poured into Macedonia, where they all joined with the Turkish army in terrorizing the Orthodox Christian population.

Local Orthodox priests, led by the Bishop of Ochrid, Natanail, reacted immediately. They set up a collection network for every pistol and knife in Macedonia, to equip roving bands of *cheti—*

guerrillas who, in October 1878, began an uprising against the Turkish occupying force. Over the next half century, the Macedonian guerrilla movement was to undergo a series of radical permutations. Macedonia was to become the original seedground not only of modern warfare and political conflict, but of modern terrorism and clerical fanaticism as well.

The first Macedonian guerrilla *rising*, as it is known, collapsed under Turkish whips and rifle butts in the suffocation cells of Bitolj prison in 1881. But while the Turks were still strong enough to crush an open insurgency, they could not prevent new insurgents and propagandists from filtering into the area.

That same year, Serbia grudgingly recognized Austria-Hungary's occupation of Bosnia, sanctioned by the Treaty of Berlin three years earlier. In return, Serbia received the blessing of the Habsburg court to pour men and equipment into Macedonia, as a wedge against both the Ottoman Turks and the pro-Russian Bulgarians. In 1885, continued Russian pressure on Turkey resulted in the union of the southern half of Bulgaria with the already independent northern half. Fearful that the Bulgarians might yet achieve their aim of a Greater Bulgaria, the Turks discovered that they could benefit by helping the Serbs against the Bulgarians in Macedonia.

In 1897, this situation broke all bounds of complexity. An uprising on the island of Crete sparked a war between Greece and the Ottoman Turks. To prevent Bulgaria from joining forces with Greece, the Turkish Sultan Abdul Hamid suddenly reversed his policy in Macedonia. Rather than continuing to help the Serbs in order to contain the Bulgarians there, the Sultan now gave Bulgaria's King Ferdinand *carte blanche* to help the Serbs contain the Greeks.

Meanwhile, in the town of Shtip, southeast of Skopje, six conspirators, including Gotse Delchev, a twenty-one-year-old schoolteacher, had founded "the Macedonian Revolutionary Organization" on the ruins of the original *cheti* guerrilla revolt. To distinguish this indigenous movement from another Macedonian underground group set up in the Bulgarian capital of Sofia, the Macedonian Revolutionary Organization soon became the *Internal* Macedonian Revolutionary Organization, or IMRO. IMRO spread rapidly in the 1890s, raising its money through bank robberies and kidnappings for ransom.

By the turn of the century, Macedonia was a power vacuum of sectarian violence. The absence of a viable central government or a defining concept of nationhood permitted various outside powers—all soon to disappear as a result of what Macedonia would unleash—to play out their rivalries against the backdrop of a magnificent, mountainous landscape. In Macedonia, Christian militias fought Muslim militias, and fought each other as well; bearded and bandoliered terrorists like Gotse Delchev planted bombs at cafés, open-air theaters, and railway stations; splinter groups murdered members of rival groups, conducted secret tribunals, executed civilians accused of collaboration with the "enemy," and took hostages, such as the American Protestant missionary Ellen Stone. "Two hundred and forty-five bands were in the mountains. Serbian and Bulgarian *comitadjis*, Greek *andartes*, Albanians and Vlachs, . . . all waging a terrorist war," writes Leon Sciaky in *Farewell to Salonica: Portrait of an Era*. Macedonia, on the day the twentieth century began, was a place of atrocities and refugee camps that people in the West were already bored by and cynical about; it represented a situation that would never be solved and to which the newspaper correspondents were paying far too much attention.

But by 1990, except as memorialized in a handful of old black-and-white photographs buckling inside dusty frames in the local museums of Skopje and other towns, all this was long past and forgotten—in the West, that is.

Macedonia, the inspiration for the French word for "mixed salad" (*macedoine*), defines the principal illness of the Balkans: conflicting dreams of lost imperial glory. Each nation demands that its borders revert to where they were at the exact time when its own empire had reached its zenith of ancient medieval expansion. Because Philip of Macedon and his son, Alexander the Great, had established a great kingdom in Macedonia in the fourth century B.C., the Greeks believed Macedonia to be theirs. Because the Bulgarians at the end of the tenth century under King Samuel and again in the thirteenth century under King Ivan Assen II had extended the frontiers of Bulgaria all the way west to the Adriatic

Sea, the Bulgarians believed Macedonia to be theirs. Because King Stefan Dushan had overrun Macedonia in the fourteenth century and had made Skopje, in Dame Rebecca's words, "a great city, and there he had been crowned one Easter Sunday Emperor and Autocrat of the Serbs and Byzantines, the Bulgars and the Albanians," the Serbs believed Macedonia to be theirs. In the Balkans, history is not viewed as tracing a chronological progression, as it is in the West. Instead, history jumps around and moves in circles; and where history is perceived in such a way, myths take root. Evangelos Kofos, Greece's preeminent scholar on Macedonia, has observed that these "historical legacies . . . sustained nations in their uphill drive toward state-building, national unification and, possibly, the reincarnation of long extinct empires."

"How do you divide up the past?" the poet Todorovski asked me. It was nine in the morning in Skopje, and he was offering me a plum brandy along with Turkish—excuse me, "Macedonian"—coffee.

"You argue over what was in a dead man's mind," I answered.

Take Gotse Delchev, whose thick handlebar moustache, sweep of jet-black hair, and grave black eyes haunt the museums and government offices of Bulgaria and former Yugoslav Macedonia. On February 4, 1872, Delchev was born in a town in the Ottoman Empire, north of Salonika; it was called Kukush by its Bulgarian inhabitants. On July 2, 1913, during the Second Balkan War, the townspeople of Kukush fled before an invading Greek army, believing that they would return in a few days after Bulgarian forces drove the Greeks "into the sea." But the Greeks burnt Kukush to the ground and its Bulgarian inhabitants never came back. The Greek town of Kilkis, which rose from the ashes, is now dominated by fast-food restaurants. "Do not talk to me about Kilkis," a red-faced Bulgarian diplomat had told me in Athens in 1985, a time when experts were dismissing Bulgaria as a loyal Kremlin satellite. "You are from America and know nothing of these things. Know only that there is no Kilkis, only Kukush; and one day, after NATO and the Warsaw Pact are no more, there will be Kukush once again."

Delchev received his secondary education at a Bulgarian gymnasium in Salonika (now a completely Greek city). Afterward, he attended a military academy in the Bulgarian capital, Sofia. The rest of his short life he passed as a schoolteacher and a guerrilla-terrorist in "Macedonia," an area that today includes parts of north-central Greece, southwestern Bulgaria, and the southeastern former-Yugoslav Macedonia. He died on May 4, 1903, in a hail of Turkish gunfire: "cloak flung over his left shoulder, his white fez, wrapped in a bluish scarf, pulled down, and his gun slung across his left elbow," according to a nearby comrade, Mihail Chakov. The skirmish occurred in the Bulgarian village of Banitsa—now the Greek village of Karie. To Bulgarians, this changes nothing: "The land remembers every one, even the murdered unborn babies who have no names," cried MacDermott, Delchev's pro-Bulgarian hagiographer.

After his death, the story of exactly who (or rather, what) Gotse Delchev was grows even more complex. In 1923, Greek authorities agreed to transfer Delchev's remains from Greece to Bulgaria. In 1947, in an effort to placate Tito (before Yugoslavia left the Cominform), Stalin pressured the Bulgarian Communists to give up Delchev's bones. Today, Delchev's tomb is under a fir tree, marked by a block of stone adorned with wreaths, in the courtyard of the eighteenth-century Church of Sveti Spas in Skopje. To suppose that Bulgarians have ever forgiven Stalin or the Russians for this act is to have no understanding of the passions that rule the Balkans.

"Do not tell me about Macedonia," the Bulgarian diplomat in Athens had raged. "There is no Macedonia. It is western Bulgaria. The language is 80 percent Bulgarian. But you don't understand; you have no grasp of our problems. . . . Gotse Delchev was a Bulgarian. He was educated in Sofia. Bulgaria funded his guerrilla activities. He spoke a western Bulgarian dialect. How could he be something that does not exist?" The diplomat had handed me a copy of MacDermott's biography—which another Bulgarian official has already given me—as well as a massive, blue-jacketed book containing nearly a thousand pages of small print, entitled *Macedonia: Documents and Material* and published by the Bulgarian Academy of Sciences. I opened the book and read:

"A survey of some of the key issues examined in this volume of documents about Macedonia convincingly shows that the Slav population in this region is Bulgarian. . . . This is the historical truth, reflected in a multitude of documents. . . ."

* * *

"The Bulgarians are well-known falsifiers of documents around the world. What can you expect of Tartars?" explained Orde Ivanovski, a state historian for former-Yugoslav Macedonia, whom I interviewed immediately after drinking brandy with the poet Todorovski. It occurred to me that, because the world media establishment had ignored the Balkans for so long (the wire services didn't even maintain stringers in Macedonia until 1992), these people never had to learn, as the Israelis and Arabs did, how to talk in code, so as not to offend Western sensibilities with their racial hatred. In the Balkans, people spoke more honestly than in the Middle East, and therefore more brutally.

Dr. Ivanovski went on: "The Bulgarians, you know, have specialized teams who invent books about Gotse Delchev. They bribe foreign authors with cash and give them professorships in order to put their names on the covers of these books. I know that the Bulgarians are now buying up advertising space in India to propagandize about Macedonia and Gotse Delchev.

"How could Gotse Delchev be Bulgarian? He was born in Macedonia. He spoke Macedonian, not Bulgarian. How could he be a Bulgarian? He was a cosmopolitan; he wanted a democratic commonwealth of nations, sort of what is emerging now in Central Europe. . . .

"Chauvinism is poisoning the soul of humanity. We Macedonians hate no one and have no pretensions. We search in the darkness for a friend." Dr. Ivanovski grabbed my forearm, then handed me a biography of Delchev published by the former Yugoslav Republic. "You must help us," he pleaded.

If Delchev could rise from the grave, what would he call himself: a Macedonian or a Bulgarian?

Experts agree that the Slavic language he spoke—and the one spoken here now—is closer to Bulgarian than to Serbian. But on account of Tito's break with Stalin, the Yugoslav government, encouraged by the Serbs, promoted a separate ethnic and linguistic identity for Macedonia, in order to sever any emotional links between the local population and the one next door in Bulgaria, whose government obeyed Moscow's every order. When Delchev lived, nobody promoted such a separate Macedonian identity.

Only about one thing do the two sides agree: Delchev, certain facts be damned, was no terrorist. "He was an apostle," said Dr. Ivanovski.

Three months after Delchev's death, on August 2, 1903, Macedonia exploded. IMRO began its new rising on Ilinden, the feast day of St. Iliya (Elijah). Elijah, in Bulgarian Orthodox tradition, is a transmuted version of Perun, a pagan god of lightning and stormy heavens, to whom the pre-Christian Slavs sacrificed bulls and human beings. Church bells rang, IMRO operatives cut the Turkish telegraph wires and burnt tax registers, and peasants sold bulls for sacrifice in order to buy guns. In the town of Krushovo, 4,000 feet up in the mountains of western Macedonia, IMRO proclaimed the "Krushovo Republic." It lasted ten days, until 2,000 Turkish troops, supported by artillery, overwhelmed 1,200 guerrillas in Krushovo; forty of the guerrillas, rather than surrendering, shot themselves in the mouth after kissing each other good-bye. The Turks reportedly raped 150 women and girls in Krushovo. Wild dogs and pigs devoured the naked corpses.

Throughout Macedonia it was the same. The two-month uprising cost the lives of 4,694 civilians and 994 IMRO guerrillas. Estimates put the total number of women and girls raped by the Turks at over 3,000.[4] In northwestern Macedonia, fifty Turkish soldiers raped a young girl before finally killing her. Turkish soldiers cut off another girl's hand in order to take her bracelets. A correspondent for the London *Daily News* at the scene, A. G. Hales, wrote in the October 21, 1903, edition: "I will try and tell this story coldly, calmly, dispassionately . . . one must tone the horrors down, for in their nakedness they are unprintable. . . ." Public protests ensued against the Turkish Sultanate throughout Great Britain and the West. Pressure from British Prime Minister Arthur James Balfour, Russian Czar Nicholas II, and Habsburg Emperor Franz Joseph resulted in the entrance of an international peacekeeping force into Macedonia in 1904.

Not by accident, the Hurriyet ("Young Turk" Revolution), which toppled the Ottoman Sultanate, originated in the Mace-

4. These statistics, based on Bulgarian and Macedonian sources of the day, were corroborated by on-scene observers of the British Relief Fund.

donian port of Salonika, where a young Turkish major, Enver (soon to be called Enver Pasha), stood on the balcony of the Olympos Palace Hotel on July 23, 1908, and acknowledged the cheers of a multiethnic crowd acclaiming "Liberty, Equality, Fraternity, Justice."

Mustapha Kemal "Ataturk," the future father of modern Turkey, was also a Macedonian, born in 1881 in Salonika.[5] Standing right behind Enver Pasha on the balcony that historic day, Kemal immediately experienced doubts about the revolution. Apart from forcing Sultan Abdul Hamid to accept a liberal constitution, the "Young Turk" officers led by Enver Pasha had no well-defined program. As with Mikhail Gorbachev and his reformist allies in the Soviet Union, Enver Pasha and the other Young Turks were determined to conserve—albeit in a looser, more liberal form— the Empire, which they perceived as being threatened primarily by a reactionary Sultanate and its near-total resistance to change. But as Kemal suspected, Enver Pasha and the Young Turks underestimated the forces of the long-repressed nationalities in the Balkans. These Orthodox Christian people wanted more than just constitutional safeguards within a Muslim-run confederation. "The Revolution," writes Lord Kinross, Kemal Ataturk's biographer, "far from arresting the disintegration of the Empire, as the Young Turks had hoped, at once accelerated it," in the Middle East as well as in the Balkans.

In October 1908, Bulgaria's King Ferdinand proclaimed his country's complete independence, which for a long time had been de facto but not de jure. That same week, the island of Crete (still part of Turkey) voted for union with Greece, and the Austrian Habsburgs annexed the Turkish province of Bosnia-Hercegovina, which they had been administering since the conclusion of the Congress of Berlin.

Put another way, Bulgarian-financed guerrillas in Macedonia had triggered a revolution among young Turkish officers stationed there, which then fanned throughout the Ottoman Empire; this development, in turn, encouraged Austria-Hungary to annex Bosnia, inflicting on its Serbian population a tyranny so great that a Bosnian Serb would later assassinate the Habsburg Archduke and ignite World War I.

---

5. Ataturk is Turkish for "Father Turk."

The Ottoman Empire's disintegration enraged fundamentalist Muslims within Turkey proper. In April 1909, army units revolted; joined by masses of theological students and turbaned clerics shouting "we want *Sharia* [Islamic law]," they demanded the restoration of the Sultan's absolute power. The Young Turks violently crushed this counterrevolution, forcing Sultan Abdul Hamid into exile in Salonika. When the Sultan learned that he was being dispatched to the Macedonian city where the revolution against him had originated, he fell unconscious into the arms of a eunuch.

The increasingly authoritarian nature of the Young Turk regime culminated with their 1915 mass murder of an estimated 1.5 million Armenians, the century's first holocaust. This government-orchestrated genocidal campaign was perpetrated because the Armenians, unlike their fellow Eastern Christians in the Balkan peninsula, demographically threatened the Muslim Turks in their historic heartland, central Anatolia. The Empire—any empire—a young and skeptical Kemal Ataturk foresaw wisely, had no future in this new age.

The development of the Young Turks into more brutal and efficient killers than the Sultan had been, together with the unwillingness of the other Great Powers to interfere, prompted Bulgaria, Serbia, and Greece to accomplish what no one had thought possible: they submerged their differences and formed an alliance.

During the years 1909 through 1912, all three of these states built up their armies. In October 1912, they declared war on the Ottoman Empire. Men and horses dragging artillery maneuvered under heavy rains through ankle-deep mud. The allies' principal goal was to liberate Macedonia.

The First Balkan War ended in December 1912 with the dissolution of Turkey in Europe. In Macedonia, the Serbian army occupied Skopje, Stefan Dushan's ancient capital, and the Greek army occupied Salonika. Meanwhile, although its army had overrun Turkish Thrace up to the gates of Istanbul and had gained a foothold on the Aegean Sea, Bulgaria found itself virtually locked out of the very region that for decades—through its diplomats, its guerrilla-terrorists, and its linguistic influence—it had often seemed on the brink of annexing.

John Reed described how, in the aftermath of the First Balkan

War, the Serbs and the Greeks tried to wipe out Bulgarian influence in Macedonia:

> A thousand Greek and Serbian publicists began to fill the world with their shouting about the essentially Greek or Serbian character of the populations of their different spheres. The Serbs gave the unhappy Macedonians twenty-four hours to renounce their nationality and proclaim themselves Serbs, and the Greeks did the same. Refusal meant murder or expulsion. Greek and Serbian colonists were poured into the occupied country. . . . Bulgarian school-teachers were shot . . . Bulgarian priests given the choice of death or conversion. . . . The Greek newspapers began to talk about a Macedonia peopled entirely with Greeks—and they explained the fact that no one spoke Greek, by calling the people "Bulgarophone" Greeks. . . . The Greek army entered villages where no one spoke their language. "What do you mean by speaking Bulgarian?" cried the officers.

Meanwhile, in Bulgaria, the government and the people smoldered. At 1 A.M. on June 30, 1913, without any warning or declaration of war, the Bulgarian army crossed the Bregalnitsa, a Vardar tributary, and attacked the Serbian forces stationed on the other side. The Second Balkan War had begun.

The battle lasted several days. The Serbs recovered the advantage and were soon helped by Greek reinforcements. Then the Romanians joined the Serb-Greek alliance and invaded Bulgaria from the north, in a campaign that saw more men die of cholera than of bullet wounds. At the August peace conference in the Romanian capital of Bucharest, Bulgaria lost everything: its outlet on the Aegean Sea, its gains in Thrace from the First Balkan War, and every square inch of Macedonia.

This disaster was to have grave consequences for world history.

When John Reed visited Sofia in the summer of 1915, the city provided a foretaste of what Beirut, Damascus, and Amman would one day be like: "Half the population of Sofia was composed of Macedonian refugees, and you could visit a camp in the outskirts of the city where sixteen thousand of them lived under tents, at great expense and annoyance to the government. . . . Every day the press was full of bitter tales brought by the refugees, and expressions of hatred against the Serbians. . . ."

In the fall of 1915, Bulgaria entered World War I on the side of the Central Powers (Germany and Austria-Hungary) in order to regain Macedonian territory from Serbia, which had aligned itself with the Triple Entente (czarist Russia, Great Britain, and France). While the Habsburg army advanced through Serbia from the north, Bulgarian troops rolled up Macedonia from the east. Rather than surrendering, the Serbian army staged a winter withdrawal, accompanied by a large civilian population, into the snowy wastes of the Albanian mountains. Without vehicles or even mules, the Serb soldiers could take no additional food supplies and had to carry their wounded on stretchers. It was one of history's most harrowing winter retreats, ranking with those of Napoleon's soldiers from Russia the century before and of Xenophon's Greek troops from Mesopotamia in 401 B.C. into the mountains of Anatolia.

French and Italian ships met the 125,000-strong remnant of the Serbian army on Albania's Adriatic coast and transported the troops to the Greek island of Corfu, where they recovered and reprovisioned. From 1916 until the armistice in 1918, trench warfare raged across the length and breadth of Macedonia, pitting the French, the Greeks, and a reorganized Serbian army, as well as British Commonwealth troops withdrawn from Gallipoli, against the Habsburg and Bulgarian armies. For the Bulgarians, World War I ended exactly as had the Second Balkan War: their nation lost all of Macedonia to the Serbs and the Greeks.

Macedonia is full of historical lessons, if only history were better learned or remembered. Just as the disintegration of the Soviet Empire under Gorbachev in the twentieth century's last decade mirrors the collapse of the Ottoman Empire under Enver Pasha in the twentieth century's first decade, the political tragedy of the Arab world in the second half of the twentieth century mirrors that of Bulgaria during the first half.

After starting and losing two wars over Macedonia, Bulgaria's King Ferdinand abdicated in 1919. For the next twenty years, until the outbreak of World War II, his son, King Boris III, presided over a political system in Sofia that was riven by coup attempts and other violent conspiracies connected to the loss of what Bulgarians considered their historic homeland. IMRO, radicalized by the defeats of 1913 and 1918, became a terrorist state within a state, and, helped by its skull-and-crossbones insignia, became

synonymous in the outside world with hate and violent nihilism.
Opium profits financed the purchase of IMRO's weaponry. The
standard fee for an IMRO assassination was twenty dollars, so
Bulgarian politicians walked around with trains of bodyguards.
This caused the *New York Times* journalist C. L. Sulzberger to
remark: "For some strange reason, the Bulgars are Europe's finest
murderers."

The terrorists, aided by Orthodox clergy, came from the Macedonian refugee population of Sofia's slums. By the 1930s, Macedonian terrorists were hiring themselves out to radical groups
throughout Europe—in particular, to the Croatian Ustashe,
whose chief paymaster was the fascist dictator of Italy, Benito
Mussolini. A Bulgarian Macedonian nicknamed "Vlado the
Chauffeur" assassinated King Alexander of Yugoslavia—the
crime that initiated Dame Rebecca's passion for that country.

World War II provided another sickening replay of World War
I and the Second Balkan War. Again, as in World War I, Bulgaria
joined a German-led alliance against a Serb-dominated Yugoslavia
in order to regain Macedonia. Again, while forces of a German-
speaking power occupied Serbia from the north, Bulgarian troops
invaded and occupied Macedonia from the east. And again, Serb
and Greek resistance forces, aided by the British, drove the Bulgarians back to the hated borders established in August 1913 at
the conclusion of the Second Balkan War. At that point, Communist totalitarianism stopped history until the century's final decade. Nothing of all this has yet been resolved.

In World War II, Bulgarian occupation troops in Macedonia
worked alongside the Nazis. Enforced "Bulgarization" of the population merely repeated the savagery practiced by the Serb and
Greek occupation troops in 1913. While King Boris's regime
helped save the Jews residing in Bulgaria proper, the Bulgarians
in Macedonia collaborated with the Nazis in rounding up Jews
for transport to death camps. Such behavior erased the pro-
Bulgarian sympathies that had existed for decades among non-
Serbs and non-Greeks in Macedonia. This helped foster a new
irredentism. Now, in addition to Bulgarian, Greek, and Serbian
claims on Macedonia, there was a home-grown "Macedonianism"
that demanded territory from Bulgaria and Greece.

"Two thirds of Macedonia is under foreign occupation and still to be liberated," explained another local poet, Ante Popovski, whom I met on the same brandy-filled morning. He chain-smoked and scribbled constantly in a notebook. His face was like a clenched fist. "The rest of Europe in 1989 achieved their national rights, but not yet the Macedonians in Greece and Bulgaria, who are under occupation."

"Parts of our nation are enjoying no human rights—a partition that is the result of imperialist *peace* treaties," said Dr. Ivanovski, the historian, referring to the "unsatisfactory" conclusions of the Second Balkan War, World War I, and World War II. By his lights, even more land should have been taken away from Bulgaria, with northern Greece also handed over to the Republic of Macedonia.

Maps were repeatedly thrust on me that day, depicting a leaf-shaped bulge of territory much larger than the present-day Republic of Macedonia. Inside the thick black border lines of this ideal Macedonian state were one-third of mainland Greece; the Greek island of Thasos, called "Aegean Macedonia"; a chunk of southwestern Bulgaria, called "Pirin Macedonia" after the Pirin Mountains there; a slice of "Macedonian" land in Albania; and former-Yugoslav Macedonia, the only "liberated" part of the country, called "Vardar Macedonia" after the Vardar River, which runs through Skopje.

A rediscovered "Macedonian" language was being promoted through volumes of books filled with poetry and history. Claims that Istanbul might even be part of Macedonia, as well as phantasmic descriptions of landscapes, exploded like storms on the sun in such poems as "Silence" by Bogomil Guzel:

> *As evening soots the gradual snow*
> *Bird and beast are silent under the heavy firs . . .*
> *Space hides in its curvature*
> *The unsuspected leap of a mountain lion*
> *And tomorrow when the sun appears with his*
> *Angry halo over an earth thawed and gurgling*
> *The air, bloodied by spurs, will scream . . .*
> *What bolt-like prayer, what suffering or wine . . .*

And on the walls near the Greek Consulate in Skopje, I noticed the graffiti: "Solun is ours!"

Solun is the Macedonian word for Salonika, Greece's second largest city. Such demonstrations of irredentism were to unleash a wave of hostility in Greece—so much so that, even when the new Macedonian state that declared its independence from Yugoslavia officially renounced all claims to Greek territory, it still wasn't enough for the Greeks, who feared that the very word *Macedonia* on the lips of these Slavs was a sign of future irredentism against Greece. When Greece demanded that Macedonia change its name in order to receive official recognition from Greece, the rest of the world laughed. The heart of the Greek argument, however, was better explained in the articles written by the scholar Kofos than it ever was by the Greek government through the media. Kofos writes that Macedonianism was an invention of Tito to serve as a cultural buttress against Bulgaria, which coveted the area. According to Kofos, this part of former Yugoslavia is actually southern Serbia. True, perhaps; but rightly or wrongly, these Slavs now consider themselves Macedonians, not Serbs, and both the Greeks and the Serbs must come to terms with that fact.

The upshot of this mess is that the Balkans have, in the 1990s, reverted to the same system of alliances that existed in 1913, at the time of the Second Balkan War: Greece, Serbia, and Romania versus Bulgaria and the Slavs of Macedonia.[6]

"I am born in Shtip, during the Turkish slavery. My father was a pupil of Gotse Delchev. I am a real Macedonian. I know what I am. I am a sparrow, not a Bulgarian, not an eagle of Serbia."

Metropolitan Mikhail raised his hand in the way of the Pantocrator ("Christ the Almighty"), whose stern image beautifies the dome of many an Orthodox church. He had ironed-back locks of white hair running down his neck. Steam appeared to emanate from his mouth as he spoke to me.

"We have some of Alexander in our blood, it is true. We have been crucified, like Jesus, on the cross of Balkan politics. . . . That is Macedonian coffee you are drinking, not Turkish coffee or Greek coffee. . . .

"Macedonia, not Serbia, is the true birthplace of the Renaissance. What is Grachanitsa compared to Ochrid? How can Giotto compare to our artists? Tell me, how can Giotto compare?"

---

6. Romania, because it shares both water resources and an important western border with Serbia, cannot afford to upset Belgrade, no matter who is in power there.

Metropolitan Mikhail then told me about his church. "You must have patience, young man. It is a long story."

I will shorten it. The two ninth-century apostles who brought Christianity to the Slavs, Cyril and Methodius, were born in Salonika. This makes them Greek, Bulgarian, or Macedonian, depending on your point of view. Metropolitan Mikhail has no doubt about what they were. Moreover, two disciples of Cyril and Methodius, Sveti ("Saint") Kliment and Sveti Naum, taught at Ochrid, in southwestern Macedonia, where it is highly likely that the Cyrillic alphabet—invented by Cyril and Methodius through their Slavic translation of the Greek Bible—was refined and first put into daily use.

Ochrid is also where the Macedonians under King Samuel founded an independent Orthodox Patriarchate at around the end of the tenth century. When the fourteenth-century Serbian leader, Stefan Dushan, conquered Macedonia, he sanctioned the independence of this Macedonian Patriarchate. "But in 1767, the Turks abolished our Patriarchate at Ochrid because we were organizing an uprising against the Sultan. Only in 1967 was an independent Macedonian Orthodox Church reestablished. Why will the Serbs, the Greeks, and the Bulgarians not recognize our church? Macedonia is where Slavic Christianity was born. We are better Christians than they. Tell me why we are friendless?"

Metropolitan Mikhail would not let me go. He needed to tell me about King Samuel, "a Macedonian feudal lord," who in A.D. 976 broke out of his stronghold at Ochrid to create an empire stretching from the Adriatic Sea in the west to the gates of Constantinople in the east.

"But Samuel also ruled in the name of Bulgaria," I countered. Michael Psellus, an advisor to several Byzantine emperors, whose *Chronographia* is the principal sourcebook of the period, referred to Samuel as a "Bulgarian." Moreover, the Byzantine Emperor Basil II, on account of vanquishing Samuel in 1014, became known as Basil Bulgaroctonos, "Basil the Bulgar Slayer."

"No, no, young man," Metropolitan Mikhail bellowed. His eyes looked heavenward. "You do not understand. The material is so immense, so vast, you will need years of study to comprehend our problem."

Among the books he gave me before I left his office in Skopje was a volume of poetry by Blazhe Koneski, who defines the search for identity and love in Macedonia as the "move of a hand thirsting towards the realm of the stars."

Zlatko Blajer, the editor-in-chief of *Vecher* (*Evening*), Skopje's biggest daily newspaper, was one of twenty-seven Jews remaining in the city from a pre–World War II population of 3,795. He sat against a mirror in a Skopje restaurant, where I met him at the end of my day of intense meetings and multiple glasses of coffee and alcohol. I stared at his reflection while he talked. Blajer's voice had the immaterial quality of a screened-off witness. He was the only one I meet in Skopje who had no book of history or poetry to give me.

"This is the most volatile area of the Balkans. We are a weak, new nation surrounded by old enemies. Several nations could come to war here as they did at the beginning of the century. For decades, the Yugoslav federation protected us. As Yugoslavia fell apart, Macedonia again became a power vacuum.

"And don't forget that we are a quiet Kossovo: twenty-three percent of Macedonia's population is actually Albanian, and their birth rate is much higher than ours. We face the same fate as the Serbs in their historical homeland.

"At the end of the twentieth century, we are trying to separate inseparable strands, to divide this one from that one, because this one may be Macedonian and that one may be Bulgarian. . . . Here the men sit back like the old men of Crete, talking about nationalism and hate while the women do all the work."

The more obscure and unfathomable the hatred, and the smaller the national groups involved, the longer and more complex the story seemed to grow. I could not help but wonder, what would Lebanon offer the student of history a hundred years from now?

CHAPTER FOUR

The White City and Its Prophet

I arrived in Belgrade by bus from Skopje and checked into the Hotel Moskva. The next morning, I performed my regular Belgrade ritual, designed to impress upon me where, historically and geographically, I was. This was always necessary, since, on account of an accident of inner-city development, foreign correspondents in the frozen decades following World War II might have had no idea where they were in Belgrade.

Although the Moskva, in downtown Belgrade, was built in 1906 and had all the endearing qualities of a grand hotel gone to seed—obliging waiters, lumpy mattresses, noisy central heating—until World War II had spread to Yugoslavia, the Srbski Kralj ("Serbian King"), not the Moskva, was *the* hotel in Belgrade. Dame Rebecca and her husband had stayed at the Srbski Kralj. So did *New York Times* correspondent C. L. Sulzberger; the author and newspaperman Robert St. John; and others who had come to chronicle the buildup to war.

From Sulzberger's description in *A Long Row of Candles*, the Srbski Kralj appeared to differ little from the Moskva. It "was a large, old-fashioned" building, "which made up with good food and affable service for its somewhat outmoded physical comforts." But what enabled the Srbski Kralj to exert its crucial effect on writers was its location: across the street from the vast park that ornaments the Kalimegdan fortress, built on a wooded headland at the confluence of the Danube and Sava rivers, where in the third century B.C. the Celts established the first human settlement in the vicinity and thus determined where the history of Belgrade and much of Serbia was to be written. Dame Rebecca noted that, from her dressing table at the Srbski Kralj, she had an eye-catching view of the Danube and Sava floodplain.

The nearby Kalimegdan fortress was built upon by Romans, Byzantines, medieval Serbs, Ottoman Turks, Habsburg Austrians (during a brief occupation), and Ottoman Turks again. Outside its retaining walls spread Beograd, the "White City," after which Belgrade was named. For eighteenth- and nineteenth-century travelers, this headland above the two rivers was, literally, the border between West and East: where the Habsburg Empire ended and the Turkish Empire began. Indeed, walking over the long, flat sweeps of green reaching to the two rivers, I have always felt the exciting sensation of stepping into a frontier region, of being at the edge of something.

In the spring of 1915, when John Reed visited Belgrade, the Kalimegdan formed the front-line defense of the Serbian army, with Austro-Hungarian troops and artillery pitched on the opposite banks of the Danube and Sava. These troops had occupied Belgrade for two weeks during the previous December before being driven back across the water; and they were to come back again, in October 1915, and stay for three years until finally defeated. Reed's visit came between the two Austro-Hungarian occupations, when the city lay devastated by typhus:

> We visited the ancient Turkish citadel which crowns the abrupt headland towering over the junction of the Sava and the Danube. Here, where the Serbian guns had been placed, the Austrian fire had fallen heaviest; hardly a building but had been literally wrecked. Roads and open spaces were pitted with craters torn by

big shells . . . we crawled on our bellies to the edge of the cliff overlooking the river.

"Don't show yourselves," cautioned the captain who had us in charge. "Every time the Swabos see anything moving here, they drop us a shell."

From the edge there was a magnificent view of the muddy Danube . . . and the wide plains of Hungary. . . .

The Srbski Kralj survived that war but not the next. Its rooms were packed with journalists when at dawn on April 6, 1941, Palm Sunday, 234 Nazi bombers began their aerial assault on Belgrade. The hotel was one of nearly 700 buildings destroyed. "I kept thinking the plane was aiming not just at the roof, but at me personally. . . . At least ten planes must have come down at the Srbski Kralj," Robert St. John recollected.

Thus I strolled down Pariska Street to the Kalimegdan Park, near where the Srbski Kralj used to be. By the park I gazed at Byzantine ramparts, the few remaining Turkish buildings, the Orthodox Cathedral, and the reconstructed, neobaroque monuments. From here—that is, from the Srbski Kralj—the city was not only handsome but comprehensible. From the Moskva it was not.

"We went through an area which is common to all parks," writes Dame Rebecca, "[where] children play among lilac bushes and little ponds and the busts of the departed nearly great. . . . Then there is a finely laid-out flower garden, with a tremendous and very beautiful statue to the French who died in Yugoslavia during the Great War, by Mestrovitch, showing a figure bathing in a sea of courage. Many people might like it taken away and replaced by a gentler marble."

The statue by Ivan Mestrovich was still there by the entrance to the Kalimegdan Park. It had survived the Palm Sunday bombing and World War II. Nor was it ever taken away and replaced by a "gentler marble." There was still the "finely laid-out" flower garden and the lilac trees where the children of Belgrade still came to play. Standing by the statue, I felt the closeness of time like a tight lump in my throat, as if the long and calcifying decades of Communism could be blotted out.

But they couldn't be, I knew. And so I walked back in the

direction of the Moskva to find out what was about to happen next in Yugoslavia.

Throughout the 1980s, I had been coming as a journalist to Yugoslavia. It was a lonely task because few were interested in what was going on in the place, or where it might be headed. On every trip to Belgrade, I paid a visit to the apartment of Milovan Djilas. After the first visits, our conversations became eerie affairs, because I realized that Djilas was always right. He was able to predict the future. His technique was a simple one for an East European, but a difficult one for an American: he seemed to ignore the daily newspapers and think purely historically. The present for him was merely a stage of the past moving quickly into the future. What appeared inconceivable to conventional analysts was always the natural outcome to him.

Djilas was already seventy when I first met him in 1981. He had been one of Tito's top wartime lieutenants in the guerrilla struggle against the Nazis. Later, he became vice-president of post–World War II Yugoslavia, and was considered to be Tito's heir apparent. Indeed, Djilas had conducted the difficult, one-on-one negotiations with Stalin that set the stage for Yugoslavia's break with Soviet Communism in 1949. Djilas's recollections of those vodka-filled midnight meetings, *Conversations with Stalin*, provided a uniquely personal glimpse of one of history's great criminals. In the early 1950s, Djilas started having grave doubts about Titoism. Djilas's demands for a democratization of the system—*perestroika* three decades before its time—led to his expulsion from the Yugoslav Communist party and to his imprisonment for nine years. In his prison cell, Djilas wrote *The New Class* and other powerful critiques of Communism that became dissident classics, as well as two novels, two autobiographical works, and several volumes of short stories. From the moment he got out of prison in the 1960s, he lived in anonymity and official disgrace. Djilas was the greatest dissident intellectual in the history of communist Eastern Europe: the grand old man of dissent before the world had ever heard of Lech Walesa. As his wizened face receded into the shadows cast by the afternoon sun in his somber, book-lined study, the past would always come into focus and the broad outlines of the future would emerge as well.

In 1981, following the start of the Albanian *intifada* in Kossovo, which nobody in the outside world had the slightest interest in, Djilas had told me that "our system was built only for Tito to manage. Now that Tito is gone and our economic situation becomes critical, there will be a natural tendency for greater centralization of power. But this centralization will not succeed because it will run up against ethnic-political power bases in the republics. This is not classical nationalism but a more dangerous, bureaucratic nationalism built on economic self-interest. This is how the Yugoslav system will begin to collapse."

By 1982, this was starting to come true, although again, few outside cared. In November of that year, the world's attention was taken up with the new leader in the Soviet Union, Yuri Andropov, who was said to collect modern Hungarian furniture—whatever that was—and who therefore might prove to be a great reformer. Djilas was skeptical: "Andropov is sixty-eight, the same age as Charles de Gaulle when he returned to power. But you will see that Andropov is no de Gaulle: he has no new ideas. Andropov has possibilities only as a man of transition, making the way for a real reformer to come afterwards."

By 1985, that reformer had emerged: Gorbachev. But Djilas was, by then, no longer impressed. "You will see that Gorbachev is also a figure of transition. He will make important reforms and introduce some degree of a market economy, but then the real crisis in the system will become apparent and the alienation in Eastern Europe will get much worse."

"What about Yugoslavia?" I asked. He smiled viciously: "Like Lebanon. Wait and see."

In early 1989, Europe, if not America, was finally beginning to worry about Yugoslavia, and particularly about the new hardliner in Serbia, Slobodan Milosevic. But the worry was only slight. This was still several months before the first East German refugees began streaming into Hungary on their way to the West, which eventually ignited a chain of events resulting in the collapse of Communist regimes across Eastern Europe. Eastern Europe was then enjoying its final months of anonymity in the world media.

But Djilas's mind was already in the 1990s: "Milosevic's authoritarianism in Serbia is provoking real separation. Remember what Hegel said, that history repeats itself as tragedy and farce.

What I mean to say is that when Yugoslavia disintegrates this time around, the outside world will not intervene as it did in 1914. . . . Yugoslavia is the laboratory of all Communism. Its disintegration will foretell the disintegration in the Soviet Union. We are farther along than the Soviets."

A thought then occurred to me: if Yugoslavia was the laboratory of Communism, then Communism would breathe its last dying breath here in Belgrade. And to judge by what Milosevic was turning into by early 1989, Communism would exit the world stage revealed for what it truly was: fascism, without fascism's ability to make the trains run on time.

It was now the last month of the decade. Eleven months had passed since I had last seen Djilas: eleven months during which the world had changed. In December 1989, Slovenia and Croatia were experiencing peaceful transitions to democratic rule, and even here in Serbia—so Byzantine, so Orthodox, so Eastern—the breath of liberalization was unmistakable. All of Djilas's books, banned for decades in his homeland, were being published in his native tongue of Serbo-Croatian for the first time. There was even speculation that Milosevic was "yesterday's man" and that he would soon fall from power. Djilas was not so optimistic. He laughed that vicious laugh of his and told me: "Milosevic still has possibilities. . . . The liberalization you see has a bad cause. It is the consequence of national competition between Serbia and the other republics. Eventually Yugoslavia might be like the British Commonwealth, a loose federation of trading nations. But first, I am afraid, there will be national wars and rebellions. There is such strong hate here."

PART II

Romania: Latin Passion Play

. . . the Devil in Rumania leads a strenuous and tireless life.
—E.O. HOPPE, In Gipsy Camp and Royal Palace

CHAPTER FIVE

Athenee Palace, Bucharest

The night clerk at the Athenee Palace Hotel in Bucharest seemed a clean-cut youth, with a cheery smile and an altogether wholesome look in his eyes. He changed my money at five times the legal rate, handing me the stacks of Romanian *lei* right at the reception desk. He then offered me a woman. When I said no, he looked confused, saying that whatever I fancied he could easily procure.

Beyond the reception desk was a colonnade of marble pillars with gilded Corinthian capitals, like the inside of a cathedral. Sitting on a couch behind one of the pillars was an attractively slender woman with dark enamel skin, black hair cut short like a boy's, and olive-pit eyes highlighted by purple mascara that matched her mini-dress.

"Would you like to buy my bottle of champagne?" she called out from the couch, holding up the bottle.

"No, thanks," I replied.

"Come." She got up off the couch and began walking toward me. "Take me to your room and we'll finish the whole bottle together."

"No, thanks."

"How can you say no? I come with the champagne. For the same price."

Later, in the hotel's basement discotheque, anther woman approached me—a greenish-blonde with a mealy face. She stood over my table and dropped a crumpled piece of paper on my plate. I opened it and read: "My name is Claudia Cardinale. My telephone number is 708254."

I shook my head "no." She picked up the piece of paper and went over to another man.

I bought two bottles of mineral water and headed back to my room. As I entered the elevator, the dark-haired woman with the champagne cornered me: "Come on, take me up to your room."

"Leave me alone, I'm with my wife," I said with sudden inspiration. "See, I've got two bottles of water, one for me and one for her."

"I don't believe you," she said, completely sure of herself. "I saw you check in tonight. You're alone, I think you don't like women."

Beneath the ice mask of Communism and violent revolution, Romania lived on, indestructible, unchanged.

John Reed had settled in at the Athenee Palace in 1915, when the hotel was only a year old. "Ten thousand public women parade," he observed, "for your true Bucharestian boasts that his city supports more prostitutes in proportion than any other four cities in the world combined."

"These were Western women," wrote Goldie Horowitz in 1941, "but about them hung the flavor of the harem."

"Bucharest," observed *New York Times* correspondent C. L. Sulzberger at the start of World War II, "was delightfully depraved.... There was small opportunity for the ample population of paid prostitutes because of enthusiastic rivalry among amateurs of all classes, from princesses down.

"Graft was the great leaven," he went on. "The very first official

I met pulled open a drawer in his desk, exposing packets of foreign money, and sought to bribe me," promising a black market rate "fifteen percent more" than "what the Athenee Palace porter gave me."

Hannah Pakula, the biographer of Romania's Queen Marie, quotes a member of the old aristocracy as saying that no word exists in the Romanian language for self-control: "the term and idea being equally untranslatable and alien to a Roumanian mind."

Nicholas II, the last Czar of Russia and Queen Marie's first cousin, had sneered: "Rumania: it's not a country, it's a profession."

Prostitution, black marketeering, and informing on one's neighbors and friends all had such a deep-rooted tradition in Romania that there was a charming naturalness and innocence about it. First you were shocked. Then, after a few weeks in Romania, you gave in to the environment. A perverse side of your nature allowed you to fall in love with the country and people. You even thought that, perhaps, the Romanians possessed a peculiar wisdom about life and survival that the rest of the world lacked. And thus you would begin to understand. . . .

Such a country tantalizes writers and foreign correspondents. In the first years of World War II, "there were seldom less than fifty correspondents housed in the Athenee Palace at any one time," according to Robert St. John, the Associated Press bureau chief in Bucharest. The Athenee Palace was the only hotel in war-affected Europe where Nazi and Allied officials slept under the same roof, where American and British journalists could engage uniformed SS officers over drinks. But it was the Romanians themselves who provided the main attraction, enthusiastically accepting the new fascist order while thoroughly corrupting it in a way that softened its effects. The Nazis, observed Goldie Horowitz, "were deliciously disquieted by the liquid-eyed daughters of princely houses who made them go to bed with them before they had a chance to check up on their Aryan grandmothers."

Horowitz was a naturalized American, born into a family of wealthy Berlin Jews. Under the pen name of R. G. Waldeck, Horowitz, a dashing and attractive-looking journalist, wrote a gossipy memoir of sexual intrigue inside the hotel, entitled *Athenee Palace Bucharest*. Robert St. John, in his own account of moral depravity in Bucharest, *Foreign Correspondent*, writes that "one of the oddest sights after the Germans appropriated the Athenee Palace dining room . . . was to see Goldie Horowitz being entertained at luncheon or dinner by high-ranking Nazi officers—some of whom would be executed as war criminals."

Horowitz's book, nearly fifty years out of print, offers an exquisitely detailed closeup of Romanian manners. Olivia Manning, the young wife of a British Council lecturer who also passed much of her time at the Athenee Palace, painted a broader picture of those manners in *The Balkan Trilogy*, a paperback bestseller that became a television mini-series. And there were others. Romania's descent into fascism in 1939–1941, seen from the lobby and rooms of the Athenee Palace, spawned an entire genre of novels and journalists' memoirs that provide a rich historical background for Romania's transition to a different sort of fascism in the 1970s and 1980s. With the historical process underway again in Romania in the 1990s, these books took on an even greater relevance, explaining much that to most outside observers must have seemed unexplainable.

The Athenee Palace lines the width of a vast square, bordered by the royal palace on one side and a Paris Opera–style concert hall, with its green lawn and gladioli, on the other. In Reed's day, the hotel had a "dazzling, neo-French facade" with turrets and caryatids. In 1938, prior to Horowitz's and Manning's arrival, the turrets and caryatids were removed, and a modernistic chrome and white stone fronting appeared. When I arrived, in the spring of 1990, this white facade was scarred with bullet holes from the revolution of the previous December.

Inside the hotel were more changes. Beyond the colonnade of Corinthian pillars, the Communist 1950s began, with a gloomy, serpentine staircase and purple wall-to-wall carpeting. The Romanian intelligence service, the Securitatae, assisted by the KGB, had turned the Athenee Palace into an intelligence-gathering factory. The Securitatae tapped the telephones, installed microphones under the restaurant and bar tables, and in all the rooms. The hotel manager was a Securitatae colonel, and all of the 300 employees were Securitatae agents, down to the charwomen who photographed every piece of paper in the guests' rooms.

In return for a retainer and extra ration cards from the Securitatae, hotel prostitutes reported everything their clients told them. But in the 1980s, even the prostitutes became desperate. On an earlier visit to the Athenee Palace, in 1983, I heard a knock on my door about midnight. I opened it: a woman stood in the darkness and slipped a strap of her blouse off in the corridor. She said she was willing to take coffee for payment.

Coffee was rare in Bucharest then. It was winter, and although I paid seventy-five dollars a night for the room, it had no heating, no hot water, and only two 25-watt bulbs. As in Africa, I knew enough to bring a flashlight and my own toilet paper. "If only we had a little bit more food, it would be like wartime" went a local joke.

Sometime in the winter of 1988–1989—nobody is sure exactly when—the Gypsy flower sellers disappeared from the streets near the Athenee Palace. These Gypsies had been the final vestige of a sentimental personal life in the city's landscape, recalling an existence, a history, before the Communist ice age.

When the ice finally cracked with fissures of blood in December 1989, the Gypsy women were the first to return: "perched like tropical birds," to use Olivia Manning's description, selling pink roses and mountains of yellow and red tulips, which mourners of the slain revolutionaries set ablaze in sacrificial offerings on the pavement. The ethereal smell of beeswax was suddenly everywhere. Denied public religion for more than four decades, the whole Romanian capital became an open-air church.

PACE VOUA, MORTI NOSTRI, read the graffiti. "Rest in peace, our dead."

The imagery was indeed surreal. No country during Eastern Europe's year of revolution in 1989 baffled the West as Romania did. Those first grainy scenes, broadcast with Romanian television's own antiquated equipment, revealed a physical world in which World War II had just ended, filled with soldiers in greatcoats and fanned helmets reminiscent of Russians at Stalingrad. The atmosphere was wintry, Slavic. Yet the people were dark, almost South American–looking; the language was a Latinate one, in some respects closer to the ancient Roman tongue than modern Italian or Spanish; and the violence, along with the religious rites that surrounded the burial of the victims, bore a theatricality and ghoulishness that revealed a people driven by the need to act out their passions in front of a mirror, over and over again.

Think about it: Beeswax candles set alight next to naked and badly decayed corpses in the street. A ruler who had himself photographed with a scepter in hand, and his foot stepping on the carcass of a boar; who built a Forbidden City of fascist architecture to encircle a wedding cake structure larger than the Pentagon; whose sycophants proclaimed him "Genius of the Carpathians," and whose people called him "Dracula" and "the Antichrist"; whose Christmas Day execution was shown repeatedly, for weeks, on local television; whose body was then rumored to be missing or deliberately hidden.

There was more going on here than the downfall of a Communist tyranny. Stalin may have provided the foundation, but the rest sprang naturally from the local soil.

Sandwiched between two other graves, half-concealed by bushes in Bucharest's sprawling Ghensea cemetery, I stared at a wooden cross over a narrow mound of earth. On the cross, written in white paint, were the words: COL. (RESERVE) POPA DAN, 1920–1989.

Thus was buried Nicolae Ceausescu, who ruled Romania for a quarter-century until the army executed him and his wife, Elena.

Fifthy feet away, squeezed between two other graves, I saw another cross, marked: COL. (RESERVE) ENESCU-VASILE, 1921–1989.

Thus was Elena Ceausescu buried.

Following an official "tip," several European reporters and I located the graves. Amid the sea of marble and stone monuments in the civilian part of the cemetery, the wooden crosses identifying two reserve colonels were indeed odd and conspicuous. A few days later, in May 1990, on the same night that vandals desecrated Jewish cemeteries in Romania, the two wooden crosses mysteriously disappeared, never to be seen again. But the Ceausescus were not the first couple to rule Romania in this century whose resting place was obscure and unmarked.

Go to Lisbon. Walk up through the twisting and peeling alleyways of the Alfama, a neighborhood first settled by the Romans, until you emerge at the church of Sao Vicente de Fora (St. Vincent Outside the Walls). Walk down the aisle of the church, but before arriving at the altar, go out through a door to your right. You are now in a nest of stone passageways, decorated with blue and white tiled paintings that depict the fables of La Fontaine. Now go left, down a long hall, into a room of marble vaults holding the graves of Portuguese royalty since the mid-seventeenth century. By the door are two coffins, neither one of which is identified, sitting on cheap, felt stands as if ready for the removal men. The coffin wrapped in the gold, blue, and red Romanian flag holds the body of King Carol II Hohenzollern, who ruled Romania from 1930 to 1940. The other coffin, wrapped in a coarse blue sheet with a white cross, holds the body of Carol's mistress of Jewish origin, Elena (Magda) Lupescu, who, as much as Elena Ceausescu, had once been the power behind the throne in Romania.

Spoiled rotten by his mother, Queen Marie, placed under a tutor who was a "morose Swiss homosexual," and afterward dispatched to his father's Prussian military regiment to finish his education, Romania's future king Carol, despite being of English and German extraction, had gone native in the worst possible way. During World War I, with German armies occupying Bucharest, the royal family besieged in the provincial capital of Jassy, and the local population blaming their foreign-born rulers for the fiasco, Carol deserted his military unit—a crime punishable by death—and eloped with a local aristocrat, Jeanne "Zizi" Lambrino. Because Romania's Hohenzollern monarchs were not allowed to take local spouses (in order to prevent any faction of the Romanian aristocracy from gaining a political advantage), Carol was forced to abdicate. A short time later, Carol left Zizi and returned to Romania. In 1921, he married Princess Helen of Greece. After two years, however, he deserted Helen for Lupescu, who then became his live-in mistress. Rather than go back to his lawful wife and the mother of his children, as the population demanded, Carol abdicated for a second time in January 1926.

In 1930, following the death of his father, Carol once again returned to Romania to take the throne, on condition that he leave Lupescu and return to his wife, Helen. Carol did not keep his promise, and Lupescu soon moved into the royal palace.

Not even Lupescu was enough for Carol, though. According

to a popular Romanian myth I heard repeated by a historian in Bucharest in 1990, Carol suffered from "the malady of Priapism," which forced him to spend long periods in bed, in constant sexual activity. "He dropped Zizi Lambrino . . . in Paris. . . . Now he picks up tarts in the Calea Victoriei or has singers brought to the Palace," writes Petru Dumitriu in *The Prodigals*, a long out-of-print historical novel about wealthy Romanians selling out their country and each other, prior to the 1941 fascist takeover.

Legend has it that Carol was so formidable in bed that he was reputed to be the only man ever to satisfy "the Crow," a famous whore of 1930s Bucharest. The Crow was tall and thin, dressed up like a witch with black eyes dilated from cocaine, and black hair cut short like a schoolboy (still the fashion, as I found out in the Athenee Palace lobby). "This black whore had to be carried out of Carol's bedroom, drooling and half-unconscious," a professor at Cluj University swore to me in 1990. The truth was likely different. In *The Prodigals*, Dumitriu recounts the following scene:

> She [the Crow] went out again and did the round of the streets . . . for some time without any luck. But then a hoarse voice called:
> "Hey, you—come here!"
> Looking round she saw a long, black car with a gleaming radiator. The door was open and the driver was beckoning to her to get in. It was the King. She had had dealings with him before. She got in obediently, knowing that she was still out of luck, for his Majesty was a bad payer.

Carol was as insatiable for money as he was for sex. Every casino and night club in Bucharest paid him monthly extortion fees. Carol sold *lei* on the black market for dollars. Once, he had a story spread that the hundred-dollar notes circulating in Romania were counterfeit. This sent the *lei* value of the notes tumbling, at which point Carol bought. Carol took a cut out of every state contract and owned stock in all major companies. When Stalin annexed Bessarabia, Carol demanded and got from his own ministers $1 million in compensation for the property he had lost, although the rest of his countrymen, many of whom had lost everything they owned, were not even allowed to make claims. Knowing that the Bulgarians were about to assert sovereignty over southern Dobruja, Carol sold the late Queen Marie's summer home there—where his mother's heart lay buried in a gold casket—to the state. After receiving the $250,000 payment, he negotiated the transfer of the territory to Bulgaria. Between 1930 and 1940, he reportedly deposited between $40 million and $50 million abroad, a huge sum for that time.

In 1938, Carol had abolished all political parties and declared a royal dictatorship. After bankrolling the fascist Legion of the Archangel Michael for years, that anti-Semitic organization turned against him on account of his liaison with the Jewish Lupescu. So Carol had the Legionnaire leaders murdered. This angered Hitler, whom Carol for a time ignored. But after the Nazi conquest of France, Carol formed his own fascist party, which passed a series of anti-Semitic laws, forcing Romania's 800,000 Jews to live virtually an underground existence. When Stalin, in the summer of 1940, demanded that Carol cede him Bessarabia, Carol appealed to Hitler for help. Hitler answered Carol by forcing him to yield the northern part of Transylvania to the pro-Nazi regime in Hungary.

The population felt these territorial losses like hammer blows. Roars of "*abdica* [abdicate]" rose from the crowds assembled in the square by the Athenee Palace. Carol "had been too clever," in his dealings with Hitler and Stalin, writes Manning in *The Balkan Trilogy*. "He had played a double game and lost."

Carol and Lupescu left Romania in the dead of night in late 1940, in a nine-car railway train filled with the country's gold and art treasures. The fascist Legion got wind of the couple's departure and tried stopping the train, but to no avail. "Would it not be fine to have *her* [Lupescu] carried through the streets in a cage, stripped for all to see?" one hungry peasant wondered aloud after touring Lupescu's opulent villa. "They should have paraded her naked through the streets and pelted her body with stones," said another hungry peasant after touring the villa of Elena Ceausescu, a half-century later.

Nazism and Communism worked to magnify the tragic flaws of Romanian political culture out of all proportion. Thus Elena Ceausescu was a monster. Although she appeared on our television screens, she nevertheless remains difficult to imagine. Lupescu, on the other hand, despite being long gone, is easy to imagine.

Lupescu was born in 1895 in Jassy, the provincial capital of Moldavia (Moldova), one of the worst places in Europe for a Jew to have been born. In Romania, if one excepts the ethnic German community in Transylvania and the adjacent Banat, the Jews *were* the bourgeoisie. To a greater extent than in any other Eastern European country, they formed the country's middle class practically by themselves, standing between the land-owning aristocracy and the mass of peasants. This made the Jews the object of intense hatred by even the most enlightened, liberal elements of Romanian society. Romania's greatest poets and intellectuals, such as Mihai Eminescu and Nicholae Iorga, were, in Goldie Horowitz's words, "first and last anti-Semites." And because Moldavia was geographically the most vulnerable part of the country, in addition to being the traditional center of Romanian nationalism, anti-Semitism there was even more extreme than elsewhere in Romania. As anti-Semitism in Moldavia turned its focus from religion to race in the early 1920s—the fascist Legion of the Archangel Michael was born in Jassy—the fact that Lupescu's parents had converted to Christianity would not have helped her much. A Jew might reaffirm his conversion a thousand times, but to the Romanian peasants a Jew was still a Jew.

Originally married to an artillery lieutenant, Lupescu had had frequent affairs with other members of her husband's unit before finally deserting him. Tall, with "flaming red" hair, green eyes, "magnolia white" skin, and "sauntering hips," Lupescu was determined to make the most of her assets. Through a cunning and painstakingly conceived plan, she arranged to be present on two occasions when Carol could not fail to notice her. In the view of Queen Marie's biographer, Hannah Pakula, it "was probably Lupescu's self-assured vulgarity" that attracted Carol to her. After landing Carol, Lupescu began to appear in public in black Chanel dresses, which Goldie Horowitz said "brought out the white of her skin and the flame of her hair."

King Carol's Romania was a Purim story in reverse. Because the racial climate in prewar Romania was far more sinister than in Old Testament Persia, Lupescu, even if she had tried, could not have employed her talents in the royal bedroom to save her people, as Esther had in the Bible. On the contrary, the Romanians felt humiliated because their king had deserted his wife for a Jew.

So as fascist Legionnaires began slaughtering Jews in Bucharest, Lupescu was on her way across Europe, from east to west, with the exiled Carol, bound for Mexico. After spending the rest of the war years there, the couple moved to Brazil, where Carol married Lupescu, giving her the title of Royal Princess Elena. Next they moved to Portugal. After Carol died there in 1953, Lupescu moved in with Carol's former Prime Minister, Ernesto Urdareanu. With Urdareanu, she lived in luxury in the Portuguese coastal resort of Estoril, sustained by the gold and other valuables she and Carol had looted in the nine-car train. Only in 1977 did Lupescu die, a thoroughly satisfied woman.

Lupescu rises straight off the pages of Petru Dumitriu's novels: grasping, ruthless, and street-smart. *The Prodigals* even includes a character, Elvira Vorvoreano, née Lascari, with "big green eyes," who, after sleeping her way into the royal bedroom, fails utterly to satisfy the king. Realizing that she will now die a vulnerable nobody, Elvira flings herself to the floor, "writhing and biting her clenched fists, uttering strange little animal cries." One could imagine Lupescu doing that, had that been her fate.

Born into a world of enemies, surrounded by violent racial hate, with no obvious means of protection, Lupescu did what she had to do: she auctioned off her body—the only thing she had to sell—to each and every bidder, playing one off against the other, all the way up to the king. As always in the Balkans, bare survival provides precious little room for moral choices.

Lupescu's story is the story of Romania. Dumitriu, the country's most gifted modern novelist, must have realized this, since all of his most vivid characters are variations of her. Romania, too, was always alone, always surrounded by enemies who wanted pieces of her.

Romanians see themselves as a Latin race, speaking a Latinate tongue, cast into a violent sea of Slavs and forgotten by the rest of the Latin world.

For Romanians, history starts in A.D. 101, when Roman legions led by Emperor Trajan conquered a territory in southeastern Europe called Dacia. For 150 years, Roman soldiers interbred with the local women, producing, according to Romanian historical theorists, a Latin race that has remained racially pure until this day. In reality, the Romans were only the first of many waves of invaders who swarmed across this land and commingled with its inhabitants. In a somewhat mean, though telling judgment, the Hungarian-born American historian John Lukacs observed: "Official Rumanian propaganda and official Rumanian historiography claim that the Rumanians are direct descendants of Trajan's legions, which is as if Ronald Reagan were to declare his descent from Pocahontas. Yet many Rumanians have something mock Latin about them; they are curiously reminiscent of the mock-European quality of Argentinians."

Still, it cannot be denied that Romanians are closer in appearance to other Latins than to the Slavs and Hungarians who surround them. The Romanian language, although infused with Slavic, Turkish, and Greek words, is a Latinate tongue. And the Romanian people, in their politics, their personal affairs, and even in the movement of their mouths and hands, exhibit a sensuous theatricality reminiscent of the Italians—a style of behavior that a traveler simply does not encounter elsewhere in Eastern Europe.

Adrian Poruciuc, an expert on Romanian history and ethnology at Cuza University in Jassy, observed: "One hundred and fifty years is only a speck of time. The Roman legions were in Britain much longer than they were in Romania. Yet what racial and linguistic traces did they leave among the English? Almost none. But look at us. That's why I think there had to be some Latin element in our race, in addition to the Romans, which we still don't know about."

We cannot rule out the possibility of another Latin influx during the murky centuries that followed the legions' withdrawal. Romania has the most unenviable geographical situation of any nation in Europe. Its historic Danubian heartlands of Moldavia and Wallachia lie east and southeast of the Carpathian Mountains, leaving them wide open to invasion from Russia and the Ukraine in the east and from Turkey in the south. Not even Poland has been so victimized. Byzantines, Visigoths, the Huns under Attila, Avars, Gepidae, Slavs, Bulgars, Hungarians, Tartars, Turks, and various others all invaded. A ninth-century occupation by newly Christianized Bulgars caused the Romanians to drop their Western, Latin form of Christian worship (brought to Romania by the Emperor Constantine in A.D. 325) and adopt the Eastern Slavonic rite; this event severed a crucial psychological link to the rest of the Latin world.

From the fourteenth century onward, the Turks kept the Romanian peasantry in a constant state of fear and harassment. Only now and then were the local *voivods* (peasant chieftains) powerful enough to strike bargains with the Turkish invaders that granted them some degree of self-rule. In 1391, Mircea the Old arranged to pay the Turks a large tribute in return for their halting an ongoing rampage in Wallachia. Sixty-five years later, Vlad the Impaler (the historical "Dracula") and Stephen the Great, spilling vast amounts of blood and engineering cunning deals with Hungarians, Turks, and others, carved out weak principalities in Wallachia and Moldavia, which collapsed as soon as they died.

Vlad's cruelty emblemized the fifteenth century in the Balkans. His favorite means of execution was impalement (hence his name): a long, sharpened stake was driven up the victim's rectum and out through his stomach. Soldiers then hoisted the victim in the air, implanted the other end of the long stake in the ground, and waited for the victim to die, which sometimes took hours. Vlad killed tens of thousands of Turks in this manner, and not a few of his own countrymen.

In 1600, Michael the Brave briefly united Wallachia and Moldavia under local leadership for the first time, but the new kingdom collapsed the next year. Even when independent, the peasants suffered—taxed and persecuted by their own chieftains almost as heavily as by the Turks. In the 1630s, the Turks placed the administration of Wallachia and Moldavia in the hands of Greek Phanariots: these were Greeks from the wealthy Phanar ("lighthouse") district of Constantinople, who robed themselves in furs, velvet mantels, and diamond-studded turbans, and who equalled Turks in their ability to bleed the peasants. Meanwhile, in Transylvania, the region lying on the other side of the Carpathians, within the sphere of Central Europe, Romanian peasants labored at the bottom of a medieval apartheid system, oppressed by Hungarians and ethnic Germans.

"The Romanian peasants are like *mamaliga* [corn mush]," goes a local proverb; "they can be boiled forever without exploding."

But whenever the peasants did explode, as in the Transylvanian peasant revolts of 1437 and 1514, and the revolts in Wallachia and Moldavia in 1784, the results were horrific: bodies torn apart with pincers, cooked, and force-fed to other victims. The pattern of Romanian history, as the anti-Ceausescu revolution of 1989 revealed, remains unchanged: long periods of docility interrupted by brief but spectacular eruptions of violence.

Turks and Hungarians weren't the only predators violating local peasants. In the eighteenth and nineteenth centuries, czarist Russia invaded Romania half a dozen times. And in 1878, after Romanian troops had helped Russia liberate Bulgaria from the Turkish yoke, Bismarck's Congress of Berlin thanked them by insisting that they cede Bessarabia to the czar.[1] In Romania, writes the Paris-based columnist William Pfaff, "there has always been a popular familiarity with betrayal, and assumption of failure."

With French diplomatic support, Wallachia and Moldavia eventually reunited under one leader, Colonel Alexandru Ion Cuza, forming an independent Romanian nation on December 23, 1861. But Cuza's administration combined rampant corruption with incompetence. Local aristocrats and peasants alike were soon demanding his head. When Romanian army officers burst into Cuza's house in Jassy in 1866, demanding that he abdicate, they found him in bed with the daughter-in-law of the King of Serbia. "Romania," writes Manning in *The Balkan Trilogy*, "is like a foolish person who has inherited a great fortune [forests, rivers, oil, mineral wealth . . .]. It is all dissipated in vulgar nonsense."

The Romanians, imagining that they would be better ruled by a foreigner, called in a Prussian cousin of Kaiser Wilhelm I, Prince Karl of Hohenzollern-Sigmaringen, to be their king. Karl would henceforth be known by his Romanian name, Carol I (the granduncle of Carol II).

In the spring of 1866, afraid of being recognized in Austria (which, along with Russia and Ottoman Turkey, wanted to carve up the new Romanian state), the twenty-seven-year-old Carol I made his way incognito to Bucharest in a second-class railway car, wearing pink goggles against the dust and carrying a satchel full

---

1. Bessarabia constitutes the eastern part of Moldavia, between the Prut and Dniester rivers.

of cash. It was an inauspicious start to a monarchy that would forge a viable and greatly enlarged Romanian state out of the morass Cuza had left behind, only to have Carol II fritter it all away.

Although John Reed dismissed Carol I as a "dinky little German King . . . in a dinky little palace," Carol I was just what the country required: an anal-retentive, workaholic Prussian who preferred spartan accommodations to luxury and paperwork to diversions of the flesh. Despite his close attachment to the Prussia of his birth, Carol's last act before dying in 1914 was to refuse to enter the war on the side of his cousin, the kaiser—a far-reaching decision that eventually led to Romania's entering the war on the side of Great Britain and America and gaining territory in the peace settlement.

Not all of Carol's decisions were wise, however. His neglect of the peasants sparked a nationwide orgy of violence in 1907 that ended with the institution of ineffectual land reforms. Another mistake was his decision to marry Princess Elizabeth of Wied, a crackpot poet, better known by her pen name of Carmen Sylva, who conducted artistic salons in the royal palace in which no editing or criticism was permitted. Elizabeth decreed that everyone at court should dress in folk costumes. She doubtless did Romania a great service (for one generation, at least) by failing to produce an heir. This forced Carol I to name his nephew, Prince Ferdinand of Hohenzollern-Sigmaringen, as his successor.

Ferdinand lacked self-confidence; throughout his life, he had difficulty making up his mind. Fortunately for Romania, he married well. Born Princess Marie of Edinburgh, a granddaughter of Queen Victoria, Marie Windsor Hohenzollern of Romania was a queen straight out of a romance novel.

Marie was beautiful, vivacious, and incurably romantic. An accomplished equestrian, she commanded her own Romanian cavalry detachment. She learned to speak Romanian fluently and took a brilliant and good-looking local aristocrat, Barbo Stirbey, as a lover. She joined her cholera-stricken troops in Bulgaria during the Second Balkan War, wading "through the filth in her riding boots, . . . encouraging the soldiers, and passing out provisions," writes her biographer, Hannah Pakula, in *The Last Romantic*. During World War I, after the Romanian royal family had withdrawn from Bucharest and was surrounded by German troops in Jassy, the Queen, unlike the other nurses, refused to wear rubber gloves in the typhus wards, pressing her bare hands to the lips of her dying soldiers. Her willingness to inspire troops from an unsafe distance certainly earned her the epithet of "Warrior Queen."

In her later years, Queen Marie worried constantly about the rise of fascism and Communism and about where the political mess created by her son, Carol II, would eventually lead Romania. Mercifully for her, she died in 1938, before her worst fears were realized.[2]

With the flight abroad of Carol II and Lupescu in September 1940, Romanians thought that their nation had finally cast out its demons. In fact, the demons of Romanian history were now about to run riot, encouraged first by Hitler and then by Stalin.

Romanian manners have always been an unfortunate and dangerous palimpsest, which is precisely what attracted authors and journalists to them in the first place. Atop the Latin bent for melodrama was a Byzantine bent for intrigue and mysticism, inherited from the Orthodox religion and from centuries of Byzantine political and cultural influence. This mystical streak was further intensified by the Carpathian landscape itself, darkened by fir forests and teeming with wolves and bears, out of which arose a pantheon of spirits and superstitions and the richest folk culture in Europe. It was no accident that Bram Stoker, the Dublin-born author of *Dracula*, situated his novel in Romania.

Corneliu Zelea Codreanu came out of this world. In 1927, the twenty-eight-year-old Codreanu heard the voice of God calling him from an icon of the Archangel Michael, a fighting saint that Balkan peasants associated with the struggle against the Muslim Turks. Codreanu, an educated peasant influenced by the anti-Semitic teachings of his university professors in Jassy, heeded this voice and formed the Legion of the Archangel Michael, whose military wing would later be known as the Iron Guard. In Codreanu's view, the Legion was "a religious order" uniting all Romanians "dedicated to a heroic existence": those alive, those

2. See the epilogue to *The Last Romantic* by Hannah Pakula.

not yet born, and those already dead. He organized the Legion around *cuibs* ("nests") of thirteen members each. To join a *cuib*, an initiate had to suck the blood from self-imposed slashes in the arm of every other member of the nest, and then write an oath in his own blood, vowing to commit murder whenever ordered to do so. Before setting out to kill, each man had to let an ounce of his blood flow into a common goblet, out of which all would drink, thus uniting the entire nest in death. Members were also obliged to wear crosses and packets of Romanian soil around their necks. Romanian fascism, like Romanian Communism, was by no means standard-issue.

Tall and handsome, Codreanu had riveting eyes and the chiseled features of a Roman statue. His followers called him Capitanul ("the Captain"). He liked to dress completely in white and ride a white horse through the Carpathian villages. There, he was worshipped as a peasant-god—the Archangel Michael's envoy on earth. When Codreanu married, 90,000 people formed a bridal procession.

King Carol II saw Codreanu as a dangerous rival, especially after Hitler told Carol to his face, during a 1938 meeting in Berchtesgarten, that he preferred Codreanu to be the "dictator of Romania." Carol, perhaps because of his overweaning arrogance, was no coward. He answered the Führer by having Codreanu and thirteen other Legionnaires strangled to death in November 1938, and then spread rumors that Codreanu had "sold out to the Jews" (exactly what Codreanu had accused Carol of doing, on account of the King's liaison with Lupescu).

But the Romanians could never believe that their "Captain" had sold out to the Jews. To the peasant masses, Codreanu was still very much alive: "a tribune who stood in the imagination of the Rumanians as both martyr and prophet," writes Horowitz. Many peasants claimed that they had seen "the Captain" riding his white horse through the forests at night, in the weeks and months following his supposed execution. Later, the Romanian Orthodox Church proclaimed Codreanu a "national saint."

Codreanu's ghost proved to be too much for Carol. The crowds who filled the vast square in front of the Athenee Palace, crying "*abdica*" in the late summer of 1940, believed that the losses of Bessarabia to the Soviet Union, southern Dobruja to Bulgaria, and northern Transylvania to Hungary were God's retribution to the Romanian nation for tolerating a king who slept with a Jew and who had murdered their "Captain." After Carol fled with Lupescu, posters appeared throughout Bucharest, bearing Codreanu's picture and the words, "Corneliu Zelea Codreanu—Present": still alive, in other words.

The 1940 revolution that toppled King Carol left his eighteen-year-old son, Michael, as a figurehead king. Real power, however, rested in the hands of a Nazi-backed military junta, headed by a tall, red-haired World War I cavalry officer, General Ion Antonescu, who suffered from bouts of syphilitic fever and was better known by the nickname of "Red Dog." Antonescu's first act as effective head of state was to appoint several Legionnaires to his cabinet and order all Romanians to go to church and "blaspheme" the ex-king.

But members of the Legion were not appeased; and an earthquake that demolished 10,000 houses in Bucharest in early November 1940 appeared to give extraordinary weight to their argument. In *Athenee Palace Bucharest,* Horowitz writes: "Perhaps without the earthquake the belated nights-of-the-long-knives would not have happened. To a deeply religious and superstitious people like the Rumanians this terrible earthquake seemed by way of divine reprisal for their failure to revenge their martyrs."

So revenge their martyrs the Legionnaires did. First they murdered sixty-four officials and henchmen of Carol's old regime; then they stormed through Bucharest's Jewish quarter, "killing, looting, burning" in the words of Robert St. John, the Bucharest correspondent for the Associated Press. Next, the Legionnaires murdered twentieth-century Romania's best-known intellectual, Dr. Nicholae Iorga. They yanked out every hair of his long, white beard and stuffed a liberal newspaper down his throat, continuing to torture him to death. (Although he was a publicly committed anti-Semite, Iorga was also, by Romanian and especially Legionnaire standards, a liberal intellectual.) Finally, the Legionnaires ordered a public funeral in Bucharest to celebrate the reinterment of Codreanu and the thirteen other Legionnaires killed by Carol two years earlier.[3] St. John described the huge crowd at the fu-

---

3. See the prologue for the details.

neral: "[T]hey seemed to be a people gone mad. . . . The memory will always remain vivid because I saw that day how frightening religious ecstasy can be when it gets out of control. . . . This was a lynch mob of 155,000 people."

St. John's fears proved to be justified. A few weeks later, on January 21, 1941, the Legionnaires went on a three-day killing spree, in an attempt to grab power from Antonescu, whom they considered insufficiently fascist. The Legionnaires burnt down seven synagogues and went from house to house in the Jewish quarter, raping and torturing women to death in front of their husbands and children. They brought one group of Jews to the Baneasa forest north of Bucharest (near the airport that is now used for domestic flights), stripped them naked in the snow, and shot them. Gypsies came the next morning to extract the gold from the victims' teeth. The following night, the Legionnaires rounded up an additional 200 Jews and took them to the municipal slaughterhouse, where they stripped them naked and put them through all the stages of animal slaughter on a conveyor belt.

"Accounts of the atrocities committed by the Legionnaires during the . . . pogrom might never have been believed by anyone, except that we saw some of it happen, we counted the corpses, we noted the mutilations. . . . The Universal Jewish Encyclopedia calls it 'one of the most brutal pogroms in history.' This is covering a lot of ground, for the statement was written after the end of World War Two," St. John explains.

The Legionnaires went down fighting—sniping from rooftops at passers-by and at "Red Dog" Antonescu's tanks and regular army troops in the snowy Bucharest streets at the end of January 1941. Those who weren't killed or captured went into exile in Nazi Germany, fascist Italy, and (especially) fascist Spain. The escapees included Horia Sima, the long-haired maniac who had become the Legionnaires' leader upon Codreanu's death and who, more than any other individual, bore responsibility for the pogrom and the massacre at the slaughterhouse. Sima was reportedly still living in Spain as recently as 1990 in complete anonymity, forgotten even by the Israeli Secret Service and the usual Nazi hunters.

The Legionnaires lost their bid for total power because Hitler abruptly deserted them in favor of Antonescu. After meeting Antonescu in late 1940 in Berlin, the Führer told his entourage that, "of all those Latins" (a category then including Mussolini, Franco, Pétain, and Laval), he preferred the red-haired Romanian general. To Hitler, Romania now meant "raw materials"—specifically, oil from the rich Ploesti fields fifty miles north of Bucharest, to feed German tanks during the planned invasion of Russia. And Antonescu, much more than the unstable Legionnaires, could be counted on to maintain the requisite order and smooth running of the local economy, which would permit the Germans to pump and transport the precious oil. As for the adjunct task of killing Jews, Hitler's choice proved doubly wise. Antonescu, soon to be called the Conducator (Romanian "Fuhrer"—a title Ceausescu would later appropriate), showed himself to be equal to the organizational problem of murdering the huge numbers of people demanded under Hitler's program of genocide.

Thus the curtain came down on Romanian history as witnessed from the lobby of the Athenee Palace. Departing the hotel at the end of January 1941, with the Legionnaires' revolt crushed and Conducator Antonescu overseeing the quiet influx of German army advisors and logistics men into Romania, Goldie Horowitz wrote: "Bucharest, the last capital of international glamour on the European continent, was now nothing but a halting place for German troops sweeping south." And, in what must have been an unconscious intimation of things to come, she added that "the wind from Russia blew sharply the day I drove to the Bucharest station. . . ."

In December 1989, for the first time since January 1941, journalists once again filled up the rooms of Bucharest's hotels, although now they favored the Intercontinental over the Athenee Palace. But the revolutionary spectacle they were witnessing bore eerie resemblances to the one observed by Horowitz, St. John, Sulzberger, and others from the Athenee Palace.

From the same vast square in front of the Athenee Palace that the Romanians had once filled to shout *abdica* at King Carol II and Lupescu, the Romanians now shouted "Down with the dictator" at Nicolae and Elena Ceausescu. Like Carol and all the medieval chieftains, the Ceausescus had played a double game against the great powers and lost. The dictator's Securitatae troops died in an orgiastic fury of violence that recalled the suicidal resistance of the Legionnaires to Antonescu's tanks and troops in the same winter streets. The Securitatae troops who survived and weren't captured were rumored to have gone into exile in Libya, instead of in Italy and Spain. And now, Ion Iliescu and his National Salvation Front—a group composed not just of former Communists, but also of mystics and demagogues with criminal records—were being hailed as the "national savior," the same words used to describe Antonescu's quasi-Legionnaire government after it had replaced King Carol's.

But few of the current generation of journalists had read the books written by a previous generation of journalists about the same place. They represented the Romanian revolution as being unique when, even in terms of Romania's own modern history, it wasn't.[4]

I stayed for only a few days at the Athenee Palace. Then I loaded my rucksack with a different set of books—mainly by British writers who had journeyed through the Romanian countryside in the early decades of the century, during the time of Queen Marie and King Carol II. There was much to be seen. After Poland, Romania was the largest and most populous country in the Soviet Union's former Eastern European empire. The Carpathian Mountains meander through the heart of the country, dividing the interior into several distinct regions. As a result, rural Romania is far more diverse and visually spectacular than Poland (or any other country in Eastern Europe) and far less explored. I wanted to know how five years of Nazism followed by four and a half decades of Stalinism had affected this landscape and the people who inhabited it.

So one morning before dawn, in the early spring of 1990, I left the lobby of the Athenee Palace and began walking to the train station.

---

4. Columnist William Pfaff and *New York Times* correspondent David Binder were among the distinguished exceptions to this generalization.

The Danube's Bitter End

The seats in the dark and freezing first-class carriage were torn and broken. There had been nothing to eat at Bucharest's North Station. Inside the train, several carriages down, I located a snack bar offering stale cakes on a greasy, sheet-metal counter and luke-warm, liver-brown coffee. I thought of Prince Yakimov, Olivia Manning's penniless Russian aristocrat—her most endearing character in *The Balkan Trilogy*—"munching the dry, soya-flour cakes and sipping the grey coffee" on a train leaving the North Station in 1940 for Transylvania, where, as another passenger told him, "no one has food."

Transylvania lay to the northwest. I planned to go there only later. My direction now was easterly, toward the Black Sea, after which I intended to make a northerly, counterclockwise arc around the whole of Romania before returning to Bucharest. The train carriage reeked of concrete dust, urine, old cheese, sausage, tobacco, plum brandy, sour body odor, and long-unwashed clothes. It was a strangely warm and cozy mixture, not quite as bad as its individual elements suggest; to greater or lesser extents, it remained with me throughout my travels in Romania. In Manning's story, the smell made Prince Yakimov think of "stale beer."

For two hours, the view from the window was the same: a grim, flat sea of dust, checkered with green fields. Here and there grain silos and apartment blocks stood in prisonlike isolation: cheaply constructed instant slums, from which mud-colored figures emerged wearing kerchiefs or brown furry hats with earmuffs. This was Romania's heartland province of Wallachia, rolling across the southern part of the country from the Jiu Valley—the country's mining center—in the west, past Bucharest, to the Danube River in the east.

The Danube is more than twice as long as any other river in Europe, touching seven countries on its 1,776-mile journey from Germany's Black Forest region to the Black Sea.[1] This makes it a unifying symbol: a river of hope, inspiration, and cliché. The Danube's "flood harmonizes every discord and nationality and its spirit is the spirit of pan-Europe," writes Walter Starkie, an Irish eccentric who traveled with Gypsies through Hungary and Romania in 1929, and whose book, *Raggle-Taggle,* I carried in my rucksack.

But I was heading for the forgotten mouth of the river, which few travelers—Starkie included—have ever bothered to visit, especially in recent decades.

For most of its journey, the Danube flows idyllically through the alpine meadows of southern Germany and Austria, and then past Budapest and Belgrade, before forming Romania's southwestern border with Yugoslavia and its southern border with Bulgaria. But not far from the Black Sea, the river changes course. Instead of continuing as an international river, its character becomes purely Romanian, flowing due north for 100 miles through Romania before turning east again and branching into myriad smaller waterways that flow into the sea.

My train reached the Danube at Cernovoda ("Black Water"),

---

1. The seven countries are Germany, Austria, Czechoslovakia, Hungary, Serbia, Bulgaria, and Romania.

a name that sounds ominously similar to Chernobyl. Here, in one of the world's most unstable earthquake zones, Ceausescu had decided to build Romania's first nuclear power station. The nuclear plant was but an addition to an already monstrous hydro-power and transport complex on the Danube—one that since 1949 had been the chief industrial "hero project" of Romanian Communism, symbolizing, in the words of a project brochure, the "socialist, man-machine alliance."

The story goes that Stalin decided in the course of a meeting with a Romanian railway workers' leader, Gheorghe Gheorghiu-Dej, that Gheorghiu-Dej should rule Romania.[2] Before setting Gheorghiu-Dej to his task in 1947, Stalin supposedly offered him some advice: "You must keep the masses occupied. Give them a big project to do. Have them build a canal or something." And so Gheorghiu-Dej, who ruled Romania until his death in 1965, announced plans to construct "the Danube–Black Sea Canal." If the canal were completed, cargo vessels would no longer have to travel the additional 250 miles (first north, and then east) beyond Cernovoda before reaching the Black Sea, since the canal would link Cernovoda with the Romanian port of Constanta, only forty miles to the east.

In fact, it was a madcap scheme. There was never any indication that river trade to and from Central Europe would have enabled Romania to earn significant money from canal fees. Between 1949 and 1953, claims novelist Petru Dumitriu, over 100,000 laborers lost their lives from accidents, overexposure, and malnourishment building the first sections of the canal. Most of the laborers were prisoners, including political detainees associated with the Jewish intellectual Anna Pauker. Gheorghiu-Dej had brutally crushed Pauker's "internationalist" wing of the Communist party, with the assistance of a former cobbler and petty thief from Wallachia (then in his mid-thirties), named Ceausescu.

In 1953, after Gheorghiu-Dej had removed all traces of political opposition in Romania, both inside the party and out, work on the unfinished canal abruptly stopped. Then for twenty years, as Romania experienced among the most meager of Communist lib-

---

2. Antonescu's fascist regime had been overthrown and the nation occupied following the Russian victory at the end of World War II.

eralizations, the project was officially forgotten. In 1973, while launching a personality cult around himself as part of a full-scale retreat into Stalinism, Ceausescu announced not only that work on the canal would resume, but that a new port near Constanta and a nuclear plant in the vicinity would also be built.

Eight years later, in the winter of 1981, I visited the canal and the nuclear site at Cernovoda, wearing my dirtiest clothes and clutching a bottle of plum brandy in a brown paper bag so that I wouldn't be conspicuous to the militia or Securitatae, who didn't like foreigners to observe what was going on. I remember the frosted grain fields, the matrix of cranes standing on platforms in the ice-clogged Danube and in man-dug craters intended for the canal and for nuclear plant foundations. The line of trucks carrying away earth extended for miles. Wherever I walked I heard the deafening roar of cement mixers. Mud, forest, and river all merged into a single, featureless desolation. I recall a street of frozen mud where hundreds of laborers clad in caps and overalls waited silently, in single file in a snow flurry, for their ration of bread, thin soup, and ten grams of butter. Militia troops, bundled in greatcoats that reached down to their knees, watched over the laborers with automatic rifles. This was what a part of the Danube looked like in the 1980s—reminiscent of Stalin's Russia in the 1930s. According to some Western diplomats, the number of "slave laborers" in Ceausescu's "Romanian gulag" at the time might have been as high as 700,000.

Now it was the early spring of 1990. The construction sites were partly deserted in the wake of the revolution, and Cernovoda looked much less grim. Nevertheless, it was still unfinished. I wondered whether Ceausescu—or Gheorghiu-Dej, for that matter—truly cared whether this pharaonic-scale project was ever completed. Perhaps the canal, like the great steel, pig-iron, and petrochemical combines—all obsolete by the time of their completion—was meant to accomplish exactly what Stalin had suggested: provide a means to keep the masses occupied, to give them something to do, while reducing them to a subsistence existence in which the human spirit ceased to exist. Elena Ceausescu admitted as much. She frequently referred to her millions of subjects as "worms," to be controlled by hard labor and food rationing.

My eastbound train crossed the Danube and then headed

north, paralleling the river. This part of Romania, between the Danube and the Black Sea, is called the Dobruja; it is where the Roman poet Ovid went into exile and died. The earth, no longer flat, became a rough sea of grey silt. Limestone bluffs overlooked massive depressions on whose dry, burnt skin modern villages and factories rose like fever welts. Seen up close, these "villages" proved to be clusters of wood and scrap-iron shacks, surrounded by rusted iron fences and meandering curtains of concrete, each resembling a scaled-down version of the Berlin Wall. The gardens between the shacks looked more like refuse heaps. The factories challenged description.

Cruel, ugly things throughout the Communist world, factories in Romania seemed to belong to a deeper circle of hell: barbed-wire and concrete-gated enclosures, filled with mountains of coal, garbage, and rusted tractor carcasses, all plastered with dried mud and desultorily picked over by the odd cow or sheep. The plant stood in the middle, like a body without a skin: a mass of bile green, intestinal pipes, fitted with rusted gangplanks that crossed over and along long walls of plate glass and smoke-blackened cement, on top of which stood an asbestos roof with scrap-iron chimneys puffing pure black smoke into the air.

Supply wagons filled with gas containers entered the gates of these factories, pulled by horses and Nilotic-looking cattle: "elephant coloured, and awkward and uncouth as cattle in the centre of Africa," noted Sacheverell Sitwell, whose 1937 *Roumanian Journey* I had with me. The Romanian landscape reminded Sitwell of "Tartary, from the innermost of Asia." And indeed, the Dobruja was still a scene from Tartary—although, unlike in Sitwell's day, no longer a pretty one.

I was on the train for five hours. Despite the cold, the broken seats, and the lack of food, it proved to be the most physically comfortable train journey I took in Romania. The last stop was Tulcea, the gateway of the Danube delta. Here the great river fissued into several tributaries and hundreds of smaller streams, creating a 1,200-square-mile protrusion of marshland—up to fifty miles long—between Tulcea and the Black Sea.

In theory, Tulcea should have been a picturesque town, with fishing boats crowding the harbor and turn-of-the-century houses punctuated by Turkish minarets and silver church cupolas. What

I found was a rank of tall tenement buildings, blocking any view of the riverfront from the turn-of-the-century houses, the mosques, and the churches. The cement faces of these tenements had been spray-painted a sickening brownish red. Outside the windows on each floor sat flower pots, but for some reason there was nothing cheerful about them. Studying the view, I realized why. These pots, although obviously meant for flowers—the bright tulips and roses that Romanians have a passion for—had been filled instead with vegetables, notably onions and garlic: things the buildings' inhabitants evidently could not find in local shops.

I entered one of the hallways of a tenement. The staircases were made of bare concrete, the doors of plywood. Every aspect of the construction was cheap and crude. Monumental spears and arches of unfinished cement occupied the pavement between the buildings, which looked less vandalized than American slums and were certainly less dangerous. But while slums in America are often sad mistakes born of landlord abuse and tenant neglect, there seemed nothing mistaken or accidental about the buildings I saw in Tulcea.

Walking down a side street away from the waterfront, I noticed a plaque that translated as "artists' union." Intrigued, I pulled open the sheet-metal door, climbed the staircase, and knocked. The door creaked open. In the crack stood a man wearing a smock over an old suit and tie. His eyes nervously asked me, "Who are you?" I asked if he knew French. He nodded. I told him I was an American writer traveling through Romania. The door opened wider.

His name was Stefan Stirbu, a fifty-one-year-old artist who had had an exhibition in 1974 in Memphis, and another in 1977 in Pittsburgh. He boiled a glass of tea for me, then proudly took out of hiding the American-produced exhibition catalogs and review clips—their slick graphics and smooth paper so unlike the grainy artwork and recycled paper used in Romanian books and newspapers. After 1977, Stirbu was not allowed to leave the country. He slowly became a prisoner in this small room in Tulcea with its soot-blackened windows. He looked at the review clips every day, to remind himself that a world still existed outside and that he had twice been there.

"In the early 1980s, obtaining the proper cloth, paint, and other materials became difficult, then almost impossible. And there was no heating at all in winter."

After the revolution, materials were a little easier to come by, so Stirbu began painting again. He painted religious icons in deep, bright colors in a naive, peasant style, all of which told the same story: how Communism attempted, but failed in the end, to destroy the Romanian family. In recent weeks, he had made dozens of these icons—about one a day. I bought one. It depicts a wooden cross stamped with the hammer and sickle, on which a peasant couple is crucified. But in an adjacent scene of resurrection, the couple stands triumphant, holding images of their farm and flock.

"Religion sustained me in the 1980s, and after the revolution religion was all I wanted to paint about."

He offered me a cot in his studio. I could stay there as long as I wanted, he said. He told me that I was the first Westerner he had spoken to since 1977. I didn't doubt him. Ceausescu had forbidden Romanians to speak to foreigners without afterward reporting their conversation to the Securitatae. Allowing a foreigner inside your home without prior permission had been punishable by a prison sentence.

Saying good-bye took a good deal of diplomacy. It being soon after Easter, I left him with the Romanian words:

"*Hristos a inviat* [Christ has risen]."

"*Adevarat a inviat* [Truly He has risen]," came the reply.

It appeared that my lightly taken decision to stop at his door for a few moments had ended a dark era in this artist's life.

Eyeing the boats in the river, I was suddenly restless. I congratulated myself on my decision to travel for six weeks with only a single rucksack, about half of whose space was occupied by old books and toiletry items, meaning that I could take only one change of clothes. How I looked didn't much matter, I figured, since I would be with Romanians whose clothes were shabbier than mine. And I was already raking in the benefits: the ability to travel spontaneously and to stop wherever I liked, without worrying about left-behind luggage, taxis, or hotel reservations. Now I decided I would jump on one of the riverboats that was filling up with passengers. I decided on a boat going to Sfintu Gheorghe (St. George) for two reasons:

- Of all the delta villages, Sfîntu Gheorghe was the farthest away, right on the Black Sea, forty miles from Tulcea down a weaving channel of the Danube.
- Not even the intrepid authors of *The Rough Guide to Eastern Europe* had been there. They were not allowed to board the boat, since Sfîntu Gheorghe had no hotel and, until recently, it was illegal to stay in Romanian homes.

Jumping onto the boat a few minutes before it pulled away from the harbor, I had the sensation of jumping into the unknown. Because the months following last December's revolution had been cold and snowy, I might reasonably hope to be the first Westerner to make it so far downriver. It was noon. The boat wouldn't arrive at Sfîntu Gheorghe until after dark, and I would then have to find a house to stay in. Who knows which door I might decide to knock on?

I paid 66 *lei*—66 cents at the black market rate, courtesy of the Athenee Palace management—for a ticket. I needn't have spent the extra 26 cents for "first-class" quarters, since they were as flesh-packed as the rest of the boat and only slightly less squalid.

The boat was virtually an overcrowded barge: a rusted skeleton with rotting floorboards and peeling paint, reeking of gasoline— the kind you read about every now and then in a one-paragraph newspaper story on an inside page as having capsized in some far-off country, with most on board drowned. All the seats had been taken hours before departure, and the aisles leading to the lone toilet were like those of a rush-hour train; there wasn't even space to crouch down on your knees. There was no water, beer, or wine to drink; just *tuica,* Romanian plum brandy (sometimes made from prunes).

The vessel was still in operation because the state had provided no funds for new boats. Because the state had restricted energy supplies, the boats to Sfîntu Gheorghe were relatively few and far between; thus every one was overcrowded. This was also why the trains were so bad, and why the country's intercity bus system had completely collapsed. Ceausescu had said that these austerity measures were necessary because of Romania's debt to foreign banks, which he had insisted on paying back ahead of schedule in order to make Romania "completely independent" (as Albania had been). But with elbows sticking in my sides and hot alcoholic breath playing in my nostrils, I didn't believe this. I believed that the debt was merely a pretext for imposing cuts in fuel and infrastructure spending that, like the canal and the apartment blocks, were part of a policy to break the people's will.

The declining conditions went so far that even the brandy suffered. In all Communist countries, the regimes forced farmers to turn over part of their crop to the state. But in no country was the quota so severe and the system so corrupt as in Romania, where farmers managed to fill quotas with the rottenest portion of their plum and prune crops. There was good brandy to drink in Romania, but it was all homemade. Filled bottles were plugged with rags or newspaper, because cork, too, was in short supply.

The struggle to get on deck was worth it. Despite the wind and the damp chill, it was less uncomfortable outside. Conditions exactly like these had scared me away from taking riverboats up the Nile in the Sudan and down the Zaire (Congo) River in Zaire, where the landscape looked similar.

Beyond the last docked boat and telephone wires of Tulcea began a brown and green sameness: the brown of the Danube in this, one of its two main channels to the sea, and the green of the *grind*—vast, moving stretches of silt that support slender willows and poplars and all sorts of reeds and climbing plants. According to *The Rough Guide to Eastern Europe*, this is "Europe's youngest, most restless landscape." Here, falcons arrive from Mongolia, ducks and cormorants from China, and cranes and snipe from Siberia, in addition to many other species of birds from India and other places. At this point in its journey, Sitwell writes, "the Danube passes out of civilization into nothingness, towards the Tartar steppe." E. O. Hoppe, another early-twentieth-century British traveler in Romania, and the author of *In Gipsy Camp and Royal Palace*, described the Danube delta as consisting of "Conrad-like stretches—the Conrad of *Heart of Darkness*."

The passengers around me intensified my feeling of having passed beyond Europe. There were Russian Lipovans, with long stringy beards and black cylindrical hats, whose fanatical ancestors had come to the delta during the seventeenth and eighteenth centuries as religious refugees, opposed to the secular-minded reforms of Czar Peter the Great. I saw blond Ukrainians, whose Orthodox Christian ancestors had settled in the delta 200 years ago to escape persecution from Ukrainian Catholics. There were also Gypsies (*Tziganes* in Romanian) cluttered with bangled and gaudy fabrics darkened from mud; according to one theory, the Tartar hordes of Batu Khan had brought them to Romania as coppersmiths in the thirteenth century.

During the 1970s and 1980s, the Gypsy population of Romania may have doubled, from 2 million to 4 million, even as the overall population of the country remained unchanged at 23 million. Despite Ceausescu's outlawing of abortions and birth-control devices—so that the Romanians could outbreed the hated Hungarians—the regimen of poverty and semistarvation he instituted not only increased infant mortality rates, but drove women to have illegal abortions in order not to have more mouths to feed. But the Gypsies just kept having babies, as if nothing had changed. They had always lived in poverty, and outside the law.

The Gypsies I saw on the boat seemed to fit the worst stereotypes of Gypsies: drunk, dangerous, with restless hands bent on theft. E. O. Hoppe writes that a Romanian Gypsy's "dearest possession" is his fiddle. "Take it from him, and he is a broken man." No Gypsy I saw had a fiddle. In *Raggle-Taggle*, Walter Starkie had written a whole book about Gypsy troubadours in Hungary and Romania. But nowhere—not on this boat nor anywhere else I traveled in Romania—did I encounter "the music with its strange cadence, its florid trills" that Starkie described. Long ago, Ceausescu had insisted that all Gypsy folk music played in public be infused with Marxist lyrics, so few played it and the tradition had gradually been lost. The worst Western pop music blared out of the transistors on this boat. But it was the alcoholism that unnerved me.

Not only the Gypsies, but almost all of the men on this boat (and the men far outnumbered the women) were drunk and getting drunker, in a very unpleasant way. After the bar ran out of *tuica*, bottles were pulled out of burlap sacks. Some of these bottles contained homemade brandy; others, medicinal alcohol. As the crowd thinned out at halts along the way, I realized that the heaviest drinkers were staying aboard and congregating in the cabin, where bad weather on deck compelled me to go, too.

The air in the cabin was an invisible wall that slammed me in the face. With the windows sealed shut, most of the free oxygen had been sucked out of the air, its place taken by carbon dioxide, vapors of brandy, and perspiration, and the vilest of tobacco fumes. A forest of empty bottles spread across the tables. The Gypsies, Ukrainians, and others were shouting at each other in a way that implied violence. They wore sweaters and sport jackets that had lost all color and shape from being worn every day and never having been washed. On their feet were cheap slippers and pointed, silver plastic shoes, among other kinds of barely describable footwear. I was hungry and tired from standing, so I took a vacant seat in the midst of these men.

I could barely converse in Romanian, but I knew French and German. Unluckily for me, the fellow opposite knew some German, too.

He leaned across the width of the table, knocking over an empty bottle with the unfocused eyes typical of drunks, shouting and spraying spit in my face: "*Ja, Ich spreche Deutsche* [Yes, I speak German], *ja, ja, ja, ja . . .*"

I tried to pretend that I didn't understand, but his life story rambled out anyway. He was born in a delta village, from a mixed Ukrainian-Romanian family. In the 1960s, when Gheorghiu-Dej and Ceausescu were constructing Romania's largest iron and steelworks at Galati, forty-five miles northwest of Tulcea (where the Danube meets the Prut as the latter flows down from Moldavia), he was conscripted for work there and never left, except to visit his family in the delta. Although married with children, in Galati he lived in a dormitory with other factory laborers. He spoke Ukrainian and Romanian, and had picked up a bit of German somehow.

When I finally opened my mouth and told him I was an American, he said, still shouting: "Ceausescu *nicht gut* [not good], Iliescu *gut, sehr gut* [very good]."

This he repeated many times, as if I couldn't hear him. Then: "*Studenten auch nicht gut* [Students, too, no good]."

"Why?" I asked.

"*Fascisten,*" he said, spraying my face with spit.

"Oh." I didn't bother to argue.

On the table, beneath the bottles, was a pro-government newspaper that had a headline about ex-King Michael (*Mihai* in Romanian). "What about Michael?" I asked.

"*Nicht gut, nicht gut,* . . . he is a Hohenzollern, Hohenzollern: a foreigner, a foreigner." He translated my question to the other men, who then began screaming words about Michael which I did not understand but which sounded quite awful. He explained to me that in 1947, Michael had left Romania on a private train filled with all the country's money and art treasures. This, of course, was very nearly what Michael's father, King Carol II, and Lupescu had done in 1940.[3] But when I explained this to the fellow, he just shouted me down with "*Nein, nein!*" I closed my eyes and pretended to fall asleep. The drinking went on.

Another of Ceausescu's legacies was this underclass straight out of George Orwell's *1984*: badly urbanized peasants who, according to a local proverb, were "neither horse nor donkey," uprooted from villages where their ancestors had lived for decades or centuries—away from every tradition they ever had—and moved to factory dormitories where everything was in short supply except alcohol and regime propaganda. Because Carol died in 1953, Michael was always the immediate threat; consequently, the Communists long ago began investing Michael with Carol's crimes. Half-starved and worked to death under Ceausescu, these men were now capable of anything. The miners from the Jiu Valley who, wielding clubs and axes, bloodied the students occupying University Square in Bucharest in June 1990, came from this societal substratum. So, in a sense, did the Ukrainians who served as guards in Nazi extermination camps. Peasant victims of Stalin's collectivization in the 1920s and 1930s, these men had become tools of the SS simply because the Germans, at the start of the war, provided some security to them and their families. With the miners, Iliescu again demonstrated how, if you provide such men with just a little bit more food and self-confidence, they make a chillingly effective praetorian guard.

In darkness, I walked ashore at Sfintu Gheorghe. There were no lights, just the bare outlines of wattle and scrap-iron huts on a bed of silt, with the sound of waves lapping. A lone baroque

3. Michael, too, has been accused of stealing wealth from Romania. But from other details this man gave me, it was clear that he was mixing the deeds of Carol II up with those of Michael.

roof was the only sign that I wasn't in Africa. The moving silt beds and the desolation kept reminding me of the upper reaches of the Nile River in Uganda and southern Sudan, where I had traveled.

Among the crowd at the dock I spotted an old man with a well-kept beard, a beret, and a walking stick. Instinctively, I blurted out in French who I was. To my relief, he understood and promised to find me a place to stay. Then a tall woman, who appeared to be in her mid-twenties, strode up to him. She didn't look as if she came from Sfintu Gheorghe: not only was she extremely attractive, with gleaming blonde hair and tastefully applied makeup, but her clothes looked Western-made. Immediately, the old man and the young woman began arguing. I was embarrassed. When she walked away in a huff, I asked the man who she was.

"My wife," he said.

He was sixty-three, he told me. But he looked older. He had once been a lawyer, but somehow or other—the specifics never became clear—he had gotten into trouble with the regime during the early years of Ceausescu's rule in the 1960s. After a spell in prison, he was forced to work in a lead factory. "My life was ruined; now I just live here and paint. I married that woman recently, but she deserted me two weeks ago.

"Wait here," he said. "I will find someone you can talk to, someone you will find interesting."

I had been waiting alone in the dark for about ten minutes when a young man grabbed my rucksack and said in excellent English: "Come. I am Mircea, the doctor here. You will stay with my wife and me. We have so much to tell you, too much. You won't sleep tonight."

Mircea lead me into a single-story cement dwelling with a tiled roof. Inside, a woman sat crouched on the floor, reading and listening to a cassette recording of 1972 vintage Neil Young.

She jumped up and shook my hand. "This is my wife, Ioanna. She is a doctor, too. We both are from Bucharest and are in Sfintu Gheorghe for a year doing national service. Please excuse the out-of-date music. It's the best we have."

The music was fine, I told him. So were the mineral water, the boiled eggs, the smoked baby shark, the tomatoes, and the fresh fruit. But what helped revive me most of all was the normal expressions on Mircea's and Ioanna's faces. Although Mircea was dark-haired with a moustache and Ioanna was blond, to me, then, they looked like identical twins. Their clear, direct eyes lacked any trace of the unfocused ignorance of the men on the boat, the gimcrack cunning of the prostitutes and hustlers, and the sadness of so many others I had encountered. Traveling in Romania was often like inhabiting the pages of a Dostoevsky novel.

"Welcome to Africa," Mircea said with a crooked laugh. "Here we are two doctors, but there is no penicillin, no beer, no running water, no anything except what the fishermen catch and what we can buy from smugglers and pirates. There are fifteen hundred people in Sfintu Gheorghe, mostly Ukrainians. There are forty diagnosed cases of cancer. Who knows from what? Chernobyl is across the Black Sea and there are no mountains in between. The river and sea here are filled with oil slicks. The dolphins are all dead and fewer and fewer birds come from Asia in the spring. I'd classify about half the town as alcoholics. The delta should be a tourist paradise. Instead, it's a social and environmental disaster zone. There were no political manifestations here last December. One day the picture of Ceausescu was taken down, that was all.

"The society is totally destroyed. It may take decades. I don't know if Ioanna and I have the patience. In the weeks after the revolution, we had the radio on all the time. We thought about our country and helping the people around us. But it is turning bad very quickly. Ioanna and I are back to thinking about ourselves, about emigrating, now that we are permitted."

I finished eating. Mircea and Ioanna took me to the home of the mayor. Finding our way required a flashlight. We passed a small Orthodox church. "The Ukrainians built it after a boat loaded with cement washed ashore a few years ago," Ioanna explained. "In a way, Sfintu Gheorghe is luckier than other towns in Romania. The sea brings us gifts. And because we are so isolated, the regime paid us little attention."

The mayor was not at home. His wife prepared dinner, however, and Mircea introduced me with such ceremony that I felt obliged to sit down at the table. Having just stuffed myself with eggs and baby shark, I now had to eat a plate of roasted pork and fish roe salad laden with garlic. There was only homemade brandy to wash it down.

A man entered and sat down to eat with us: middle-aged, rotund, with bulging arteries on his forehead and neck. He wore wide suspenders. His face was flushed and his breath smelled of alcohol. Masticating loudly, he began lecturing me in an almost operatic fashion, thrusting his jaw out like Mussolini. Mircea translated.

"It is all the fault of Roosevelt. Everything here," waving his hand. "He sold Romania out at Yalta. Otherwise Romania would be like France today."

"What he says is true," Mircea added, suddenly a bit angry. "Because of Roosevelt, that God-damn cripple, we suffered for forty-five years."

"Roosevelt was near death's door at Yalta; he died a few weeks later," I started to explain. "The agreement he negotiated with Stalin called for free elections in Eastern Europe. It wasn't his fault that the Red Army's presence in these countries made the agreement unenforceable. Blame Stalin, blame Hitler for beginning the war in the first place. But don't blame Roosevelt."

"Roosevelt, he was the traitor," the man in suspenders said, practically spitting at me.

"And now we are being sold out again," said Mircea. "This Bush, we don't trust him. Only Reagan was good for us."

At the mention of "Reagan," everyone around the wooden table—the mayor's wife, the man in suspenders, Mircea, Ioanna—all stopped eating and nodded their heads in a sort of approving benediction. You couldn't argue with these people who had been through so much and who could imagine the world only from their own narrow, dark vantage point.

"The 'evil empire.' I remember hearing Reagan's speech on the VOA Romanian broadcast," Mircea said. The others nodded their heads and kept looking at me. "He was the only one of your presidents to speak the truth. But this Bush, *ah*, just another Roosevelt. You watch, Romania will be sold out again. We always are."

"The world from the Prut and the Danube doesn't look as nice as it does from the Potomac," the man in suspenders said to me in a very accusing tone. "We are cursed by the Prut, it is not our true eastern border. Russia must be completely defeated." He gave the air between us a karate chop. "Bessarabia is ours, not Gorbachev's. Why does Bush like so much Gorbachev? Because your Bush wants to help this Russia against Romania."

"Is this man the mayor?" I whispered to Mircea.

"No," Mircea whispered back. "In fact, I don't know who he is."

After dinner, Mircea took me for a walk along the beach, at the point where the channel of the Danube my riverboat had been plying empties into the Black Sea. It was a cloudy night without stars, and I could make out nothing in the landscape. But close to the beach, the air was filled with the croaks of what seemed like millions of frogs, as well as the screams of a multitude of birds that I could hear but not see. I felt as if I were inside a bubble of darkness, and all of these sounds were really being made by human voices, ricocheting against the outer membrane that they were trying in vain to penetrate.

"You must understand," Mircea said, in the way of an apology. "We have been beaten over the heads for centuries. How are we supposed to be optimistic? You tell me that the situation in Europe is much more hopeful now than it was in 1945, and in my mind I believe you. But my instinct as a Romanian tells me that I should not believe you."

"How can you talk like that, considering what happened last December? Don't tell me you expected that?"

"Look around you. What do you see? Ceausescu has been executed—that I am glad about—but the damage he did will help to defeat us. And those bastards are still in power."

We reached the beach. The lapping of waves obscured the sounds of the frogs and the birds. Mircea pointed out the spot where the waters of the Danube met those of the Black Sea. But I saw only darkness.

"In Ceausescu's time, every so often, someone would swim out to sea at night where a boat was anchored, and try rowing to Turkey. Most drowned. A few made it."

I was a good swimmer, but swimming out into that freezing black void looked terrifying. "You'd really have to be desperate," I said.

"No more so than any of us," replied Mircea.

As we walked back to the house with our flashlights, it was impossible for me to be so gloomy and pessimistic. I was filled with a traveler's sense of awe at everything I had seen and heard during this first, long day on the road in Romania. The idea that I could even come to Sfîntu Gheorghe and meet Mircea would have been inconceivable a few months back, when Ceausescu was still in power. For over a decade, I had been making friends in other Eastern European countries. Now, finally, I could begin to count friends in Romania. Surely this was a sign of something good?

Mircea mentioned that two West German ornithologists, studying the effects of pollution on birds, had made it to Sfîntu Gheorghe a few weeks before me. I felt sure that, in the coming weeks and months and years, many other visitors would come here from the West. Forty-five years after the end of World War II, the nightmare was over. What I was experiencing was the morning after. But like God's "first day" in Genesis, that foggy, throbbing morning might last a long time.

CHAPTER SEVEN

Moldavia: "Conditioned to Hate"

My next train journey took me north, along a route parallel to
Romania's border with the Soviet Union: from Galati, a river port
on the Danube, to Jassy, the provincial capital of Moldavia.

By the time I secured a seat in a second-class carriage, puddles
of brownish water had formed on the floor, dripping down from
wet clothes and plastic and cardboard suitcases held together by
rope. Rain water also ran down the inside cracks of broken windows. It was a double-decker carriage, with standing room only
on both levels and no cushions on the metal seats. As the
train started up, cold wind and rain swept through the carriage.
There was much coughing and sniffling. As in Africa and Asia,
people blew their noses with their fingers. Children cried con-
tinually.

Tulucesti, Foltesti, Tirgu Bujor. Each town in Moldavia looked
exactly like the one before it, bathed in lignite fumes and other

forms of pollution that brought no development in their wake. As uncomfortable as I was, the scene I saw through the window nearly made me wish that I might never leave the train. It was as though someone had taken a billowing, yellow-green Oriental carpet, and poured tar all over it.

The turbaned church domes, the absence of automobiles, the processions of horse-drawn peasant carts (called *leiterwagens* by Bram Stoker in *Dracula*) waiting to cross the road as the train passed, and the horizontality of the landscape, in which one long, sweeping hill gave way to the next, might in other circumstances have created a romantic traveler's picture of Europe meeting the Asian steppe. But all this existed on and under a film of mud and floodwater on which garbage floated, without a single paved street in sight. For miles, my eyes followed the path of an elevated sewage pipe. This scabby and rusted pipe, about three feet in diameter, passed alongside blocks of houses and through playgrounds, fields, and factory yards, merging with feeder pipes at each town. The most indelible image I have of southern Moldavia is of a shepherd driving his flock across a mountain stream underneath this elevated sewage pipe, tied together in places by bundles of blackened rags.

The train passed through a series of tunnels. Because the overhead light fixtures had no bulbs in them, some people lit candles inside the tunnels, which dramatically illuminated their black, liquid eyes. There was a solemn, almost devotional cynicism to these eyes, reflecting, as though by a genetic process, all of the horrors witnessed by generation upon generation of forebears.

I now had to change trains.

In Romania, observed the Irish traveler Walter Starkie in 1929, train platforms are "a euphemism" for "narrow spaces between the railway tracks." I waited in a driving rain on such a platform: a series of concrete slabs, each no more than two yards wide, separating one track from another. Two trains—one carrying freight, and the other passengers—approached from opposite directions, creating crosswinds that nearly caused me to lose my balance and be hit by one of several metal bars protruding from the freight train. The rest of the crowd knew to stand sideways, shoulder-to-shoulder, exactly in the middle of the slabs. Their faces were stoic. This was something they had been doing all their lives.

The next train I took was even more crowded than the first one. The crowd pushed me into a corner, where I stood in the narrow space between two sets of seats. I concentrated on the path of the same elevated sewage pipe, in order to suppress the need to urinate. This worked well for about fifteen minutes. After an additional fifteen minutes had passed, my need to urinate became intolerable.

"Toaleta," I said, to the crowd in general.

A young man lifted his eyebrows as though to offer me his condolences, pointing with a finger to the opposite end of the carriage. People were crushed chest to back, ankle- and knee-deep in baggage. Yet with barely a mutter, this tough-looking crowd somehow made a path for me. *"Multsumesc* [thank you]," I kept repeating. I arrived at the toilet cubicle only to find a family of Gypsies camped inside with their luggage. The Gypsy women filed out. The Gypsy men made it clear that they planned to remain, to guard their burlap sacks. Without protest, I just did what I had to do.

The window glass by the toilet was completely missing, and rain was falling inside the cubicle. But at least the air was fresher. On the wall above the toilet seat, someone had scrawled, *"jos nomenklatura* [down with the nomenklatura]."

Nine hours after leaving Galati, I arrived in Jassy—hungry, cold, caked with mud, and a bit humiliated. What would day after day, year after year of this do to my thinking? I wondered. But I knew the answer already: I thought of Mircea and the man with the wide suspenders.

Jassy often appears on maps as "Iasi," pronounced *"YASH"* by Romanians. Sitwell noted that "Jassy is the town, in all Roumania, which occurs most often in history."

Since the Middle Ages, Jassy has been the most important town in Moldavia, a territory that stands lengthwise against the Ukrainian steppe with barely a foothill for protection, as though it were a line of naked prisoners facing an icy wind. Jassy witnessed six invasions by Russians in the eighteenth and nineteenth centuries. In the 1850s, when Bucharest was still a small town, Jassy was a hotbed of Romanian nationalism. Here, in 1859, Alexandru Ion Cuza proclaimed the first Romanian state of modern times. In the 1870s and 1880s, Romania's greatest poet, Mihai Eminescu, lived in Jassy and wrote "Satire III," about "long and hook-nosed" foreigners:

> *This poison froth, this dung-heap, this foul and filthy brood*
> *Have they indeed inherited our nation's masterhood!*

Nicholae Iorga, Romania's greatest intellectual, who in his old age would be tortured to death by the fascist Legionnaires for not being sufficiently nationalistic and anti-Semitic, grew up in Jassy at the same time Eminescu was writing his poetry. And Lupescu grew up here a short time later, at the turn of the century. During World War I, Queen Marie and the other members of the royal family took refuge in Jassy after the Germans captured Bucharest. Between 1916 and 1918, Jassy served as the capital of free Romania. After the war, Professor A. L. Cuza (no relation to the Cuza who had declared independence in 1859) taught at the university in Jassy. Professor Cuza would later brag that he had given his first anti-Semitic speech the year Hitler was born (1889). One of Professor Cuza's disciples was Corneliu Zelea Codreanu, the founder of the fascist Legion of the Archangel Michael. Codreanu began his political career in Jassy in the 1920s, organizing anti-Semitic demonstrations on the campus of Cuza University (named after the Cuza who had proclaimed independence).

Behind much of this hate lay a lingering fear and sense of vulnerability. Until 1918, Jassy lay only ten miles from the Russian border on the Prut River. On the other bank of the Prut lay the eastern half of Moldavia, known as Bessarabia on account of a Wallachian feudal family, the Bessarabs, who first settled the region. In the peace settlement that followed World War I, Romania reclaimed not only Bessarabia, but also a northern fragment of Moldavia from the dismembered Austro-Hungarian Empire. But the fact of having an additional fifty miles of territory between it and the Soviet border—now demarcated by the Dniester River instead of the Prut—was not enough to dampen the nationalist fires that burned in Jassy, after World War I, stoked as they were by the democratization of Romanian party politics, the worldwide economic depression, the rise of fascism across Europe, and the misrule of King Carol II in the 1930s.

In June 1940, Stalin grabbed back Bessarabia; for the next five decades, the border was once again moved to the Prut, just over Jassy's horizon. In the wake of the December 1989 revolution, Jassy's residents were finally free—for the first time in half a century—to express their feelings about all of this.

The Traian Hotel was a great Empire-style wedding cake on the edge of Jassy's central square. The scene in the lobby and adjoining restaurant was one of corroded grandeur: big, dark stains on the red and brown carpets; metal champagne buckets filled with phlegm and mountains of cigarette ash; men and women huddled in overcoats with greasy faces and cigarette-stained fingertips; a Gypsy boy going from table to table, begging; waitresses, whose white socks partially covered their hairy legs, sitting by themselves in the corner, ignoring the customers.

A peroxide blonde arrayed in cheap costume jewelry, with massive breasts and badly applied makeup, guarded the reception desk. Feeling filthy and cold, I asked her in French if there was a single room available.

"*Vous,*" she sneered. "*C'est trop cher pour vous* [It's too expensive for you]." She told me to go to the Hotel Unirea, a veritable flophouse next door.

When I asked how much a single at the Traian was, she said it was $63.

"Oh, I can afford that," flashing her my American Express card. She turned the card over to examine both sides. Her stare was uncomprehending.

"*Voluta,*" she demanded, rubbing her thumb against her forefinger, using the Romanian word for Western currency. I showed her a wad of United States dollars. She smiled and gave me a room key. There were no bellhops.

The room, with its white Empire furniture, lush red upholstery and purple wallpaper conveyed the bawdy sensuality of a brothel. There was no soap, no toilet paper, and (as I found out) sometimes no water in the taps. I called the reception desk. I was told that toilet paper would be sent up immediately. Soap, however, was in short supply. I called room service. I was told that the restaurant was out of red wine, beer, and mineral water. Only white wine was available—warm, since there was no ice. Pork was the only meat in stock. It was cold and difficult to cut.

Romania was an original mix: a population that looked Italian but wore the expressions of Russian peasants; an architectural backdrop that often evoked France and Central Europe; and service and physical conditions that resembled those in Africa.

By early evening, the rain had stopped and sunlight was breaking through the clouds. I went for a walk.

Had I been able to block from sight the repeated insults and provocations of Communist-era construction, placed at strategic visual points throughout the city, Jassy might still have appeared as a leafy and monumental cityscape: a faithful, albeit provincial, copy of Vienna, with a university-town ambience. The garden in front of the gilded, neobaroque National Theater (built in the late nineteenth century, and one of Romania's most beautiful edifices) was delineated by statues of poets, composers, and pedagogues of old, including one of the nationalist poet Eminescu. But the maze of hedges these statues looked out over had not been trimmed, giving the garden a forlorn appearance, like that of a man who had forgotten to shave. Adjacent to the garden was the hard-angled brick cement of the now-defunct Communist party headquarters.

The nearby Metropolitan Cathedral of Jassy was built in 1833 in a neoclassical style. It sat on a leafy green platform overlooking a vista of smokestacks in the lower city. But the cathedral did not even dominate this platform. Wedging it in from the side—a deliberate, concrete blitzkrieg aimed at all religion and tradition—was a gigantic apartment block: a slum monstrosity-to-be, still under construction, so close to the cathedral that some of the overhanging girders almost touched it.

In the cathedral lay the reputed bones of St. Friday, in a gold coffin whose lid was open. I watched a throng of Romanians wait in line to touch and kiss the skeleton. What struck me was the fervor and terror of the faces waiting in line. Not merely were the people repeatedly crossing themselves, but they were doing so with their knees on the floor, and some of them were sweating profusely. They were truly drenched in sweat, even though the air felt colder in the cathedral than outside. Several worshippers scribbled notes to the saint—but not just one note. Each supplicant seemed to be writing as fast and intensely as he or she could, note after note after note. Only in Shiite holy places in the Middle East had I experienced such a charged and suffocating religious climate, rippling with explosive energy. It frightened me.

"Romania is too far off to be helped by the West. The messier and bloodier the disintegration of the Russian Empire is, the better for us. That's the only way for us to become democratic and to be reunited with our brothers in Bessarabia."

Petru Bejan was an editor of *Timpul* (*The Times*), a weekly newspaper born a few weeks after the December 1989 revolution and published by students at Jassy's Cuza University. *Timpul's* masthead bore the religious pronouncement *Adeverat a inviat* ("Truly He has risen"). The issue Bejan gave me to inspect contained several articles about the addition of Bessarabia to Romania in 1918 and about the "cultural genocide" perpetrated by the Russians in Bessarabia since World War II. There was also an article about Orthodox saints and a column devoted to Eminescu's poetry.

Bejan told me that a "second revolution" was necessary in Romania, in order to root out "all traces of coercion, bureaucracy, and socialism. They can't buy us off with coffee, eggs, and meat." Bejan claimed that General Ion Antonescu, the pro-Nazi Conducator and World War II ruler of Romania, was a patriot who had always acted in Romania's best interests.

Bejan's office was full of old typewriters. He wore a purple shirt and a thin brown tie that appeared to be made of imitation leather. His hair, short and unwashed, and his expression, so posed and so severe, made him look like a 1917 Russian revolutionary. His green eyes were like those of a prisoner in a mine shaft, intently focusing on a small circle of sunlight above, not knowing quite how to reach it.

I left the offices of *Timpul* and went to those of *Opinia Studeneasca* (*Student Opinion*), another weekly put out by university students in Jassy after the anti-Ceausescu revolution. I had trouble finding *Opinia Studeneasca*, and sought help from a student I met in the street, who told me that he had been a technician on the Danube canal project at Cernovoda. In the course of a conversation about the revolution, this student claimed that Ceausescu "is not dead, only in hiding." Apparently, Ceausescu often employed a look-alike for public occasions, and this look-alike was the man executed. "If you looked closely at the face in the video film, you could see it wasn't Ceausescu's." I replied that people's faces can change dramatically after they die. "But not that much," he countered. I recalled a passage from *Dracula,* in which Bram Stoker noted how "every known superstition in the world is gathered into the horseshoe of the Carpathians, as if it were the centre of some sort of imaginative whirlpool."

It was near midnight, raining. A large room at *Opinia Studeneasca* was filled with students, who sat around a table with a few old typewriters, like those I had seen at *Timpul.* Nobody was typing, though. They all talked unceasingly in a low, conspiratorial tone. All smoked cheap, unfiltered cigarettes. But these students bore little similarity to the American campus intellectuals of the 1960s. The ones here were a tough lot, with holes in their shoes and hand-me-down clothes that really were hand-me-downs. They had the grimy hands, the dead-looking hair, and the bumpy and sallow complexions that came from a life of enforced poverty. Their eyes resembled those of a person alone in a dark alley at night; the fears of these students were real and physical.

"Students died in the streets last December, but the Communists and the Securitatae remain. The corrupt professors who accept bribes from foreign students in return for giving them passing grades are still teaching at the university in Jassy, protected by the Securitatae," explained Cristian Mungiu.

Mungiu had a friendly face. He smiled easily, had black wavy hair of ordinary length, and wore a Western-made dungaree jacket. Unlike the others in the office of *Opinia Studeneasca,* Mungiu could have been mistaken for a university student in America. He told me, "In Romania today there is a lack of political culture that no one can imagine. . . . Ceausescu is dead, but Iliescu is almost as bad, and will become worse. These people, Petru Roman [then the Prime Minister] and Slyviu Brucan [a former Romanian Ambassador to the United States and Communist party intellectual] are autocrats now enjoying the soup of power."

Mungiu felt afraid and humiliated. He was afraid because "the Securitatae is still in power." He was humiliated because the December revolution should have begun in Jassy, not in Timisoara.

On December 14, two days before the first demonstrations in

Timisoara, university students here had organized a public protest in the main square by the Traian Hotel. But the Securitatae found out about it and occupied the square, keeping all trams, taxis, and other vehicles from stopping nearby. "We were easy to crush," Mungiu remarked bitterly. "If only we could be like the students of Timisoara. Timisoara is now the revolutionary city of Romania. It is close to the West. Jassy has a great and proud tradition of nationalism, yes, but we are too close to Russia, to the East. All the influences upon us are Oriental, bad."

A few days later, I met Mungiu again at the offices of *Opinia Studeneasca*. This time he was with his older sister, Alina, a medical doctor, who planned to quit her career in medicine in order to become a writer. She was about to publish her first novel.

Mungiu told me about his family. Here and there his sister interrupted to correct a small detail.

"Both my grandmothers, as well as my mother, were born on the other side of the Prut in Bessarabia. My grandfather was a prisoner of the Russians in World War II, when Romania was allied with Germany. The Nazis were not bad to us, not bad at all. Believe me, we lived much better under the Nazis than we ever lived under the Communists.

"My grandfather escaped twice from a Russian prisoner-of-war camp. The first time he was caught and sent back to the camp. The second time he walked for many nights before being captured again, near the Prut. The Russians were about to execute him when something happened, I don't know exactly what, and a fellow Romanian saved his life. For ten years after World War II, he and my grandmother listened to Radio Free Europe every night. They expected the Americans to liberate Romania from the Russians. They were convinced that America would do something. You Americans bitterly disappointed them.

"When the Romanian army was forced to withdraw from Bessarabia near the end of World War II, my other grandmother had forty-eight hours to leave her house, her parents and her brother, and everything she owned. Later, she learned that the Russians had executed her father and her brother. She blamed the Americans for this, for not helping Romania against the Russians.

"Even now, when my older relatives get together, they talk

constantly about Bessarabia, about what is changed there, about what the Russians did to their former neighbors in the village.

"At school, they taught us that King Carol II and Antonescu lost Romanian territory by making alliances with the Nazis. But we learned the real truth from our parents. Therefore, we know that Antonescu was a great patriot, a hero. The Russians and the Romanian Communists were the villains."

I asked him about the Jews.

"The Jews were not patriotic. Romania was allied with Nazi Germany, but Romanian Jews helped the Russians. You see, the Jews controlled everything here in Jassy during the war. Even at the end of the war they were very powerful."

"But there was a pogrom in Jassy at the beginning of the war. How could the Jews be powerful after that?" I asked.

"Many Jews survived the pogrom. They were still powerful in the local economy."

"How old are you?" I asked.

"Twenty-two."

"Do you believe everything that your grandparents told you?"

He was silent for a moment; then he said, "I believe all their facts, yes. But I suppose that their interpretations are not always correct."

"For instance," his sister Alina interjected. "It is understandable that the Jews would help the Russians. I don't blame them for that. Everyone here—us, the Jews—are all trapped between great historical forces. In Romania, everyone protected themselves through devious alliances."

Because of the country's obscure geographical position in Europe's back-of-beyond, events in Romania, no matter how terrible, have always assumed a remote, sideshow quality to people in the West. The Holocaust in Romania was no exception to this rule. Goldie Horowitz and the other journalists left the Athenee Palace in January 1941, but history here continued its sinister march, even though there were no longer Western observers to write about it.

Having used his troops and tanks to smash the putsch attempted by the Legion of the Archangel Michael in Bucharest in January 1941, Conducator Antonescu's next order of business was to recover Bessarabia, which Stalin had unilaterally annexed seven months before, in June 1940, under Carol II's watch. This could only be done through an alliance with Nazi Germany. Antonescu made it clear to Hitler that Romanian troops would enthusiastically join in an invasion of the Soviet Union if liberating Bessarabia were part of the deal. The Nazi invasion of the Soviet Union began on June 22, 1941. On June 25, as the Romanian army crossed the Prut to liberate Bessarabia, some Romanian soldiers deserted and took refuge in local houses—including, perhaps, some Jewish houses. A wild rumor spread through Jassy that, in fact, all the deserting soldiers were being protected by Jewish families. Furthermore, these soldiers were said to be not Romanians at all, but Soviet paratroopers who had landed during the night on the outskirts of the city. The rumor, false in every particular, ignited a pogrom. Over the next few days, the Romanian army killed 4,000 Jews in Jassy and the surrounding villages. The army then evacuated an additional 8,000 Jews from the Jassy region. The soldiers crammed them all into padlocked cattle cars, which, in the general confusion and absence of clear orders, rolled around the Moldavian countryside for several days, until all 8,000 occupants died of thirst and asphyxiation.

The Jews who remained in Jassy lived through the rest of the war in terror of more death transports and pogroms. But no such events followed—on this side of the Prut, that is.

From the moment his troops crossed the Prut, Antonescu became obsessed with gaining territory. Even after his army had reached the banks of the Dniester (the river running parallel to the Prut, fifty miles to the east, that forms Bessarabia's eastern border with the Ukraine), Antonescu was still not satisfied. He ordered his troops to continue advancing eastward, across the Dniester into the Ukraine itself, where Antonescu proclaimed a "Transdniestrian Republic." Since Nazi Germany wanted to destroy the Jews, and since Romania was an ally of the Nazis, Antonescu assumed that the Jews living in the path of this Romanian army advance were a potential fifth column. This belief was strengthened by stories and rumors Antonescu had heard about Bessarabian Jews helping the Russians, and about Jewish children throwing hand grenades at Romanian troops. "The Jews are receiving the Red army with flowers," Antonescu said.

In 1941 and 1942, Antonescu oversaw the deportation of 185,000 Jews from Bessarabia and the northern tip of Moldavia (also recently liberated from the Russians) to Transdniestria, where forward units of the Romanian army were setting up the only non-German-run extermination camps in Europe. From late 1941 until the middle of 1942, in this obscure and remote theater of the war, the Romanian army murdered every one of these people, stripping them naked, and shooting them in subzero temperatures. On a few occasions, when soldiers were low on bullets, they shot only the adults and buried the children alive.

It was too much even for Adolf Eichmann, the SS officer in charge of carrying out the extermination of European Jewry. In early 1942, Eichmann pleaded with Antonescu to halt the killings temporarily so that the job could be done more cleanly by Einsatzgruppen (special mobile SS murder squads) after the Nazis completed the conquest of the Ukraine, which Eichmann assumed would take only a few more months. But the Romanians were in a killing frenzy. Unfortunately for the Jews of Bessarabia and the extreme north of Moldavia, Antonescu ignored Eichmann.

By the late summer of 1942, however, the Romanian-run extermination camps in Transdniestria began to close down. Antonescu, whatever his faults, always had a sharp nose for the political winds just over the horizon. He had early understood the necessity for an alliance with Nazi Germany. And later, in 1944, he would foresee his own downfall. Now, just as the siege of Stalingrad was getting under way in September 1942—a turning point in the war—Antonescu began considering the possibility that Hitler might not win after all. Building bridges to the West required introducing a radical shift in Romania's Jewish policy, Antonescu realized. As the Soviet army, in 1943, was rolling back all the territory it had lost to Romania, first in Transdniestria and then in Bessarabia, Antonescu began building a reputation among international Jewish organizations as a pro-Nazi leader who would cooperate with attempts to save Jews and would even help smuggle them to Palestine.

Political considerations, though, cannot adequately explain this incredible behavioral leap. The historian Raul Hilberg, who documented the Holocaust in Romania in his 1961 book, *The Destruction of the European Jews*, asserted that in no other country during

World War II, except Germany itself, did national character play such a role in determining the fate of the Jews as in Romania.

Sadly, Romanian history has been a long and continuing hustle—the making of one desperate deal over the head of another in order to stave off disaster. Antonescu's pattern of actions toward the Jews differed little from the one he and his countrymen exhibited toward the Nazis and the Russians. As Hilberg pointed out, Romanian soldiers quickly earned a reputation within the Nazi military hierarchy as brave and, indeed, ferocious troops. But in 1944, when victorious Russian troops crossed the Prut into Romania proper, Romania not only switched sides to fight the Nazis, but did so with enthusiasm. Romanian troops quickly impressed Allied officials with their aggressiveness in fighting their former German and Hungarian allies in Transylvania, a territory the Romanians now sought desperately to recover: just as they had earlier sought to recover Bessarabia.

Explosive and short-lived paroxysms of passion have also characterized Romanian history. This trait, when combined with the ability to make expedient and contradictory deals, on top of Antonescu's fits of syphilitic fever, sheds light on Romania's Holocaust record. According to Hilberg's analysis, the Romanians simply got tired. The invasion of Bessarabia had begun in a flush of nationalist and anti-Semitic rage. Exultant at their deep advance into the Soviet Union, Antonescu's troops went wild. Though technically a program of extermination, the emotional trajectory of the Romanian army's actions in Transdniestria was more characteristic of a pogrom: a lot of savagery, particularly against children, in a relatively short space of time. Coincidentally or expediently, Antonescu and his army became exhausted with killing at about the same moment that the war was beginning to turn against Romania and the Nazis. This left him fed up with the whole business of slaughtering Jews. His hatred for them was completely spent. "I will have a bad reputation for these terrible murders," he muttered in mid-1942.

But the Conducator need not have worried about his subsequent reputation. Although deposed in 1944 and executed as a war criminal by the Communists in 1946, Antonescu was, in 1990, considered the most popular figure in twentieth-century Romanian history, towering above any member of the former royal family.

In 1990, King Carol I and Queen Marie were barely remembered, even though they had kept the country out of an alliance with the kaiser's Germany in World War I, setting the stage for Queen Marie's postwar maneuvering that resulted in the recovery of Bessarabia, northern Moldavia, and Transylvania in 1918.

The deposed King Michael was still suffering from the effects of decades of Communist disinformation, which had rubbed off on intellectuals as well as on the peasant underclass.[1] As a young figurehead king, Michael had conspired against Antonescu and the Nazis when it was unpopular and dangerous to do so. When only twenty-two years old, he had skillfully engineered Antonescu's overthrow in 1944, and afterward had led the political battle against the Communists. Despite paltry support from the United States and other Western nations, Michael desperately maneuvered behind the backs of the Russians until they finally forced him to leave at the end of 1947. Thereafter, Michael lived a dignified exile in Switzerland, supporting his family as a test pilot and technical consultant. Michael was the first Hohenzollern to speak Romanian as his native tongue, without an English or a German accent.

But Antonescu elicited only praise from Romanians—as a "patriot" who always acted in Romania's best interests and as a "victim" of the Communists, who unfairly convicted him of war crimes when everyone knew that either the Russians or the Germans had murdered the Jews in Transdniestria. The consensus in Romania was that Romanians had had nothing to do with it.

Whatever their views on World War II history, Petru Bejan, Cristian and Alina Mungiu, and the other students at Cuza University in Jassy that I interviewed displayed no current animosity toward Jews. Their anger was now directed against Arabs. I'll have to explain:

The longer Ceausescu remained in power, the more his style

---

1. By 1992, however, a shift in attitudes was finally apparent, as throngs of Romanians greeted Michael in the streets of Bucharest. This positive reconsideration of the ex-king is likely to gain momentum, perhaps leading to his permanent return to the country.

of rule began to resemble that of Carol II. Carol, by his own example, encouraged the prostitution franchise. Ceausescu supported comparable activities, but less directly. For political reasons, Ceausescu allowed large numbers of Arab students to attend the universities in Jassy, Bucharest, and Cluj. The Arabs quickly won a reputation for missing classes and for directing their energies elsewhere. The Romanian students I spoke with—as well as Western officials whom I interviewed over the years on this sensitive subject—strongly believed that a significant number of the Arab exchange students were engaged in black-market activities, particularly in running drugs from Turkey and Bulgaria through Romania to the West, with the direct connivance of the Securitatae. The drug-running left many young Arabs, not to mention the Securitatae, in possession of sizable amounts of hard currency. In the words of one Romanian professor, the Ceausescu era saw the lobbies of the Traian and Unirea hotels in Jassy, of the Intercontinental in Bucharest, and of the Hotel Napoca in Cluj become "knock shops," where "Romanian prostitutes publicly competed and humiliated themselves for the attention of these Arab boys," whose pockets were full of dollars.

"We hate the Arab students. We know that our civilization—despite the regime—is a European one. But the Arabs come from a lesser civilization and have no respect for ours. They just bought and humiliated us and our women. They buy off professors, too. Everybody at the university knows that the Arabs are the weakest students. In their own countries these students were poor. Here they are rich," Mungiu raged.

Another student told me that the Arabs "are like new feudal lords imposed upon us. When they need a sheep or a goat cooked for one of their religious festivals, they go to a village and pay the peasants to do it. There is nothing wrong with this. But you should see the expressions on their faces. The Arabs act like these peasants are *theirs*."

I pointed out that Romanians should not judge Arab culture by the students who were sent to Romania, since Arab countries have always sent their best students to the West, and the weakest and least serious ones to Eastern Europe.

I was not believed. "The Arabs oppress us," one student shouted back at me.

Adrian Poruciuc, an assistant professor at Cuza University and an expert on Romanian folklore, used a Danubian parable to explain what was happening in Romania:

A young hero lops off the head of an evil dragon, but the blood that gurgles out of the dragon's neck spreads pestilence throughout the countryside for years. "Think of the students in Timisoara who began the revolution last December as the young hero," Poruciuc counseled, "and everything else you see and hear around you—the people's ignorance of their own history, the insensitivity and the intolerance, and the drunken violence—as the dragon's blood.

"In Moldavia especially," Poruciuc went on, "Romanians have been caught in the pincers of three empires: Austria-Hungary, Ottoman Turkey, and Russia—czarist or Communist, it made no difference. The people here have been conditioned to hate."

Although an intellectual, Poruciuc came from a peasant family in a small village in Moldavia. We drank a bottle of white Moldavian wine in the Traian restaurant. "This was among the best Romanian wines," he said. "It is not filled with chemicals like the others."

I talked to him about Elias Canetti's theory of crowd symbols. "The Croats have their Catholic Church. The Serbs have the medieval monasteries and Kossovo Polje, the Jews have the Exodus from Egypt, et cetera. What would you say is the crowd symbol of the Romanians?" I asked.

Poruciuc was silent for a moment. He poured a whole glass of wine down his gullet. "I love such questions," he said. A knowing glint registered in his eyes.

"The Carpathian mountains and forests are the first natural fortress against the Pontic steppe [the steppes of southern Russia and the Ukraine]. In the Middle Ages, the Latin Romanians protected their church against invaders by, in effect, transporting the church deep into the forest; just look where our monasteries are located. Our church, like all the Orthodox churches, became the hearth of our culture during the Turkish oppression. But psychologically speaking, the church was more. It became the supreme symbol for one's hearth and home, whose security was always being threatened by plunder and starvation. *The home, the family seated around the humble table with food on it, that is the Romanian crowd symbol.* Thus you must protect the sanctity of your home and not let it be destroyed.

"We are a people whose hatreds, when they are analyzed, can be reduced to the fear of an empty stomach. The utmost pride of a Romanian during the Ceausescu years was to provide food for his family table.

"Ceausescu's rule was like that of the Turks. Inside their minds, our people are still in the forest, only now unbolting their doors, looking this way and that, very suspiciously."

CHAPTER EIGHT

The Land Beyond Dracula's Castle: The Painted Monasteries of Bucovina

Bram Stoker never visited Romania. But at the British Museum he did his research well. In *Dracula,* first published in 1897, Stoker located the "Castle Dracula" at the top of a mountain plateau, "just on the borders of three states, Transylvania, Moldavia, and Bukovina, in the midst of the Carpathian mountains; one of the wildest and least known portions of Europe."

Bucovina (as it is now spelled) is actually the northern part of Moldavia, annexed by the Habsburg Austrians in 1774. They labeled their new acquisition Bucovina—"beech-covered land"—on account of the territory's beech (*Buche*) forests. Complicating matters further, Bucovina is itself divided into a northern part and a southern part. The northern part was summarily annexed by Stalin in June 1940 along with Bessarabia, only to be reclaimed (like Bessarabia) in 1941, by Antonescu's army, which then transported the Jews of northern Bucovina to Transdniestria to be murdered by Romanian soldiers. Just as in the case of Bessarabia, Soviet troops recaptured northern Bucovina in 1943. The southern half of Bucovina, however, has always been part of Romania. Stoker situated Count Dracula's castle in the area where southern Bucovina joins both Moldavia proper and the northeastern tip of Transylvania. Jonathan Harker, one of Stoker's fictional narrators in *Dracula*, journeyed by horse-drawn coach up to the Castle Dracula from the Transylvanian side of the mountain pass. But the coach and its other passengers continued on past the castle, and then down the other side of the pass into southern Bucovina. This region, unrolling from the back windows of Count Dracula's mythical castle, was still, nearly 100 years after Stoker published *Dracula*, "one of the wildest and least known portions of Europe."

On the eve of World War II, in an observation about Bucovina that was as true in 1990 as it was then, Sacheverell Sitwell wrote: "In no other district that I have ever visited, be it in Spain or Portugal, in Sweden or the Gaeltacht of Western Ireland, is there this sensation of remoteness . . . a land of green meadows and firwoods. It is at an inconceivable distance from newspaper and tram."

After leaving Jassy, on Adrian Poruciuc's advice I headed for the forests of Romania's far north—southern Bucovina, that is—which, due to the very geographical remoteness noted by Stoker, Sitwell, and other long-dead writers, had escaped the worst social and environmental ravages of Communism.

As in other parts of rural Romania, I saw hay-ricks and horse-drawn *leiterwagens* bearing peasants in sleeveless sheepskin vests, white homespun linen, and black fleece headgear. Elsewhere in the country, such things were juxtaposed against ugly factories and cheap apartment blocks to form a picture of industrial poverty. In Bucovina, however, they were details in an idyllic picture of early-century Europe.

Among the wide ranks of beech trees, the soft hills were garlanded with pines, birches, and massive, black-pointed firs. Poplars and linden trees lined the roads, and apple trees filled the adjacent fields. Enjoying the absence of polluting factories and the blessing of blue skies after days of rain, I felt as if the black-and-white part of my Romanian journey had suddenly ended and the Technicolor sequence had begun.

Nestled between the Carpathian Mountains and the Soviet border, southern Bucovina had been largely forgotten by Ceausescu. Collectivization hardly took place here, and most of the agricultural land remained privately owned. These factors, along with a tradition of tidiness that locals say was bequeathed by the Austrians, whose rule ended only in 1918, is why nearly every aspect of the landscape cried out with pride of ownership.

In place of concrete walls, I saw freshly painted picket fences. Peasants had decked out the long manes of their horses with red pompons. Hand-carved wooden lintels and metal latticework adorned the farmhouses. There were elaborately designed scarecrows, and naive wooden crosses under shingle roofs along the road, which, as Starkie writes in *Raggle-Taggle*, "speak the sweet humility of a religion that belongs to the peasant."

During several days of travel in Bucovina, I noticed only one or two tractors; the peasants here used hoes and scythes. But of all the regions of the country I had seen and was later to see, the countryside of Bucovina—checkered with corn and potato fields—appeared the most prosperous and the least underdeveloped.

John Reed rode through southern Bucovina in a horse-drawn carriage that had been lent to him by a Jewish farmer: "Here the earth mounted in magnificent waves. . . . Through valleys whose sides fell like a bird's swoop were vistas of checkered slopes and copses soft with distance. Far to the west the faint blue crinkly line of the Carpathians marched across the horizon. Tree-smothered villages huddled in the immense folds of the land— villages of clay houses unevenly and beautifully molded by hand, painted spotlessly white . . . and elaborately thatched."

Miraculously, little had changed. The forests of Bucovina seemed to exist in a paradisiacal time warp. Here I traveled by foot and a lucky hitchhiker's forefinger (used instead of the thumb in Romania). Hitchhiking in Romania is not the daring means of travel that it is elsewhere. In this case, Ceausescu's madness worked in my favor. The shortage of cars, the horror of train travel, and the collapse of the intercity bus system had forged an informal, nationwide carpool network. In rural Romania, everyone hitches, including children and old ladies. Most drivers were obliging. Intent on trekking much of the time, I was actually frustrated to see a car pull up even when I didn't have my finger out. The custom was to pay the driver about 10 percent of the taxi rate for the distance. But when drivers found out that I was an American, they usually refused to take my *lei*. Several months after the revolution, meeting a Westerner was still a novel experience for Romanians who lived off the beaten path.

After a few days of such wandering, I wanted to inspect the monasteries of Bucovina that Poruciuc had mentioned to me, and talk to the nuns there. To do that, I needed a translator. I found one through the local tourist office in Suceava, Bucovina's principal city. The translator's name was Mircea, the same as that of my friend in Sfintu Gheorghe. To avoid confusion, I will henceforth refer to him as Mihai ("Michael"), because, as he later told me: "My father and mother wanted to name me Mihai instead of Mircea. But under the Communists, the name Mihai aroused suspicions because of King Mihai [Michael] in Switzerland. Before God, though, I am Mihai."

A modern town, rebuilt from the ruins left by World War II Soviet bombing, Suceava is one of the few places in Bucovina that has little ambience. Still Suceava is certainly not depressing like other Romanian towns and cities. There are many parks, the quality of construction is (by Romanian standards) high, and the inhabitants do not look so beaten down. "Bucharest is farther away from Suceava than it is from Jassy, and the Austro-Hungarians have been a good influence," Mihai explained.

At our first meeting, Mihai took me to a local bar in Suceava, decorated in a tasteless style that featured machine carpets on the walls as well as on the floor. In this weird and impersonal setting, Mihai went through the same ritual as other Romanians I had met: he poured out the story of his life.

Mihai was born in 1959 in Tirgu Mures, a town in Transylvania that has historically been a battleground between Romanians and Hungarians. Mihai's father was Romanian; his mother, Hungarian.

Before World War II, Mihai's father went to work as a bookkeeper in a wood-pulp factory whose owner was Jewish. During the war, Tirgu Mures, like most of Transylvania, was occupied by Hungary, an ally of Nazi Germany. The Jewish owner was taken to a concentration camp and never returned. After the war, as the Communists under Gheorghiu-Dej were consolidating their power, they took over operation of the wood-pulp factory, retaining Mihai's father as the bookkeeper.

"The new managers were from a very low class of society," said Mihai. "They were just thugs, people with no education, who cared nothing for the factory except what they could steal from it. They ran the factory down and sold the best pulp on the black market. My father, because he kept the books, knew exactly what was going on. But of course, he could do nothing. You in the West have no idea what it's like to be ruled by peasants.

"This went on for years. But my father never got used to it. He was a nervous man, he kept a lot inside him. One day at work he lost control. He shouted at the manager, 'I know what you've been doing. I don't like you or your party. You've destroyed a fine factory that a man had worked hard all his life to build.'

Police came to Mihai's house in the middle of the night to arrest his father. This was in 1964, Gheorghiu-Dej's last year in power. Mihai was then four and a half years old. He was asleep and doesn't remember his father's arrest. Mihai's most vivid memory of early childhood came three days afterward, when the police returned to do an inventory of his father's possessions.

"My father liked to read. He had many books. I remember men taking away all the books and papers from his study. They took his watch, his ring. We had a Persian carpet hidden inside a pillow case. The police came with a neighbor of ours, who had once slept at our home as a guest and knew where we kept the carpet. He told the police where it was, and they took it.

"My father spent a year in prison, 366 days because it was a leap year. He sat in his cell and did nothing. The prison guards did not allow him to read."

After his father's arrest, Mihai and his mother went to live with her Hungarian family, who put pressure on Mihai's mother to divorce his father.

"Because my father was Romanian, my grandmother always wanted to break up my mother's marriage. Now was her chance to do it. My mother didn't know what to do. She went to a friend, a Romanian lawyer. This lawyer told her, 'No problem. Start divorce proceedings against your husband, just as your relatives ask.

The proceedings will take over a year. Before they are completed, your husband will be out of jail and you can drop the whole thing.' That's just what my mother did.

"When my father got out of jail, my mother and I went back to live with him. But neither of my parents could find work. My father's old friends were afraid to speak to him. It must have broken his heart. My father died a few years later, in 1969, thinking Ceausescu was a good guy who would eventually change the system, since Ceausescu had criticized the Soviet invasion of Czechoslovakia [that took place in 1968].

"The summer of 1971, that was the turning point. Ceausescu made his first trip to China and North Korea. I'll never forget it. *Butch Cassidy and the Sundance Kid* was playing at the local movie theater. Ceausescu returned to Bucharest on a Sunday or Monday, I forget exactly. On Wednesday, *Butch Cassidy* closed down and was replaced by a Soviet documentary. We knew then that something had changed. It took you Americans another ten years to realize it.

"Imagine, others go to Asia and come back with ideas about trade and electronics. Ceausescu came back with the personality cult of Mao and Kim il Sung."

Little of his father's tragedy penetrated Mihai until he was a teenager. "I was in a café with some friends, when a drunk man began insulting me for having a criminal father. Then I began hating my parents. Now I hate myself for hating them."

Mihai learned not only Hungarian from his mother's family, but German as well. At a philology institute in Suceava, he mastered English and French. That wasn't enough, however, to get Mihai a job at the local tourist office, none of whose employees spoke any other language other than Romanian. The tourist office was run by a close friend of Emil Bobu, a close advisor of Ceausescu who came from Suceava (and was sentenced to life imprisonment after the revolution). Mihai had to settle for a job as an English translator of technical pamphlets at a machine tool factory.

"You see, under Ceausescu, someone who knew foreign languages was at a disadvantage. He aroused suspicions. The last kind of person the authorities wanted at the tourist office was a person who could communicate with foreigners. After all, who knows what he might say to them? And being the son of a former political prisoner made me doubly suspect."

When the Securitatae began shooting student demonstrators in Timisoara on December 17, 1989, Mihai told his wife: "It's all over, believe me; as soon as the Romanians see the blood of their children, they'll go wild."

In rapid succession, Mihai's life began to change. The negative items on his résumé suddenly became assets. Foreigners began arriving in Suceava—not many, just a few French journalists and Swiss Red Cross officials. But who could communicate with them? The embarrassed officials at the tourist bureau sent for Mihai. The foreigners paid Mihai in hard currency, which, on account of a new law passed a few weeks after the revolution, Romanians were now legally entitled to own and place in a savings account. The head of the tourist office was fired. Mihai became the deputy director. But he was soon spending most of his time as a private guide. The flow of foreigners to Suceava remained a trickle, but every one of them went to Mihai, paying him fifty dollars a day.

When it emerged that Ceausescu's social war against birth control had resulted in a large pool of orphans, other foreigners began contacting Mihai for help in adopting these orphans. Mihai arranged the paperwork in return for a hard-currency fee.

And Mihai had ideas of his own. When I met him, he was trying to establish a Suceava branch of Rotary International, "to teach people here that making money isn't enough; some of what you make you must give to charity."

Mihai wasn't sleeping much. "I can't. All my life has been a hard preparation for this moment." He went on: "Don't you see— the forests, the monasteries. Suceava is surrounded by the most beautiful countryside in Romania. This is a tourist's paradise, but there is no infrastructure for tourism. I will build one."

Mihai's immediate goal was to save enough foreign currency to buy a Western-made mini-van, in order to guide small groups instead of just individuals. "Once I have the van I'll be on the way to having a real company, which a foreign firm can then buy into, or even buy out, making me the local manager, of course."

Mihai also wanted to take his family to America:

"Don't misunderstand me. I don't want to emigrate. Why

should I be a poor Romanian immigrant in America when there is so much opportunity to make money in Suceava? But I need to touch the Alamo, to touch the Lincoln Memorial, to make sure that such things are real. I want my son to see America, to know what a society of dreams-come-true is like. You think I am not sincere? I know more about your American history than you do. And if I don't, I still appreciate it more."

Mihai was of average height and build. Like many Romanians, he had black hair and dark eyes. His clothes were shabby. It was the expression in his eyes and his way of speaking that distinguished him. Mihai was a fellow on the make. He came on to you, aggressively and unashamedly, with a product to sell: in his case, translation and guide services. His eyes were on fire with ambitious, meat-and-potatoes calculation, like those of a Russian cab driver in New York.

Although Mihai had an encyclopedic knowledge of Moldavian history, emotionally he seemed ahistorical. I tried to provoke him with charges against Antonescu. He was not really interested. Even Ceausescu did not interest him much. Why waste emotions on the past when there was so much to do to improve the present? Mihai had found the Promised Land inside his own country. He was one of the only Romanians I met in Romania who had no energy to waste on hate.

Mihai explained to me how, in the late fifteenth century, Stefan Cel Mare ("Stephen the Great") forged an independent and Latin-speaking Moldavian state in the midst of the Ottoman Turkish Empire. To teach the Christian religion and Moldavian history to their illiterate, peasant subjects, Stephen and his nobles built monasteries deep in the forest, safe from the Muslim Turks. They decorated the monasteries with traditional paintings, not just on the inside, but on the outside walls, too. The next morning, Mihai and I set out in his car to see these "painted monasteries," as they came to be known.

After forty-five minutes of driving, we reached the monastery of Humor. Humor is the smallest of the "painted monasteries," surrounded by ramparts of wood rather than of stone. It was built between 1532 and 1536, by noblemen under Petru Rares, Stephen the Great's illegitimate son.

Immediately I fell under Humor's spell, seeing its artistic visions of suffering and redemption as though they were a distant memory, in which the miles of beautiful forest Mihai and I had just covered counted for the backward passage of time. The grainy world of industrial poverty in the rest of Romania seemed light-years removed from this realm of sparkling copper, lacquered wood, and pure mineral and vegetable dyes.

Despite the wet climate and the passage of nearly 500 years, the paintings on the outer walls of Humor's church were in a magnificent state of preservation. The fan-shaped roof, extending far out over the walls to cover the paintings from the rain, suggested the protective intimacy of a peasant's home. So did the ring of pine trees surrounding the main church. But the most important factor in preserving these paintings has been their use of pure dyes: madder for red, cobalt and lapis lazuli for blue, sulfur for yellow, and so on. As Sitwell wrote, after visiting Humor in 1937, "these exterior frescoes in the Bucovina were executed with all the medieval care and attention that was devoted to miniature paintings."

The predominant color at Humor was madder red, with sulfur yellow and cobalt blue playing supporting roles. Across the bottom of the outside walls were the earthly prophets, in the middle the Orthodox Church fathers, and across the top the fighting saints—notably Saint George and Saint Michael. The anonymous medieval artists placed the Bible in a specifically Moldavian setting. For instance, the devil who tempts Abraham was dressed up as a Turkish houri. The scene of the Last Judgment, on the back outer wall, depicted the fallen angels as Turks and Habsburg Austrians, while the angel blowing the Lord's trumpet was a Moldavian shepherd.

In a lovely valley a few miles down the road from Humor, Mihai and I located a Jewish cemetery, whose grounds and crooked tombstones were guarded and well-maintained by a family of Gypsies living in an adjacent cottage. This cemetery was not a sad place. The dates on the tombstones indicated that the dead here had lived long lives and had been spared knowledge of what was to happen during World War II, when their fellow Jews in nearby northern Bucovina would be transported to Transdniestria.

"It is hard for me to believe that Romanians would ever harm a Jew," Mihai remarked. "Perhaps the Communists, the kind who mistreated my father, would do something like that, but not the simple people or our soldiers."

I was in too tranquil a mood to pursue the matter.

We came to the monastery of Voronets, concealed in a valley of towering beech trees on the other side of the Moldova River. Voronets, founded by Stephen the Great himself in 1488, is the oldest of the painted monasteries. The plan of the outer walls was similar to that at Humor and the other monasteries, except that the predominant color at Voronets was a blue so blue that it has come to be known as "Voronets blue." The fresco of the Last Judgment here was even more spectacular than the one at Humor. Hell was an endless tunnel of blood filled with drowning spirits. On the Scales of Justice, a few good deeds, represented by angels, outweighed many more bad deeds, depicted by monkeys and dragons.

Inside the church, the stone portal leading to the icon screen was rather low. I had to tilt my head to pass under it. "It is exactly the height required by Stephen the Great, a crown on his head, to pass underneath" without stooping, Mihai explained. Stephen the Great, alas, was only about five feet four inches tall. "*Nu mare de stat* [Not great by size]," said Mihai, quoting a sixteenth-century Moldavian chronicler.

Humor and Voronets were uninhabited, unlike the next monasteries we came to.

Moldovitsa monastery was built in 1532, the same time as Humor. Built by King Petru Rares himself, instead of by his nobles, Moldovitsa is larger than Humor, with long lines of stone ramparts rising over the trees in the forest. The reigning color at Moldovitsa was sulfur yellow, which glowed with the same force as gold leaf when struck by the sun.

"Now, do you understand why our national flag is red, blue, and yellow?" asked Mihai. "Because they are the reigning colors of our great monasteries: red for Humor, blue for Voronets, and yellow for Moldovitsa."

Pine and fir scents mingled with the dew to produce an aroma that approached the ethereal quality of beeswax. We met Mother Tatulici Georgeta Benedicta in the courtyard. She had been living at Moldovitsa monastery for twenty-three years, and had peculiar orange-green eyes. Mother Benedicta pointed out a group of local schoolchildren touring the monastery. "This was never allowed during the rule of the tyrant. Soon nuns will go back to live at Humor and Voronets. Why should those monasteries be empty when the rule of God has returned to Romania? You see, Romania is specially protected by the Holy Virgin. That is why forty-five years of Communism did not destroy us."

Mother Benedicta told me how, after hearing the first news about the demonstrations in Timisoara, she and the other sisters had come to the church at night to pray until dawn. They did this each night until "the Drac [Devil] fled Bucharest." The fact that the Drac was executed "on the same day that our Lord was born" constituted proof, in Mother Benedicta's view, that God had chosen Romania as the place where the millennium would be ushered in. Mother Benedicta did not deny "the past sins of our people." Her point was that, in the "Kingdom of God on earth" that would now be established in Romania, good deeds would be pursued with the same passion as bad deeds had once been.

"The people must cleanse their souls. Faith must be reborn. And it is happening. During Easter, people packed the church and the courtyard. Never before have I seen such a crowd. At midnight, we rang the bells. Everyone lit candles. There were thousands of candles. People cried. Nobody left until dawn. It was like the first Easter on earth. Before, I only believed that He had risen. Now it was a fact that he had."

Sucevitsa was the last of the painted monasteries I saw with Mihai. It was not built until 1584, long after the others, during a truce with the Turks. This relative stability emboldened its founders—two Moldavian nobles, Iremia and Simeon Movila. With its triple-tiered towers and ramparts, Sucevitsa is by far the largest of the monasteries. "There is no doubt that the first view of Sucevitsa," writes Sitwell, "is the revelation of something entirely new to experience. The Byzantines, at the height of their spiritual adventure, had the faculty of presenting a vision of the heavenly state. . . ."

Encased in a beech-and-fir forest, the reigning color of Sucevitsa's outer walls was dark green, representing, according to Mihai, "the dark green of the forests of Bucovina." The same Last Judgment, Ladder of Virtues, Tree of Jesse, saints, church fathers, and prophets were shown here as at the other monasteries. Only here, the scale was grander.

The nuns' quarters were inside the ramparts.[1] The Mother Superior, Adriana Cojocariu, invited Mihai and me to stay for lunch. We sat down by a long wooden table in a stone-walled room that was large and very cold. A sister served salami, goat cheese, a vegetable and pasta soup, sauerkraut, plum brandy, and rosé wine. It was the best meal I was to have in Romania: everything on the table was homemade on the grounds of the monastery. To warm myself, I drank several tumblers of plum brandy before attacking the rosé.

The Mother Superior sat down at the other end of the table. She was old, with a big wart on her nose and a large mouth. She had come to the monastery in 1948 and had spent practically the entire period of Communist rule inside Sucevitsa's massive walls. "Always, we had visitors. People would come here for a day or two, just to meditate, to give them psychological strength to deal with the world outside."

Her interpretation of December's revolution was the same as Mother Benedicta's: "God did everything through the hands of the youth and the innocent, repeating the scene of two thousand years ago when Herod killed the children of Palestine. Now the laws of the state are unnecessary, because we will have the rule of God."

The Mother Superior continued to speak from the other end of the table, her voice echoing against the empty stone walls:

"The revolution was a gift from God to the Romanian people. The Romanian people must now repay this gift by opening their hearts to people of all faiths, especially to those who suffered here in the past.

"Romania is one of the world's oldest Christian nations. Andrew, one of the Lord's twelve apostles, preached in Constanta. Five hundred years ago, the Moldavian monasteries were an example of what a small people could do. We can once more do a lot for the world."

Stirred up, it seemed, by the plum brandy and the rosé, Mihai added: "We have been *somebody*. We will be *somebody* again."

A sister brought in Turkish coffee and gooey sweets.

---

1. These monasteries have been traditionally inhabited by nuns.

"From now on we will have no problem with the weather," said the Mother Superior. "Under the tyrant, we were forbidden to take the icons and bones out of the treasury. Now, when the weather is too dry, we take the icons and bones outside in order to pray for rain. And it rains.

"Also, the storks have returned. For years, until this spring, we did not see the storks."

Later, Mihai explained that, soon after the revolution, the authorities in Suceava closed a synthetic-fiber factory that had been causing much of the atmospheric pollution in the region. Perhaps that was why the storks had come back.

There was one more monastery to visit, not a painted one— its exterior walls had no frescoes—but an important monastery nevertheless.

The next day, Mihai drove northward for two hours, until we came to a road paralleling the Soviet border that lay only three miles away through the fir forest. He followed this road to the battlements of Putna monastery. Stephen the Great had built Putna in 1466, before construction of any of the other monasteries. Here, inside the main church, on July 2, 1504, he was buried.

Stephen the Great firmly established Moldavia's northern and eastern borders on the Dniester River, currently fifty miles inside the former Soviet Union. On the Dniester, Stephen built a series of forts to protect his Latin holdings from the Russians and Turks. Mihai rattled off the names of these forts: "*Catatea* ['Fortress'] Alba, Tighina, Orhei, Soroca, Hotin." Because Putna was deep in the forest and far from enemy lines, Stephen gave orders that he be buried here, where his grave could be protected. Since 1940, however, except during the brief period when Antonescu occupied northern Bucovina, Stephen's tomb had been situated practically on top of the Soviet border.

We entered the church: Moldavia's pantheon. In the first chamber, inside marble tombs, were the remains of kings Petru Rares and Bogdan the One-Eyed; Petru Rares's wife, Maria; and Stephen the Great's daughter, also named Maria.[2]

Using a flashlight, Mihai led me into the last chamber before

2. Bogdan lost an eye in a battle with the Crimean Tartars.

the altar. On the left were the tombs of Stephen's second wife and their two sons, who died of disease as children. On the right, in a simple tomb of Carrara marble, was the tomb of Stefan Cel Mare. Draped over the Carrara marble was a Romanian red, blue, and yellow tricolor, on which fresh flowers had been placed. High over the tomb hung an unlit chandelier decorated with seven ostrich eggs, all hatched during Stephen's lifetime.

The cold, bare stone surroundings produced an austere and solemn effect. Over the portal of the nave was a dim and unsmiling oil portrait of Stephen. "No artist in Romania," Mihai noted, "will dare to paint a portrait of Stephen smiling, until all of Bessarabia and northern Bucovina are united with the rest of Moldavia under the Romanian flag, so that Stephen's grave and the others are again deep inside Moldavian territory, protected from the Slavs." Mihai's tone had still not changed: it was dry and informational, as if to say, "This is the way the people feel, like it or not."

CHAPTER NINE

Transylvanian Voices

It is on the plain that the regime really sank its teeth into the population. As in the Middle Ages, the mountains provided a measure of defense. Crossing westward over the Carpathians from Bucovina, I saw few signs of collectivization. The landscape was defined more by wood and natural stone than by concrete and scrap iron. I walked for long stretches downhill and even rode in the back of a *leiterwagen* for a few minutes, before realizing that I could make faster progress on foot. Only occasionally did a car pass on the road. I knew I was catching a glimpse of the Romanian countryside in a deliciously exciting moment of history: in the aftermath of a revolution, enabling me to travel freely, but before the process of modernization had begun.

Tirgu Mures was the first town in Transylvania I stopped at. I arrived in the morning, when the sun was burning off the mist from the surrounding hills, revealing the outlines of steep roofs, spires, leaden domes, and statues around a spacious green expanse called the Square of the Roses, lined with baroque and gothic facades. Unlike in Jassy, there were Catholic churches; and not only Romanian, but Hungarian, too—a tongue that conjured up Central Europe and not the Balkans—was being spoken in the streets. Surveying the square, I found an intimacy and a lack of strangeness that derived from a strong and generally uninterrupted process of cultural development, symbolized by the verticality of the architecture. Here was a coffeehouse culture, even though there had been no coffee for many years. I was back in Central Europe, albeit at the very rear door.

In the West, the very word *Transylvania* conjures up images of howling wolves, midnight thunderstorms, evil-looking peasants, and the thick, courtly accent of Count Dracula, as portrayed by Bela Lugosi. In fact, however, the historical figure on whom Dracula is based, "Vlad the Impaler," had his castle on the plain of Wallachia. Stoker's story, meanwhile, falls more into the realm of Bucovina and Moldavia than of Transylvania.

I am not being pedantic. Wallachia, Bucovina, and Moldavia belong to the East: the world of Orthodox Christianity, of peasant superstitions and mystic ecstasies. But Transylvania is, in essence, part of the same world that has had nothing but derision for the East: the West.

In the impassioned view of historian John Lukacs, Transylvania's Western identity is "the key to its history" and its "human fauna." Lukacs pleads:

> Transylvania had its high Middle Ages, cathedrals, Cistercians, a whiff of the Renaissance, its Baroque, its Enlightenment—the historical ages that made Europe . . . that did not exist in Russia or in Rumania, Moldavia, Oltenia, Wallachia, Bessarabia, Bulgaria, Serbia, Macedonia, Albania, Thrace, Greece, the Ukraine.

As Lukacs and others have pointed out, the Turks conquered all of the Balkans and half of Hungary in the Middle Ages, but they did not conquer Transylvania. While the plain of Athens below the Parthenon—not to mention Moldavia and Wallachia— dozed under an Oriental, Ottoman sleep, Transylvania was proclaiming the Enlightenment, with freedom and equality for both

Catholics and Protestants. William Penn was so impressed that he considered naming his American Quaker colony "Transylvania."

The religious freedom was only relative, however. The mass of native peasants—the Orthodox Romanians, that is—did not enjoy the benefits of this Enlightenment. They labored at the bottom of a medieval apartheid system, in which the Hungarians and the Saxon Germans, whether Protestant or Catholic, enjoyed all the rights. (Count Dracula had a Romanian name because he was from Moldavia. In Transylvania, the Hungarian elite never permitted the formation of a Romanian nobility.) Romanians, therefore, are not impressed with Transylvania's historical role as an eastern beacon of the West and of Central Europe; no more than black South Africans are impressed with the white community's role as a beacon of Western progress and efficiency on the African continent.

The cultural conflict has been further poisoned by Transylvania's particular importance in both Romanian and Hungarian tradition. For Romanians, Transylvania (Ardeal, "the land beyond the forest") is the birthplace of their Latin race, since the ancient Roman colony of Dacia was situated in present-day Transylvania. For the Hungarians, Transylvania (Erdely) was the site of their most famous victories over the Turks and of the democratic uprisings against Austrian rule that led to creation of the Austro-Hungarian Dual Monarchy in 1867. Janos Hunyadi, who defended Central Europe against the Ottomans; Matthias Corvinus, the greatest king in Hungarian history who brought the Renaissance to Hungary; Janos Bolyai, one of the independent inventors of non-Euclidean geometry; and Bela Bartok, the composer, were all Hungarians from Transylvania.

In the treaty of Trianon that followed World War I, in addition to Bessarabia and northern Bucovina, Transylvania was handed over to the Romanians.[1] The Romanian names of cities took their places alongside the Hungarian ones: Kolozsvar was now also called "Cluj"; and Marosvasarhely was called "Tirgu Mures." In these cities after World War I, the Romanians built Orthodox Cathedrals that dwarfed the Hungarians' Catholic and Protestant churches. The Orthodox Cathedral of Tirgu Mures, sitting at the

---

1. Trianon was a palace in Paris.

top of the square, included a mural painting in which Jesus, dressed in the costume of a Romanian peasant, was being whipped by men dressed as Hungarian nobles and soldiers. In addition to beeswax candles and poorly produced postcards, books were sold inside the cathedral that told about the persecution of the Romanian Orthodox Church during World War II, when the Hungarians reoccupied Transylvania.

Hungary, like Romania, was governed by a Hitler-allied fascist dictatorship during World War II. The cruelties it perpetrated in Transylvania against the local Orthodox population (and particularly against the Jews), nearly equaled the barbarity exhibited by the Romanians elsewhere. Because the Romanians switched sides after Hitler began losing the war, they were able to take back Transylvania. After the war, the Romanian Communist regimes that ruled Transylvania, especially Ceausescu's, returned it to the medieval apartheid system, only this time with the Orthodox Romanians on top.

Ceausescu forbade all public use of the Hungarian language and of Hungarian names for cities and towns. He shut down Hungarian newspapers. He closed hundreds of Hungarian schools and completely Romanized the Hungarian faculties at the university in Kolozsvar-Cluj, which nineteenth-century Hungarians had developed into one of the world's finest universities. And not only did Ceausescu forbid the use of the name Kolozsvar for Cluj, he changed the name of Cluj to "Cluj-Napoca," in reference to an ancient Dacian settlement in the vicinity—a quasi-historical connection that appealed to his crypto-fascist, blood-and-soil sense of nationalism. To alter the demographic balance, Ceausescu prohibited abortions and the use of birth-control devices among Romanian women, and he forbade Hungarians from giving their children Hungarian names at baptism. Finally, he moved hundreds of thousands of Moldavian and Wallachian farm and factory laborers into Transylvania, while forcibly relocating Hungarians from their territory to other parts of Romania. The border between Hungary and Romania—two Warsaw Pact allies—was for decades the meanest frontier crossing in Europe, certainly scarier than the Berlin Wall. Travelers would be stopped for hours in the middle of the night, no matter what passport they carried, while suspicious Romanian police searched every suitcase for

Magyar (Hungarian-language) publications, among other subversive items. In 1983, I had to bribe a Romanian border guard to avoid having my typewriter confiscated.

The 2.1 million Hungarians in Romania constituted non-Soviet Europe's largest ethnic minority and were double the number of West Bank Arabs living under Israeli occupation. But while ethnic Hungarians during the Ceausescu years suffered repression as bad as or worse than that endured by Palestinian Arabs—the 120,000 Jewish settlers on the West Bank were few in comparison to the numbers of Romanians that Ceausescu settled in Transylvania—the American media establishment's knowledge of Transylvania until the December 1989 revolution was limited to an image of Count Dracula.

As events unfolded, Ceausescu's repression of Romania's ethnic Hungarian minority provided the spark for the revolutionary fire in December 1989.

Reverend Laszlo Tokes, the Hungarian pastor of the Calvinist Reformed Church in Timisoara (Temesvar in Hungarian), had been openly preaching against the regime and its discriminatory policies. Timisoara is not in Transylvania, but in the Banat—a western frontier region of Romania where intercommunal tensions between Hungarians and Romanians were never as severe as in Transylvania. Thus, when Ceausescu's regime moved to send Tokes into internal exile, not only Hungarians but Romanians, too, joined the street protest in Timisoara, starting a chain of events that led ten days later to Ceausescu's execution.

In Transylvania, however, the weight of history, coupled with the sociological effects of Ceausescu's policy of mass population movements, quickly crushed the nascent intercommunal goodwill between Romanians and Hungarians engendered by the Timisoara uprising. "Please, let's not talk about Tokes," said a Romanian teacher of English I met in Tirgu Mures. "Even I, as open-minded as I am, have limits. The man is nothing but a Hungarian chauvinist. Did you read what he said, 'that for Hungarians under Ceausescu, Romanian became a language of oppression.' How could Romanian ever be a language of oppression?"

"The paradox is that we have suffered together," reflected Ion Pascu, a neurologist and rector of the medical institute in Tirgu Mures. "But now, suddenly, everything is poisoned."

Transylvania's very atmosphere was a paradox: the people were more Westernized than in Moldavia or Wallachia, but gutter prejudices infected the most sophisticated talk in sidewalk cafés. In a sense, Transylvania in 1990 was like Vienna or Berlin in the 1930s. I arrived in Tirgu Mures in late April, a few weeks after gangs of Romanians and Hungarians had come from the outlying villages to rumble with knives and clubs in the Square of the Roses, leaving several persons dead and over 250 wounded.

While tanks grimly patrolled the Square of the Roses in Tirgu Mures, some 50 miles away in Cluj (officially "Cluj-Napoca"), Liberty Square was filled with Romanian students on the afternoon that I arrived. They had covered the plinth of the statue of the Hungarian King Matthias Corvinus with the Romanian flag, having cut out the Communist symbol from the flag's center. The students sang the drum-rolling song "Awake Romania," written by Andrei Muresamu during the 1848 uprising against Transylvania's Hungarian rulers. The demand of the students: a second revolution, to rid Romania of the neo-Communist National Salvation Front.

For me, no city in the whole of the Balkans is quite as intoxicating as Cluj, with its steep, gabled roofs and its yellow baroque facades lining narrow streets of cobblestones that, in the early evenings, when the weather is warm, smell of the dust of the nearby countryside. There is an Indian-summer quality to this provincial outpost of Central Europe. Drunk on love and brilliant talk in the days when Cluj was called Kolozsvar, Hungarian romantics argued long into the nights at the cafés off the main square. To me, their spirits lingered still, as palpable as the memory of a good coffee or the taste of a particular kiss.

Patrick Leigh Fermor, the noted British traveler and Balkan scholar, thought that Mozart's *Don Giovanni* was performed in Cluj before it was in Budapest, and that Liszt gave recitals here. I settled in at the Continental Hotel on the main square, known in pre-Communist days as the Hotel New York, a yellow-and-white baroque building with silver cupolas. To its neo-Roman café, set about with gilded Corinthian columns, Fermor had come to drink and talk with Hungarian friends in July 1935. In his travel memoir about Hungary and Transylvania, *Between the Woods and the Water,* Fermor recollected hearing "the muffled lilt of the waltz from *Die Fledermaus*" drifting into the café from the hotel dining room. In 1990, no waltz music—and no Gypsy tunes either—emerged from the dining room; only the deafening metallic roar of what, to the rowdy and drunken men at the tables, symbolized the freedom and prosperity of the West. Unlike in Fermor's day, no one sat in a dinner jacket, sipping cocktails. The diners wore overcoats, and empty bottles of plum brandy and beer, watered down and rumored to be spiked with detergent, covered the stained and smelly tablecloths. Gypsies approached travelers in the lobby, offering Western cigarettes, pink-colored balloons, and prostitutes.

But despite the social and cultural destruction that the Communists had wrought by moving Romanian peasants into the city and native Hungarians out, the spirit of Cluj and Kolozsvar somehow survived. Starkie, in 1929, saw Cluj as "an ideal city for the contemplative traveller. Here might be the Oxford of the East of Europe, with its students and its traditional buildings." Though the once-great university was no longer what it had been in Starkie's day, it remained the city's determining presence, as my own experience demonstrated.

At a dinner party I attended on my first night in Cluj, I met Nigel Townson, an English teacher at the university, who, in 1990, was the only lecturer in Romania affiliated with the British Council. The British Council supports English libraries and lecturers throughout the world. Although strictly a cultural organization, with no official links to the British Foreign Office, the British Council's use of British Embassy facilities in many countries has given it an ambiguous image: people in the host country sometimes think that British Council lecturers are spies. Novelist Olivia Manning was married to a British Council lecturer, R. D. Smith, who served in Bucharest in 1940 and 1941. The absurd yet dangerous notion entertained by contemporaneous Romanians that he and the other bumbling bookworms on the British Council staff in Romania were spies provided the basis for the plot of *The Balkan Trilogy*.

Ceausescu also thought that British Council lecturers were spies. Under his rule, the conditions of their employment became so stringent that the 1980s saw a gradual reduction of British Council staff. Eventually, Nigel, the lecturer in Cluj, was the only practicing link to the characters of *The Balkan Trilogy*.

Nigel lived up to my every expectation. Just like Guy Pringle, the fictional British Council lecturer in *The Balkan Trilogy*, Nigel had a large build, wore wire-rimmed glasses, and was deeply immersed in the lives and problems of his Romanian students, worrying about whether this one would get a scholarship to study in England, and whether that one would pull out of a depression. Nigel read a book of English literature a day; he spoke Romanian, Portuguese, German, and other languages. He, his fiery Serbian wife, and their daughter lived in a typical Romanian apartment block on the outskirts of Cluj, putting up with typical Romanian hardships. The reappearance of eggs or beer in the local store, for example, would excite Nigel as much as it would his neighbors. Life wasn't easy for Nigel, but he had a better elemental grasp of what Romanians and their country were like than any pampered foreign diplomat could ever hope to have.

Without Nigel, I would not have met some of the people in Cluj that I did—people who, in spite of themselves, brought me face to face with an unpleasant truth: the Western Enlightenment in Transylvania was still a primarily Hungarian affair and had little effect on the local Romanian population.

Sandra Danciu translated the books of the late Greek author Nikos Kazantzakis from Greek into Romanian. My first morning in Cluj, I went to her apartment for coffee.

"Did you read *Zorba the Greek*?" she asked. "Then you know about the Devil himself being inside the monastery. It is so with us. In Alba Julia, for example, the confession stall in the church was bugged. . . . I don't remember one honest ruler in Romanian history. In Romania, evil always triumphed. And now the Hungarians are making all this trouble. It is true, they really are chauvinists. The way they talk about *their* Magyar culture, you'd think it was saints' bones."

I asked her about what happened in Cluj on December 22, 1989, the day Ceausescu fled Bucharest.

"I don't like to remember that day, because I associate it with despair. Even though Ceausescu is dead, we are still not released from our own selves."

"Can you just describe what you saw and felt?"

"The night of December twenty-first I couldn't sleep. I prayed. That day there had been a demonstration in the square, where the army killed many people. At six-thirty the next morning, December twenty-second, I got up and took my daughter for a walk, to see what was happening. I don't know what drove us to do it. It was a compulsion. There were traitors everywhere; it was so dangerous. Soldiers and Securitatae patrolled the streets. But I dared to measure them with hate with my own eyes. I wanted revenge for the tragedy of my people. I'll never forgive them, never. They are unworthy of any sympathy.

"My daughter and I were not the only ones on the street trying to find out what was happening. There were others. Everyone was going to the square where there is the statue of Michael the Brave. Doina Cornea was there, speaking to the crowd.[2] All of us swore against death to the spirit of Michael the Brave that we would come to his statue, every morning at the same time, until Ceausescu fell. Then we all went together to the Orthodox cathedral.

"We passed between two rows of tanks. Maybe they'll kill us, I said to my daughter. Then, I remember, a young priest came out of the cathedral. He was very serious, very intellectual. I felt his words reach the sky: 'Tatal nostru carele esti in ceruri . . . [Our Father who art in heaven . . .].'

"Later, the whole crowd moved on to the Liberty Square. There, someone shouted from a window, 'Tyrannul a fugit Bucuresti [The tyrant has fled Bucharest].' At that moment, I loved every beggar, every soul on the street. . . .

"Ceausescu's execution was like a cleansing of the soul, a bloodletting, the first spiritual exercise of our nation. . . . So bloody, so pure, our minds swayed between Christ and Ceausescu. But it was no good; it was still not enough. It was like I wanted to eat his flesh. No, we were not released that day."

"Who was the young priest who came out of the cathedral?" I asked.

"His name is Father Ion Bizau. You can find him always at the cathedral."

I discovered Father Bizau in the nave of the cathedral, holding a loaf of bread. He wore the black cassock and black, cylindrical hat of an Orthodox priest. I introduced myself. He smiled and,

---

2. Doina Cornea was a well-known dissident in Cluj.

for no reason that I could fathom, put the loaf of bread in my hands, motioning for me to follow him. "Come, you will be my guest for lunch."

Father Bizau kept smiling at me. He had dark hair under his black hat, and a long red beard. He appeared to be about my age, in his late thirties. His expression was meek, like that of someone who had been fasting for a day or two. Father Bizau was a small man. But when he gave me the loaf of bread to carry, I noticed that he had huge hands, very sinewy and with prominent veins. I immediately thought of the statue of David by Michelangelo in Florence, where the hands are also out of proportion to the rest of the body. I vaguely remembered reading somewhere that Michelangelo deliberately exaggerated the hands of his heroic subjects, as a symbol of virility and divine favor.

Inside Father Bizau's house there was a lot of screaming. Father Bizau and his wife had two small children. (Orthodox priests can marry, provided they do not serve in a monastery.) "Little Ion is six," Father Bizau told me. "Dumitru was born only last October. For twelve years we couldn't make a child. Then came Little Ion. When Dumitru was born last October, I took it as a sign from God that something good was about to happen here. Come into my study where it is quiet."

Father Bizau's study was lined with books. I noticed Shakespeare, Camus, Plato, O'Neill, Baudelaire, and Joyce, in addition to religious books and works by Romanian writers.

"A priest reads Camus—an existentialist, an atheist?" I inquired.

I then learned that when Father Bizau wanted to scream, he hissed softly, while holding out his huge hands to the sky: "Camus is more a man of God than any of the men who ruled us since the time of King Ferdinand and Queen Marie. Without God and Job, there could be no existentialism! Job's analysis of his own sufferings—that is not existentialism! Come, let us have bread and *tuica*," taking the loaf from my hands and tearing it into pieces on a table. "You see, the *tuica* bottle has a Hungarian label. That is good. Romanians and Hungarians must learn to love each another."

"People tell me that you were an important figure in the revolution here last December."

"I am not important," Father Bizau answered. "All of us collaborated by our silence. We are all responsible, not only for the crimes here, but for those of the other Communist regimes in Cuba, Ethiopia, North Korea. It is we who are responsible for the famine in Ethiopia. . . .

"For decades, our King, Michael Hohenzollern, a man who is not a pagan or a thief like our Communist rulers, was not permitted to set foot on Romanian soil. But a bandit like Yasser Arafat was allowed to come here! Tell me, how was this possible? How?" Father Bizau spread his arms wide and crinkled his forehead like a martyred figure in an icon.

"Drink, drink," he ordered me. "This is plum brandy made by the Romanian church and kept in a Hungarian bottle. You see," he went on, "the mission of a priest is to say what is right and what is wrong. To say which side is light, and which side is darkness."

His wife served lunch for us in the study: red wine, roast pork, and eggs. "Will you join me in a Christian prayer?" he asked.

"Certainly, but I am not Christian."

"What are you, a believer I hope?"

"I am Jewish."

"Then you must say your own prayer. And my wife must take away the pork and make something else for us."

"No, no." I became very embarrassed. "It's fine. I'm not religious. I mean, please. . . ."

His look was disapproving.

"Tell me," I began, changing the subject as I started to eat the pork and drink the wine, "what happened when the crowd came to the cathedral on December twenty-second, 1989."

"The Communist party headquarters are across the square from the Cathedral. Well, when I saw the crowd of people between the tanks, coming to the church from the direction of the party headquarters, I cried. I cried. For this was not a man's work, I knew. The people of Romania were leaving the place of the pagan and returning on their knees to *God's house*. On my knees I fell, and I said: '*Tatal nostru carele esti in ceruri* . . . [Our Father who art in heaven . . .].' "

"And now?"

"Now, there is so much work to do. The people still lack faith. They are suspicious of Doina Cornea and Laszlo Tokes—he, because he is Hungarian. Tokes is a hero, but no one will say a kind word about him. The truth is in our souls. But we are still afraid to speak it. We are a religious people, but we have become a spiritually disfigured people."

Father Bizau sent me away with a bottle of homemade plum brandy. He invited me to eat lunch and dinner at his home every day until I left Cluj. I had met him less than two hours before and had come without an appointment.

Walking back, quite drunk, to the Continental Hotel, I thought to myself that Romania was one of those places overflowing with passion, where you met the best and the worst people, and that perhaps the nuns in Bucovina were right: a savior could only emerge from a place where this much evil had been committed.

"I think it's time you had a talk with Gheorghe," said Nigel, flashing a wicked smile. "I have a feeling that you and Gheorghe will really hit it off."

I met Gheorghe and Nigel for lunch at a restaurant near the university. Gheorghe was tall with a very athletic build. He had short-cropped, gray-flecked black hair and a small black mustache. There was a certain charisma about him and a certain caginess, too. When I took out my notebook, Gheorghe said, "I would rather you don't use my real name." Therefore, "Gheorghe" is not this fellow's real name. Later, as I took out my wallet to pay the waiter, Gheorghe remarked, "I can see that you changed your money on the black market—by the way the bills are folded."

The waiters all knew Gheorghe. They served us quickly and politely, making sure to change the tablecloth and give us well-polished glasses: something rare in Romania.

But even if the waiters had not known Gheorghe, I suspect that the service would have been good anyway. Gheorghe is that enviable type of person who can walk into a crowded restaurant and get served quickly. Gheorghe would later brag to me, wagging his finger: "This is a country of lines. But never, never in my life have I had to wait on a line."

Gheorghe was in his early forties. His face was never without a worried look. He lived by the notion that the minute you stop worrying and stop assuming the worst, the worst will happen. In Romania, that's a good strategy to live by.

I can best explain the impression that Gheorghe made—the vibes he gave off—by comparing him to a character in *Doctor Zhivago*: Victor Kamarovsky, played in the film version by Rod Steiger. At the beginning of *Doctor Zhivago*, Kamarovsky is a prominent member of the Russian aristocracy, conniving for the czar and seducing the daughter of a friend, a woman less than half his age whom he gets pregnant. Kamarovsky next appears near the end of the film, after the 1917 revolution. Now working for the Bolsheviks, he has the same worried look on his face. "The Bolsheviks trust you!" exclaims Yuri Zhivago (Omar Sharif) naively. Kamarovsky sneers, as though talking down to a child: "They trust nobody. They find me useful."

Gheorghe was formerly a member of the Romanian Communist party. He now belonged to Vatra Romaneasca ("Romanian Hearth"), a secretive nationalist organization that, according to reports and hearsay, was a 1990s version of the Legion of the Archangel Michael, in addition to being a post–Ceausescu era refuge for members of the Securitatae, who still ran Romania behind the mask of Iliescu's National Salvation Front. Gheorghe also edited two newspapers in Cluj: one newspaper supported the National Salvation Front; the other, a student paper, opposed the Front.

Gheorghe made his mistakes, though. In London, where he went on a scholarship in the mid-1970s, Gheorghe did some freelance work on the side: selling used cars to Arabs, and arranging with a Romanian diplomat to sell Moldavian wine from the Romanian Embassy's cellar to local collectors. When Gheorghe returned home to Romania for a short visit, he was told that his passport had been invalidated. "I had seven hundred pounds in the bank in London; that is a lot of money for a Romanian. The bastards never let me out again," clicking his tongue and raising his eyebrows, the Oriental way of showing disdain.

There were rumors in Cluj that Gheorghe was a colonel in the Securitatae. But I don't believe that Gheorghe was anything more sinister than a classic hustler and survivor, awash in cynicism and pessimism, who despised both the system and those naive enough to openly oppose it. Gheorghe was a type who never starts revolutions but who always figures out how to benefit from the new order, whatever that new order is.

Gheorghe spoke English, as well as German and other languages, and was a self-taught expert on the novels of John Steinbeck. "Steinbeck is the only writer who could ever do justice to what the Communists did to the peasants. What happened in Romania from the 1950s—that is the story Steinbeck had been preparing all his life to write. *The Grapes of Wrath,* ha," Gheorghe said with a disgusted laugh, "that is a child's story compared to what happened here."

Gheorghe was looking out for number one: himself, his beautiful, red-haired wife, Augusta, and their son. Within a few weeks of the revolution, Gheorghe began giving private English lessons, as well as joining Vatra Romaneasca and getting involved with the National Liberation Front. With the money, he bought a satellite dish on the black market that he installed outside his living room. The family now watched "Satellite News" from London, "Love Boat," and other programs, while Gheorghe calculated which side was going to win in post-Ceausescu Romania and whether he and his family would be better off in Cluj or someplace abroad.

Augusta was pushing Gheorghe to leave for America, for anywhere "where the family can live like human beings and not like savages. Now that we are allowed passports, let's get out while we have the chance. Here, you never know what's going to happen next." Gheorghe was not sure. Gesturing with his hand, he said, "I'm middle-aged already. I don't want to start all over. What?" lifting up his black eyebrows, "What will I be in America? Some immigrant slob working twenty-four hours day so my wife can go to the shopping malls and have a microwave. No," wagging his finger. "I will wait and watch. Perhaps there will be some opportunities here."

Nigel was right; Gheorghe and I hit it off famously. Nigel left after lunch, and Gheorghe and I went to his apartment to meet his family. Over the next day or so, we talked almost nonstop. Our conversation was fueled by Gheorghe's supply of homemade plum brandy. I was often in no condition to take notes. But I remember whole passages of Gheorghe's monologues.

"Of course I was a Communist party member! Do you think I'm stupid?" thrusting his jaw out and showing his palms to the air. "How do you think I learned English, German? How do you think I got the money and permission to travel to England and

America in the 1970s, where I learned about Steinbeck? By being a dissident? Sure I played the game. The only people who traveled and got good educations in Romania were those who belonged to the party. That's why there is no alternative, for the time being, to the National Salvation Front. Romania is not like Czechoslovakia or anyplace else in Central Europe. This is a nation of sub-peasants. The only qualified people are former Communists.

"And believe me, there is nobody who hates Communism more than a former Communist. You see, we Romanians have one advantage over the Yugoslavs. The Yugoslavs, because of their World War II partisan tradition, actually believed in it—in Communism, I mean. We," he said, raising his eyebrows in a knowing, superior manner, "never believed in anything. It was one big racket. That's why we can be trusted and why the Communists in Yugoslavia fucked up so bad.

"Bob, I will now tell you something that you can be sure about. Those people in the square, in Cluj, in Bucharest, those students who want to get rid of Iliescu and all the Communists: if they succeed—or more likely, if there is a sudden fear that they might succeed—then there will be a bloodbath. Because every single person in this country who is not in the square feels safer with Iliescu than with those students."

Gheorghe said that to me in early May of 1990. A month later, riot police cleared University Square in Bucharest of student demonstrators. But the students quickly retook the square. Emboldened, thousands more students surrounded the government's headquarters nearby. Neither the police nor the army intervened this time, and there was speculation that Iliescu might be forced to resign. Within twenty-four hours, though, thousands of miners arrived in Bucharest from the Jiu Valley in western Wallachia. The miners, armed with clubs and axes, staged a massacre. At the local hospital, nurses refused to treat the students. Few Romanians, to the horror of foreign diplomats and journalists, showed any sympathy for the wounded students.

Gheorghe went on: "Let me tell you what's going to happen. Iliescu will be elected president in a landslide. [He was.] Then, gradually, over the next two years, the National Salvation Front will fall apart from within. While the Front is falling apart, new opposition parties will emerge that will be more mature than the ones we have now. Romania will eventually have a real non-

Communist government. But it won't happen until the mid-1990s, and the politicians who will make up this non-Communist government are still sitting on the sidelines. I am with the Front. The minute the Front starts collapsing, I will have nothing more to do with it."

"What about Vatra, Gheorghe?" I asked. "Is Vatra the new Legion of the Archangel Michael?"

"Vatra Romaneasca, you mean. It is interesting. Vatra was formed after the revolution, when Romanians suddenly awoke and realized we have to stand together against the Hungarian threat. But although I am a member, I still don't know what, exactly, Vatra is and where it is going. It could be an avalanche. Remember that the Legion of the Archangel Michael began in exactly the same way Vatra began—as an idealistic, back-to-the-roots national movement that was above politics and therefore incorruptible. About Vatra, I will wait and see."

Gheorghe talked for hours about Ceausescu. I remember only the highlights:

"Ceausescu was the worst sort of Romanian; he was a Wallachian peasant, something between a Turk and a Gypsy. That is crucial to understanding how his mind worked. You think he wanted to pay off the foreign debt for the sake of national responsibility? Who in their right mind pays off a debt ahead of schedule? He figured, 'Once the money is paid off, the country is all mine and I can do what I want with it.' Just like a peasant paying off a landlord: once the mortgage is paid, the house is his. He can add rooms, or burn it down, whatever. That's how Ceausescu's mind worked.

"Ceausescu kept donkeys as pets. Think of that." Gheorghe pointed his finger to his head and started twisting it. "The donkeys dictated policy. You know, in 1965, when Ceausescu emerged as the new leader after Gheorghiu-Dej died, nobody had heard of him. He was unknown, which is to say that his work, up until that point, had been in the area of internal security. Ceausescu was like Stalin, a petty thief who mastered the bureaucracy, someone who is cunning without being intelligent. We have an expression in Romania, '*Hirtia suporta maimult ca betonul*—Paper is harder than stone.' It is only with pencil and paper that you can really torture and murder on a mass scale.

"Stalin at least had some education. He studied in Georgia to

be an Orthodox priest. That is why Stalin's speeches, which became the style for all Communist speeches, sounded like Orthodox
liturgy. But Ceausescu was uneducated. He left school at fifteen.
He had a speech defect. His father beat him. The story is that
once, when Ceausescu was thrown in jail for stealing, he was put
in a cell with Communists. They saw a use for him. That's how
Ceausescu became a Communist—another racket." Gheorghe
lifted his eyebrows and shrugged his shoulders. "Ceausescu grew
up in Scornicesti, in Oltenia, the most backward part of Wallachia.
It's one of those towns where everybody looks like everybody else,
retarded like," he said, twisting his finger in the direction of his
head, "like in your Appalachian Mountains.

"You Americans built him up. Nixon invited him for a visit in
1968. All right, I admit, back then we all thought that, maybe,
he'll be better than Gheorghiu-Dej. After all, Ceausescu criticized
the Soviet invasion of Czechoslovakia. You see, we were all scheming, looking out for ourselves, and Ceausescu sucked us all in. It
was like quicksand. What an idiot I was to come back here in 1974.
I should have stayed abroad. In England or America, I'd be rich
now.

"But when Carter invited him to America in 1976, that was
unforgivable. That was like rubbing our faces in shit. By then, we
all knew who Ceausescu was. I remember reading the paper here
during the visit that somewhere, I don't know, in Maryland or
Pennsylvania, they named a supermarket in Ceausescu's honor.
Carter's advance men probably told Ceausescu anything to make
him happy, and he believed it, and he wanted us to believe it.
You Americans, when you want to humiliate a nation you really
know how to do it." Gheorghe made a spitting motion. "And you
wonder why in the 1970s I was a Communist. . . ."

"Did we do anything right?"

"You had one good man, one."

"Who?"

"Your Ambassador, Funderburk."

I looked up at Gheorghe, startled.

David B. Funderburk was appointed the United States Ambassador to Romania by Ronald Reagan in 1981, shortly after
Reagan was first elected President. Funderburk's was a political
appointment, one of the most interesting and controversial Reagan made. Funderburk was a protégé of Senator Jesse Helms, the

North Carolina Republican whose extreme right-wing views on abortion, prayer in the schools, and other issues Funderburk loudly and proudly shared. But Funderburk also had other aspects to his résumé that were more relevant to the task at hand and the media paid less attention to. He spoke Romanian; he had studied in Romania as a Fulbright scholar; and he wrote his thesis on how the British and French policy of appeasement in the 1930s helped to place Romania at the mercy of Hitler and Stalin, giving the Romanians little choice but to be pro-Nazi at the beginning of the war and pro-Soviet at the end. Funderburk was not a fatcat who wanted an ambassadorship in return for a campaign contribution. Funderburk, a young and severe-looking man with black hair and black-framed glasses, was a scholar on a crusade, and he was interested in one job only: the Ambassador's post in Bucharest.

The U.S. State Department loathed Funderburk, and Funderburk reciprocated in kind. In the 1970s and the 1980s, Romania was the only country in Eastern Europe over which there was a fundamental policy dispute in Washington, a mini-war almost.

Romania and Hungary were the only two Warsaw Pact nations upon whom the U.S. government bestowed the trading status of a Most Favored Nation. In Hungary's case, this caused little controversy; by Eastern European standards. Hungary had a liberal economy and a liberal human rights record. The United States labeled Romania a Most Favored Nation for different reasons. Ceausescu, in the State Department's view, had a "maverick" foreign policy that did not completely toe the Soviet line. For example, he recognized Israel and had close relations with China. The "pinstripes," as Funderburk called his enemies at the State Department, felt that, however meager the value of the "maverick" foreign policy was to the United States, canceling Romania's favored status would only remove what little influence Washington had over Ceausescu, leading to an even worse human rights situation in Romania. To this line of argument, Funderburk's reply was, in effect, "Worse? How much worse can it get in Romania?"

The story went around Washington that Funderburk was an amateur, who knew nothing about diplomacy, and who did not even speak Romanian that well. "He's made a bad situation worse; a new ambassador is needed to get things back on track in Bucharest," one think-tank expert had explained to me.

But that wasn't the opinion of some of the Foreign Service

officers at the Bucharest embassy, one of whom said flatly, "Funderburk does speak pretty good Romanian. More importantly, he understands what this place is really about." Another U.S. official in Bucharest said, "I don't care what anybody says about him; after watching him deal with the Romanians, I feel only the deepest respect toward Ambassador Funderburk."

Funderburk resigned in 1984 in a very spectacular fashion. He publicly referred to Ceausescu as a *"schmecher,"* a Romanian slang term for a "con artist," who was successfully "conning" the State Department with a foreign policy that was less independent than it seemed. Though Funderburk's outburst caused only sighs and huffs at the State Department, it went down well with Gheorghe.

"When your Ambassador Funderburk used that word, *schmecher,* I can't tell you how good it made me feel. It was the first time I felt that there was hope, that somebody outside knew what was going on here. *Ah"*—Gheorghe nodded his head in admiration—*"Schmecher,* that's just what Ceausescu was.

"Maybe you liked Ceausescu because he had relations with Israel," Gheorghe said sarcastically. "What bullshit! He had relations with Israel so he could sell Jews the way he sold Germans to West Germany: four thousand dollars a shot for an exit visa—a racket. The money went to Ceausescu's brother, Marin, to deposit in Switzerland. The one who, they say—*they say*—committed suicide. Don't you see, the brother [Marin Ceausescu] was, how do you call it . . ."

"The bagman."

Gheorghe smiled. "Yes, the bagman. Why do you think he spent so many years stationed at the Romanian Embassy in Vienna? He was taking the money to Switzerland. They say he hung himself in the embassy basement. They tortured him for the bank account numbers, then they hung him."

"Who tortured him, other diplomats?" I asked.

"Yes, other diplomats, why not!"

"So the Romanian government now has the numbers of Ceausescu's Swiss bank account?" I was trying desperately to follow Gheorghe's logic.

"No." Gheorghe closed his eyes and threw up his hands. *(How naive these Americans are.)* "After they killed Marin, they went to Switzerland to withdraw the money. By now they're in France or somewhere. You think that a Romanian, after he kills another Romanian for money, is going to give the money to the Romanian government?" Throwing up his arms again, he added, "He's going to keep it for himself!"

I traveled by train through the velvety green hills of "Muntenia," Wallachia's mountainous northwest bordering Transylvania, to the town of Curtea de Arges, where there was a monastery.

A stern-faced nun guarded the church's entrance. On the right, as you walked into the church, were the white marble tombs of King Carol I, his wife, Elizabeth of Wied (Carmen Sylva), and Neagoe Bessarab, the sixteenth-century Wallachian prince whose family settled Bessarabia. On the left was the tomb of King Ferdinand. Ferdinand's tomb, like those of Carol I, Elizabeth, and Neagoe Bessarab, was ornately carved and marked with his name and royal insignia. But there was another tomb on the left side of the nave, next to Ferdinand's: unmarked, with only a simple cross engraved on it. Ordering that his mother's grave be unmarked was one of many slights that King Carol II committed against his mother, Queen Marie.

Atop that simple marble slab, the nuns had placed a sign: MARIA, REGINA ROMANIEI 1914–1938.

I watched as a group of schoolgirls picked some flowers from the garden. When the sister's back was turned, the girls sneaked under the rope and, in fearful silence—afraid to breathe almost—placed the flowers on the tomb of Neagoe Bessarab, a figure whom they had doubtlessly learned about in school.

Outside the church, I approached the girls and mentioned the name of Maria Regina. The girls shrugged. They did not seem to know who I was talking about. I kept imploring, using alternate wording. Definitely, they did not know who she was.

So ironic, I thought. Queen Marie, more than any other individual, secured the accession of Transylvania (as well as of Bessarabia and northern Bucovina) to Romania after World War I. She had slept on the battlefields of the Second Balkan War and World War I, right beside her soldiers, and had dressed like the pagan warrior goddesses of Dacia. By sheer force of will, this British-born princess had recast herself as a Romanian and had given her subjects a better sense of what it was to be Romanian than any of the native-born fascists and Communists who came after her.

I grabbed a yellow flower from the garden. Slightly embarrassed, I waited, like the girls, for the sister to avert her gaze. I then placed the yellow flower atop the marble, under which Romania's last good and decent ruler, Marie Windsor Hohenzollern, lay buried. Walking away, I looked back and saw the stern-faced sister smile.

Rebecca West *(UPI/Bettmann)*

Archbishop Aloysius Stepinac *(UPI/Bettmann)*

Kemal Ataturk *(The Bettmann Archive)*

Milovan Djilas
(Author photo)

The Athenee Palace Hotel in Bucharest *(Author photo)*

John Reed *(UPI/Bettmann)*

President Nicolae Ceausescu and his wife, Elena
(UPI/Bettmann Newsphoto)

Nicolae Ceausescu's falsely identified grave *(Author photo)*

Queen Marie of Romania *(The Bettmann Archive)*

King Carol II of Romania (while still Prince Carol) with Magda Lupescu *(UPI/Bettmann Newsphoto)*

Corneliu Zelea-Codreanu *(UPI/Bettmann)*

Mircea ("Mihai"), the author's guide in Bucovina, standing between two farmers *(Author photo)*

The painted Monastery of Humor in Bucovina *(Author photo)*

Father Ion Bizau of Cluj, with a couple he is about to marry *(Author photo)*

Lorenz Loock (bottom left) and his family, in front of their house in Sibiu *(Author photo)*

Sunday at the Heroes' Cemetery *(Author photo)*

Guillermo Angelov *(Author photo)*

Rila Monastery in Bulgaria *(Author photo)*

Prime Minister Andreas Papandreou and Dimitra Liani
(Reuters/Bettmann)

Transylvanian Tale: The Pied Piper's Children Go Back to Hamelin

An hour's hitchhiking back into Transylvania brought me from filthy lodgings in Curtea de Arges to a spic-and-span room, with hand-tooled furniture, at the neoclassical Imperatul Romanilor (Roman Emperor hotel) in Sibiu, for the same price.

It was like coming up for air. The clay tiles and metal spouts in the bathroom had been polished to a shine. A bar of soap lay inside a new wrapper. The hotel café served cappuccino with whipped cream. The restaurant, lined with marble and gilded mirrors—the same one in which Liszt and Johann Strauss had gained sustenance—offered greaseless soup and clean salad. The Romanian waiters, like the Romanian maids who attended my room, worked quietly and efficiently, and didn't whisper in my ear about exchange rates and prostitutes.

Looking out a hotel window, as Walter Starkie had more than sixty years before, "I rubbed my eyes in amazement. The town where I found myself did not seem to be in Transylvania, for it had no Roumanian or Hungarian characteristics. The narrow streets and gabled houses made me think of Nuremberg. . . ." I walked into Republic Square adjacent to the hotel and beheld a flagstone expanse encircled by colorful baroque facades, with heraldic wooden signs and steep tiled roofs that were covered with moss and had dormer windows. I looked down side streets shaded by overhead archways, and saw the panoply of spiked onion domes atop the "stalwart towers" that Patrick Leigh Fermor, in 1935, had marveled at. With the addition of a fresh coat of paint on the house fronts and a few exorbitantly priced boutiques, this square in Sibiu could have passed for one of several in Germany. I had come to the southeast extremity of the German and Austro-Hungarian worlds, yet I was right smack in the middle of Romania. Never before in my journey did the sensory paradoxes of Romanian travel seem so real and magical. Indeed, the story told by this architecture bordered on the fantastic.

When the children of medieval Hamelin, in Lower Saxony, were led underground by the Pied Piper, they reemerged 1,000 miles to the southeast, deep in the Carpathian Mountains, within range of the Black Sea. The fairy tale, immortalized by Johann Wolfgang von Goethe, the brothers Grimm, and Robert Browning, is actually based on the twelfth-century German colonization of Transylvania. Browning writes:

> And I must not omit to say
> That in Transylvania there is a tribe
> Of alien people that ascribe
> The outlandish ways and dress
> On which their neighbours lay such stress,
> To their fathers and mothers have risen
> Out of some subterranean prison
> Into which they were trepanned
> Longtime ago in a mighty band
> Out of Hamelin town in Brunswick land,
> But how or why, they don't understand.

"Brunswick land" is Saxony, an area in central Germany. Although the original German settlers in Transylvania were probably Flemings from near the Dutch border, the label of "Saxon" stuck. In the fairy tale, the Pied Piper was a ratcatcher whose music was so bewitching that the sound of his pipe lured all the rats in Hamelin to the bank of the River Weser, where the rats drowned themselves. When the piper was not paid by the towns-folk for this service, he got his revenge by playing a tune that entranced the children of the town. Then he led them all under-ground, never to see their parents or homes again.

The widespread belief that Gypsies steal children (not to men-tion the Gypsies' reputation for playing enchanting music) indi-cates that the figure of the Pied Piper was based on a Gypsy, who piped the children all the way to his home in Transylvania.

In truth, it was the Magyar king, Geza II, who recruited the Saxons to settle in what was then medieval Hungary's eastern flank against the Byzantine Empire. There, the Saxons founded seven fortified cities, or Siebenburgen, all masterpieces of provincial baroque architecture. Before Cluj was called Cluj, Cluj-Napoca, or Kolozsvar, it was called Klausenburg by its original Saxon in-habitants. Brasov was orginally founded as Kronstadt; Sighisoara, as Schassburg; and so on. And the most powerful of all these towns was Hermannstadt, named after a Saxon baron. Only later did Hermannstadt also become known by the Hungarian name of Nagy-Szeben; and only later still, by the Romanian name of Sibiu (after a nearby river).

Despite the Romanian appellations on maps, these towns are still known to Germans and Austrians by the grave, Teutonic peal of the original place names. Such was the influence of these dour, hard-working Saxons on regional travelers that, when Jonathan Harker, in Stoker's novel *Dracula,* traveled east through Transyl-vania on his way to Count Dracula's castle, he naturally alighted not at Cluj, but at "Clausenburg."

"I found my smattering of German very useful here; indeed, I don't know how I should be able to get on without it," Harker jotted in his diary.

The Saxons entrusted themselves to nobody, building tight and efficient communities behind their fortress walls. In Saxon eyes, the less contact they had with the Romanians, the Hungarians, and the Jews, the better. Romanians and Hungarians called Tran-sylvania by the poetic terms Ardeal and Erdely, which refer to the forest; but to the Saxons, Transylvania has always been known simply as Siebenburgen—Seven Fortresses.

The Protestant Reformation fortified the Saxons' awareness of their German roots. They became, in historian Lukacs's view, "the grimmest Lutherans in all of Christendom." The collapse of the Austro-Hungarian Empire in 1918 and the immediate transfer of the Siebenburgen to Romania furthered the Saxons' sense of ethnic isolation, rendering members of their community especially susceptible to Nazi propaganda in the 1930s. Under Hitler, the status of the Saxons was raised to that of Volksdeutsche—an untranslatable term full of blood, soil, and racial implications, that means something akin to "German folk." Saxon youths served in large numbers in the Waffen-SS as German forces swept across Eastern Europe during World War II. In particular, they congregated in the SS Prinz Eugen division, responsible for the most ferocious of wartime atrocities in Yugoslavia.[1] Lukacs calls the Saxons the "proudest followers of the Führer." As recently as 1981 driving through a Saxon village in Transylvania, Lukacs observed: "a young boy in lederhosen, seeing my Viennese license plate, gives the Hitler salute."

Regarded as fascist, petit-bourgeois, and non-Romanian, the Saxon community, numbering several million, became prime victims of the post–World War II Romanian Communist regime. After the war, the Romanians conspired with the Soviets to send all Saxon men between the ages of eighteen and fifty, and all Saxon women between eighteen and forty-five, to work in the coal mines of the Donets Basin of the eastern Ukraine and in Siberia. Only a quarter of those deported ever returned to their homes in Romania. Another quarter went directly to West Germany after their release. The remaining half simply vanished inside the Soviet Union, presumably dead by the early 1950s of disease, exposure to the cold, and overwork.

From the 1960s onward, Ceausescu treated the Saxons as he did the Hungarians, making every attempt to destroy their cultural life. He sold the Saxons off slowly, for hard currency, as visa hostages to West Germany, just as he was selling off Romanian

1. The Prinz Eugen division was named for Prince Eugene of Savoy, an early eighteenth-century Habsburg military hero.

Jews to Israel. According to Ion Mihai Pacepa, Ceausescu's intelligence chief, who later defected to the West, Ceausescu once confided that "Jews and Germans," along with oil, were Romania's "best export commodities."

By the late 1980s, only 200,000 Saxons remained in Transylvania. When passports and exit visas became easily available in the aftermath of the 1989 revolution, these Saxons began leaving in droves for Germany.

In 1989, in the German city of Munich, I interviewed an elderly Saxon immigrant from Romania, Dorothea Pastior. "I can trace my mother's family in Kronstadt [Brasov] as far back as the seventeenth century," Mrs. Pastior began, "but I'm sure our roots in the Siebenburgen go back further. My mother met my father while he was on military maneuvers with the Austro-Hungarian army near Kronstadt. . . .

"My girlhood was perfect. We Germans lived in our own protected social world. We had little to do with the Romanians or the others, and they had little to do with us. It's funny, we lived alongside each other, but we had little desire to know their language or to know much about them. Our schools were so much better than theirs. In Saxon schools, school attendance was mandatory before it was anywhere else in the Habsburg Empire, and certainly before it was in Romania. The economic crises of the 1920s did not affect us, since our community was self-supporting. In fact, Germans from Germany used to send their children to holiday camps in the Siebenburgen because we had enough to eat.

"In Kronstadt, we had a very *burgerlicher* [bourgeois] life-style. My father sang in the church choir. We put on our own Wagner operas. We had our own national pride . . . there was a mass psychology among us that encouraged many of the young men to enlist in the Waffen SS. Whenever the sad news came that one of my schoolmates had lost a brother in the war, she would stay away from school for a few days, then come back wearing black. Otherwise, the war was far away. The Hitler years were quite pleasant.

"The breaking point in my life, when everything went from good to bad, was when the German army was defeated in 1945."

Soviet soldiers, their bayonets drawn, entered Mrs. Pastior's home, taking her father and her fifteen-year-old brother away on a forced labor conscription. Her brother escaped. Her father died in 1946, while working in the mines of the Donets Basin. Only in 1973 was the family officially notified of his death. The years in between were an unsparing procession of suffering. The Romanian authorities evicted her and her relatives from their home. They were made to live in a single room for fourteen years.

"I have no war guilt," said Mrs. Pastior, nearly in tears. "I am what I am, and that's German. And I've suffered plenty for it."

"Seven hundred years ago there was nothing here but wild forest land. We came from the Rhine at the bidding of the King of the Magyars. Here we settled and made this town what it is to-day," said an old Saxon man to the traveler E. O. Hoppe in Sibiu in 1923.

I entered the Brukenthal Museum on Republic Square, founded by an eighteenth-century Austrian governor of "Her-mannstadt." Walking through the rooms after several weeks of travel in Romania, my eyes gazed with delight at the original Rubenses and Van Dycks, the gilded mirrors, the Biedermeier furniture, and the French windows, all set against a background of maroon silk wallpaper. It occurred to me how, to a person growing up in this milieu as did that old Saxon man and Mrs. Pastior, the material effects of Romanian civilization—naive icons, blood-red wooden crosses, eggshells painted in a florid, Oriental style—could easily seem repulsive and barbaric.

Near the square I also found an old bookshop, perhaps the same one Hoppe had found in 1923, when he admitted to having "many a time crossed and re-crossed a street at the tempting sight of old bindings." After weeks of suffering Romanian bookstores, with their half-empty metal racks studded with cheaply produced paperbacks on technical subjects by Eastern Bloc authors, finding this place was yet another delight.

Although only 7,000 of Sibiu's 170,000 inhabitants in 1990 were Saxons, the Saxons seemed to confer not just an atmosphere on the town, but also a way of doing things. I found that the hotel, plus many of the shops and eating places, operated at (for Romania) an unusually high standard of efficiency. The Saxons might deny that their proximity to the Romanians had helped the Saxons in any way, but it had clearly helped the Romanians a great deal.

One evening in the hotel I met Beatrice Ungar, a young and intense-looking Saxon journalist at the *Hermannstadter Zeitung*, the local German weekly—founded, like the Romanian newspapers, immediately after the revolution. However, unlike Romanian journalists, Ungar and her colleagues at the *Hermannstadter Zeitung* were using their newly won freedom to open the lid on their own community's past. "Both we and the Romanians collaborated with the Nazis," Ungar stated. "Both we and they have things to feel guilty about. But the difference is that, while we openly acknowledge our guilt and are willing to look at it, the Romanians deny everything."

The next morning in Republic Square I was haggling with a Gypsy over the price of a newspaper. A young man rode up on a battered and rusted bicycle, and made the transaction for me. He was unshaven and dirty, and wore a white shirt that was torn and stained. His flaxen hair and intelligent-looking blue eyes betrayed him as a Saxon. His name was Lorenz Loock, and he invited me to his home for dinner that night.

Lorenz and his wife, Katharine, lived in one room off a courtyard that was located on a partly demolished street near the railway station. There was so much dust and garbage in the vicinity that I felt as if I were back in North Africa. The three of us sat on broken stools in the courtyard. Lorenz poured homemade plum brandy into glasses; then took some pieces of wood he had found in the street and put them in a metal can. Using the brandy alcohol to light the match, Lorenz started a fire, throwing bits of pork and fish in.

"This is what I have to show for eleven years of hard work in this Gypsy country. I pay eight hundred *lei* a month for rent, electricity, and water [there was one tap in the courtyard]. I make ten *lei* an hour as a technician. After buying food, we have nothing left to save at the end of the month."

Lorenz showed me a large plastic and cardboard suitcase. It was already filled with his and his wife's clothes: that was all the couple would be taking to Germany, when they left Romania in a few days, forever.

"It was good here only in the *Hitlerzeit* [the time of Hitler]. The Nazi soldiers were nice to the Saxons, yes, unlike the Russians and the Romanian *soldaten*. When I was in the army, the Romanians treated the Saxons as pigs. They carried guns, we did the hard labor. You know that the Nazis even gave chocolate to the *Kindern* [Saxon children]?

"But now, all Gypsies around." Lorenz grimaced. By Gypsies, he meant both Gypsies and Romanians. "All the demonstrations in the square and this talk of elections, this is all Gypsy business. Before December, there was Gypsy Communism; now there will be Gypsy democracy. It is the same. You cannot change the Gypsies. I am a Saxon man, I care nothing about this place."

Lorenz drank fast, and kept refilling all of the glasses with more brandy. His wife—a Saxon, too—talked little. Lorenz took out a box of family photos and handed me a copy of his wedding picture. "This is yours," he insisted, "in honor of our friendship." The grainy black-and-white photo was taken in 1986. It looked like it had been taken fifty or seventy-five years ago.

Lorenz walked with me back to the hotel. Pools of moonlight fell on the cobblestones, and on the gothic and baroque buildings. The darkness concealed Romanian poverty. Speaking German with Lorenz, it was easy for a moment to imagine that I was no longer in Romania, but somewhere in Germany or Austria.

"Just Gypsies here now," Lorenz kept repeating. "But you know, in Germany, the Germans will call me a Gypsy because I am from here. I don't care. I just want to work, to make real money, to have a car, a washer, a video, yes. . . ."

On my last day in Sibiu, Lorenz and I went to collect his passport. At the passport office, people crowded around a small window where a clerk was calling out names. After waiting just a few minutes, the clerk called out Lorenz's name. Lorenz pushed his way through the crowd, gave the clerk a receipt and was handed two Romanian passports (one was Lorenz's; the other, his wife's). To me, the whole procedure seemed quick and ordinary.

Pushing his way back through the crowd, Lorenz's eyes were beaming. "You don't know how many years I've waited for this moment." Lorenz spent several minutes inspecting every page, feeling them between his fingers. "Now I know I am really leaving this place."

We then walked to the edge of Sibiu, where we hitched a ride to the village of Lorenz's parents. The village's official name was Rusi, Lorenz explained. "But its real name is Reussen," founded in the Middle Ages by Saxons.

Reussen was north of Sibiu, on a barely traveled country road that took us through a verdant and hilly landscape. A cluster of eighteenth- and nineteenth-century houses with red-tiled roofs, dominated by a baroque church on a hillside, appeared on the right. Lorenz asked the driver to stop. My pleas—about pockets bulging with *lei* that I had no use for—fell on deaf ears. Lorenz insisted on paying the driver. As we walked up the dirt path, the fragrance of camomiles and peppermints mixed with the heavier odors of manure and farm animals. Lorenz and I found his mother and father working in a potato field. Looking up at me, shielding their blue eyes with thick and sunburnt hands, they shyly said hello. Lorenz began speaking with them, but I could barely understand a word. They spoke in the Saxon dialect—already formed in the fourteenth-century, two centuries after the first German settlers came to Transylvania—in which the pronunciation of the German words was twisted beyond recognition by any but the most trained of ears. Lorenz took the passports from his pocket and waved them in his parents' faces. They all smiled. His mother and father each took one of the passports and tested it thoroughly between their fingers, inspecting every page.

I looked around. It all seemed so idyllic. Lorenz's parents grew their own potatoes, maize, garlic, onions, radishes, and celery, as well as other vegetables and fruits. In a yard shaded by apple trees, they kept a few sheep, pigs, roosters, and rabbits. In a cellar, I later learned, they had barrels of fermenting wine and plum brandy.

"Almost everything we eat and drink we make ourselves. In the shops there is nothing," Lorenz's mother explained to me. She had iron-gray hair and a ruddy and weathered face. Her hands were like a man's. She looked about sixty, but who could tell? Lorenz was twenty-six, but looked forty. His father claimed to be fifty-eight and easily looked seventy-five.

"My father drinks a lot, that's why he looks so old," Lorenz said.

"He drinks more than you?" I asked in astonishment.

"Oh much more. I don't drink that much. It is you who are not used to drinking."

Lorenz's parents laughed at this. But they did drink a lot. The rest of the afternoon I struggled to keep up with all three of them, slugging back brandy after brandy, washed down with wine. They did not become drunk, however, and later went back into the fields to work.

The house consisted of two rooms. The toilet was in an outhouse by the barn. Placards bearing simple Christian sayings in German were on the walls.

"We survived this long in Romania; there's no reason for us to leave," Lorenz's mother said. "But for Lorenz, there is no future in Romania. This is not a country with a future."

"But life in this village seems so nice," I said.

"Yes," Lorenz answered. "We have some relatives in Germany. They send my parents marks to bribe the Communists. That's why they never took our crop. With the Gypsies, you must always bribe."

His parents nodded in agreement. Lorenz's mother mentioned that she would vote for Iliescu in the election.

"But he is a Communist," I said. "The National Salvation Front is the Romanian Communist party without the Ceausescus."

"Yes," said Lorenz's mother. "But with Iliescu we know what we get. With the others, we don't know. You cannot trust this country. The Romanians don't like the Saxons. We work. They don't. When the Russians came, in 1945, we ran and hid in the forest for weeks. The Romanians helped the Russians to find us. My sister was caught and was taken to Russia to work. She died there."

Lorenz's mother opened a tin of Spam sent from Germany, to eat with the plum brandy and wine. I could have fallen asleep in the chair from so much drinking in the hot and dusty afternoon. But Lorenz and his mother wanted me to see the village church.

The church had been built in the eighteenth-century. Lorenz and I climbed to the top of the baroque bell tower, made of wood that had badly corroded and sorely needed repainting. Under the Communists, repairs had been forbidden, and now only a few Saxons were left in the village. Lorenz said the tower used to have a clock, but it was stolen by the Turks following a battle against the Habsburgs. Inside the church was spare and spotless—like any church in Germany, except for the rotting wood beams. Wind rustled through the holes in the ceiling, eerily sounding notes on the organ, making me think of the passage of time: of an era when the wooden pipes echoed with the notes of Bach chorales. By the altar I noticed a memorial plaque, listing the two dozen or so members of the community who had fought for the Austro-Hungarian army and died in World War I.

"What about a plaque for the Saxons from Reussen who died fighting in World War II?" I asked Lorenz.

Lorenz said he didn't know, and put the question to his mother. She just shrugged, wearing an expression that was hard to read. Her face seemed full of frustration and ambivalence. I instinctively knew that it would have taken days of drinking with her to figure out how she really felt about this. She mumbled something in Saxon to Lorenz, who told me: "The *Hitlerzeit* was good for us, but it was a mistake. It is better to forget."

Lorenz and his mother showed me the tombstones in the village cemetery. Each grave had flowers on it. Some were several hundred years old; others were recent, including a young cousin of Lorenz who had died on account of a back-alley abortion. I realized that, in a few more years, the "smattering of German" that Jonathan Harker had found so valuable in Transylvania would be useful only for reading such tombstones in Saxon cemeteries. Once the generation of Lorenz's parents died, this cemetery would be like the Jewish one in Bucovina: guarded and maintained by Gypsies who would be paid by a Saxon immigrant association in Germany. Yes, one day, the Gypsies would even take over Lorenz's parents' home. I wondered if Lorenz realized this. Perhaps that was why he always used the word "Gypsy" as a swear term: out of bitterness.

On the way back to Sibiu, Lorenz kept repeating that all he wanted to do in Germany was to make money. "Whatever work there is there, I will do, so long as I earn marks, not *lei*." He laughed, triumphantly.

Romania's loss would be Germany's gain: another case of the rich getting richer and the poor poorer. The Saxons, along with the Jews, were the only people in Romania with a tradition of bourgeois values: standing, economically, between the wealthy nobles and the mass of downtrodden peasants. But just as Romania was beginning to emerge from Communism, just as it desperately needed the Saxons to act as a motor driving Romanian society in the direction of middle-class capitalism, the last Saxons of working age were leaving for Germany.

And not only Romanian Saxons were leaving for Germany. So

were millions of other ethnic Germans—from Silesia and Pomerania in western Poland, and from East Prussia, the Volga region, and Soviet Central Asia. All were like Lorenz, willing to work, work, work: to take the jobs that prosperous Germans didn't want, and to make themselves middle class in the process.

I thought of the great flood of Irish, Italian, Polish, and Jewish immigrants into America in the first decade of the twentieth century, and what they did for the strength and prosperity of their newly adopted country. Germany was going to be a much more powerful nation than even the addition of East Germany would have indicated. The era of Soviet domination in the Balkans was about to give way to an era of German domination. German economic imperialism, I realized, offered the most practical and efficient means of bringing free enterprise, democracy, and the other enlightened traditions of the West to Romania. Romania's only hope, it seemed, was Germany. European history at the end of the twentieth century was made up of Lorenzes, and it was full of ironies.

CHAPTER ELEVEN

Last Glimpses:
Timisoara and Bucharest

The train took me westward, out of the low mountains of Transylvania and onto a flat and monotonous plain. This was the Banat:[1] the *marchland* close to the borders of Hungary and Yugoslavia, where Romanians, Hungarians, Serbs, Jews, and ethnic Germans had all lived.[2]

Romania's history and character have been largely defined by mountains. Blood guides mountain life. The Carpathians not only cut off Moldavia from Transylvania, and Transylvania from Wallachia, but one group from the other. In the Carpathians, this village is Romanian, that village Hungarian, another German, and so on. But on a plain, in a frontier area where national borders

1. *Banat* is originally the Persian word for a Turkish military governor who ruled over a "Banat."
2. Because the ethnic Germans in the Banat were originally from Swabia, they are called Banat Deutscher rather than Saxons.

often changed over the centuries, the different groups intermingle. As in Central Europe, an element of social cohesion results. Thus, society here presented a more formidable edifice against the destructive fists of Communism.

Moreover, because the Banat was next door to Hungary and Yugoslavia, its inhabitants could watch those countries' television, and get an idea of what life was like in societies not ruled by a Ceausescu.

As the principal city of the Banat, Timisoara was called the "forehead" of Romania. Romanians from Jassy, Cluj, and even Bucharest had for years seen Timisoara as Romania's gateway to the outer world, the Romanian city farthest from the East and the closest to the West. Timisoara was the least Romanian of Romanian cities.

When the revolution erupted in December 1989, people throughout Romania were obviously surprised. Centuries of cynicism had conditioned them to believe that the situation could only get worse, not better. Yet one thing did not surprise them: that the revolution had begun in Timisoara. "It could only have started in Timisoara," was a refrain I heard over and over again (although the students in Jassy had hoped the revolution would start there). This simple and obvious fact of history and geography, however, was unnoticed by the journalists reporting on Romania's revolution, who saw the uprising only in terms of personalities.

Nobody I interviewed in Timisoara was pure anything. Every person claimed at least one member of another ethnic group as a relative. Many people I interviewed had such diverse parentages that it would be almost impossible to define what they were. A journalist I befriended at the German *Neue Banater Zeitung (New Banat Newspaper)* had a father who was "a Serbian Communist" and a mother who was "a German Nazi."

"And then got along?" I asked.

"They argued about politics," he said.

"Who knows what other blood I have in my veins," he added, noting that Romanian, Hungarian, Bulgarian, and Jewish forebears were all a possibility. "Here there is more cosmopolitanism, less hate. All the hate was directed against the regime. The food rationing during World War I and World War II was better than the rationing under Ceausescu. Under the kaiser and Hitler there was fresh bread and the occasional orange. Under Ceausescu, such things did not exist."

I had come to Timisoara with no contacts—no names or phone numbers in my notebook. Yet, in one morning, after asking at the hotel reception desk for the phone numbers of various local newspapers, I had interviewed several people. The offices where I conducted these interviews were clean, had secretaries, ashtrays that had recently been emptied, and modern art rather than icons or posters of rock stars on the walls. More significantly, nobody I interviewed got angry, or said anything really outrageous.

I got bored quickly in Timisoara. Although it was as poor as other places in the country—with badly dressed people, peeling building facades, and restaurants with only one or two dishes on the menu—in Timisoara, I no longer felt that I was in Romania. Romania was an echo of Dostoevsky's world: the inside of a ghoulish, Byzantine icon, peopled by suffering and passionate figures whose minds were distorted by their own rage and belief in wild half-truths and conspiracies. In Timisoara, Romania was less a reality than a powerful memory.

After Timisoara I returned to Bucharest. The Diplomats Salon of the Athenee Palace was open in the evenings. A table required an advance reservation, or rather a bribe, since whoever stuffed more *lei* into the hands of the head waiter got the place. Unlike the rest of the hotel, the Diplomats Salon was a perfect throwback to an earlier era: that of *Athenee Palace Bucharest* or *The Balkan Trilogy.*

Eight crystal chandeliers hung from the ceiling around a domed, yellow-and-green-tinted skylight. The light of the chandeliers reflected against the polished glass mirrors. The baroque columns had been inlaid with gold leaf, and the curtains trimmed with gold lace. A Gypsy played soft music on a violin. Waiters served Black Sea caviar and French champagne, which at the black-market rate for *lei* was quite reasonable. Journalists, in Bucharest that May of 1990 to cover the first free elections in fifty-three years (since Carol II had proclaimed a royal dictatorship), occupied most of the tables. There were also a few young and earnest couples from England and America, who had come to

Romania hoping to find a child to adopt. According to reports, some 40,000 abandoned children languished in Romania's orphanages—medieval-style asylums where children were interned to die of hunger and disease. The problem for prospective foster parents was not to find adoptable children, but to negotiate the hurdles of a corrupt bureaucracy in order to get the children out of the country. Everyone talked excitedly, exchanging the names of lawyers and local fixers, along with the latest political rumors. Prostitutes crowded around the salon entrance, pressing foreign males to invite them for dinner.

I ignored the elections: the victory of Iliescu and the National Salvation Front was a foregone conclusion. Walking around Bucharest on my next-to-last day in Romania, I realized that, despite the most maniacal attempts to erase the past, the ghosts of local history met me square in the face.

Ceausescu's last five years in power had been one hellbent orgy of destruction. Much of the southern part of Bucharest, beyond the Dimbovitsa River, including sixteen churches and three synagogues—architectural masterpieces all—had been bulldozed. On the ruins rose the "Civic Center," Ceausescu's Forbidden City of Stalinism, built in such a fury that the residents of the old eighteenth- and nineteenth-century neighborhoods had been given only a few hours to pack and leave with all their belongings before their homes were blasted into oblivion.

A boulevard wider than the Champs-Elysées, lined by white marble apartment buildings with neoclassical, quasi-fascist facades, now led to the House of the Republic: a cheap marble wedding cake containing sixty-four great halls and a thousand rooms. Larger than the Pentagon, the House had consumed so much marble that there was now a black market in gravestones in Bucharest. For miles around, nothing remained but a wasteland of tacky construction: the wish-fulfillment of a vindictive peasant.

Eeriest of all, however, was not what had been destroyed, but what had survived the bulldozers' wrath.

At one end of the Civic Center, right on the edge of the destruction, was the *abator*—the Bucharest slaughterhouse—boarded up and no longer in use, yet still (almost miraculously) standing: a collection of red-brick, barracks-style buildings, with rusted pipes and scrap iron smokestacks, where the Legionnaires had committed arguably the single most gruesome act of the Holocaust, in January 1941.

At the other end of the Civic Center, about 100 yards from the line of destruction, was the Church of Ilie Gorgani. By the entrance hung a framed summary of the Church's 300-year history, listing everything of relevance except the fact that, in this church in 1940, Codreanu and the thirteen other executed Legionnaires had been declared "national saints." By the altar in 1990, bedecked with tulips, was a portrait of Teoctist, the Patriarch of the Romanian Orthodox Church. Dismissed immediately after the anti-Ceausescu revolution, he had recently been reinstated. More than any other figure, Teoctist was a symbol of the Church's collaboration with the Ceausescu regime.

I spent election day with two Icelandic journalists, Thorir and Atta Gudmundsson, looking for Ceausescu's grave. In the midst of our search, in the southern part of Bucharest near the Civic Center, I was approached by an old man in a black beret.

"You're a journalist, no?" he asked in German, rudely inspecting me as though I were personally familiar to him.

"Yes," I answered. The man's eyes were small and penetrating: they were not going to let me get away. I looked at him closely.

His trench coat was torn in many places and so soiled that it took me a few seconds to realize that its original color had been white. Underneath the trench coat was a torn sweater of some dark and indeterminate hue, and beneath the sweater a shirt, the collar of which was almost completely ripped away. His neck had a bad rash on it.

What staggered me, though, was the way he stank. He had a putrefying odor that signaled humiliation and approaching death. It was the carrion stench of old people who live in conditions where it is not easy to wash or to change clothes.

His small eyes gleamed sardonically. He knew he smelled bad, and he appeared to like the fact that I was bothered by it.

"You're a Jew, from America," he barked. It was not a question, but a clear statement.

I was speechless.

"Me too; I'm a Jew. The Jews have to stick together. Your

friends?" motioning to Thorir and Atta. "Goyim, eh. But nice. I think they are nice people. They like Jews, I mean."

By this time, Thorir and Atta had come up to us. They spoke German and could therefore understand everything. We asked him—might as well give it a try—if he knew about the rumor of Ceausescu's body being buried in an unmarked grave in Ghensea Cemetery.

"Maybe," the old man said. "You want to see graves, I'll take you to graves."

Thorir, Atta, and I looked at each other. "Why not," we decided. He was interesting, I said to myself. Embarrassed by his outburst, I was falling deeper into the cynical thought-mode of a journalist.

We helped him into Thorir's car. He had a terrible limp, but no cane.

He directed us to one of the "heroes' cemeteries," where the students killed by Ceausescu's Securitatae troops in December 1989 had been buried. "You go, take your pictures. I'll stay in the car," he said.

Election day, May 20, 1990, was a Sunday, and the heroes' cemetery was crowded. It was a heart-wrenching scene. The parents of the dead were piling flowers atop the dirt mounds. One old woman beat her fists uncontrollably against a wooden cross. An old man just sat on a block of cement next to the grave of his son, wearing no expression. It would make a powerful photo, I thought. I asked the man if I could take his picture. He looked up at me blankly, completely lost in his own misery. I snapped away. The graves of so many young persons all in one place was unnerving. It seemed so contrary to nature.

I walked back to the car. "It's terrible," I said. Our mysterious old guide just nodded. His expression was distant. I suspected that he felt little sympathy or emotion for these people.

"Did you vote today?" I asked him.

"I voted. For Iliescu, for the Communists."

"Why?"

"Iliescu has Jews close to him. Petru Roman, he's a Jew. Sylviu Brucan, he's a Jew, too. In this kind of country, you don't take chances. Satisfied?" he said abruptly, seeing Thorir and Atta walking toward the car from the back of the cemetery.

"Did you get good pictures?" he asked us all.

"Yes," I said.

"Maybe you have some *voluta* [hard currency] for me? Say, ten dollars?"

I reached for my pocket.

"No." He made a stopping motion with his hand. "Later, maybe, you'll give me a present. We Jews, we must help each other."

After we were all in the car, he said: "Now you'll see graves," as if the graves we had just seen didn't count, or were only a warmup. "Go straight," he said to Thorir, who was driving. "There is a flower market straight ahead. I must buy flowers for my parents' graves."

Atta and I looked at each other.

On account of the old man's bad limp, Atta offered to buy the flowers for him. But he insisted on going with her, since he always bought flowers from the same man. It took him ages to cross the narrow street.

Back in the car, holding the flowers in his lap, he directed us to the edge of a junkyard, next to a disused section of railroad tracks, where Thorir parked.

"You're sure the cemetery is this way?" I asked.

"Yes," he said, smiling for the first time. "I come here every week."

He led us on foot along the tracks, one foot dragging behind the other, at an excruciatingly slow pace. The physical pain he felt in walking seemed outweighed by the enjoyment he got from taking someone here. In the distance loomed the Civic Center.

"You always come this way?" I asked.

"Yes, always. Usually, I come alone."

The tracks, concealed under weeds in many spots, seemed to lead his mind back into the past. Limping along, he told us that he had been born in northern Bucovina and had moved with his parents to Bucharest only a short time before the Romanians began transporting the Jews of northern Bucovina to the Transdniestrian death camps. In Bucharest, he and his parents had lived in the old Jewish quarter (demolished by Ceausescu to make way for the Civic Center). As it happened, shortly before the Legionnaires' pogrom of January 1941, he and his parents had moved out of the Jewish quarter and taken an apartment near an Orthodox Church. When the Legionnaires had rounded up the Jews to take them to the Baneasa forest and the slaughterhouse, they had overlooked his parents' house.

Both of his parents had lived into old age. He was their only child. When he lifted his beret to adjust it, I saw he had only a few, white whiskerlike hairs on his crinkled and skeletal head. With his old coat hanging down nearly to his ankles, he looked like the quintessential concentration-camp survivor—although, as he had just told me, he had never been in a concentration camp.

"Your family was very lucky. You barely missed every calamity," I said.

He shrugged his shoulders and grimaced. *"Das ist das* [That is that]." Nothing registered on his face.

"Here," pointing to the gate of the Jewish Cemetery, which suddenly appeared on the left, an oasis of order and cleanliness in the midst of a wasteland.

He took a dirty black yarmulke out of his pocket and thrust it into my hands. "You'll need this, but I don't have another for your friend."

Thorir pulled his jacket over his head. The old man looked at Thorir, very satisfied.

"Here," he said. "Look."

On the left, inside the gate of the cemetery, stood a forest of stone. Each monument was carved in the shape of a tree trunk with its branches lopped off at the base, like a torso without arms and legs. The monuments were of all different sizes, each with its own unique shape. The effect was grisly. I looked at the in-scriptions, commemorating the 185,000 Jews from northern Bu-covina and Bessarabia massacred in Transdniestria. Each monument stood for a particular town or village.

The old man smiled as we took pictures.

"Come," he said.

He brought us to two long rows of graves, each row about the length of a football field. All the graves were cut in exactly the same severe shape: their uniformity and closeness to each other suggested a frightening vision of infinity. Some of the graves had a small black-and-white framed photo of the deceased. I saw one picture of an elderly man, another of a young girl. The date of death on every grave was the same; JANUARY 21–23, 1941.

"They can't deny the *abator* [slaughterhouse]," he said, nodding his head and smiling with a triumphant, jack-o'-lantern grin. "Whatever they tell you, eh, here is the proof."

Then abruptly he said, "Good-bye. I'll see my parents alone."

I handed him back his yarmulke. "No, you keep it. It's for you."

Like him, the yarmulke smelled of death: a black and circular memory.

PART III

Bulgaria: Tales from Communist Byzantium

When I make involuntary comparisons between the life of a normal citizen in the West and the life of a normal Bulgarian, the difference seems so great that the life of the Westerner could be represented by a child's simple drawing whereas in the life of the Bulgarian reality is inextricably mixed with the symbolic and the abstract. We are subjected to the impact of far more factors and forces than the Western citizen can imagine. While the citizen in the West is constantly striving to acquire ever more, our main instinct is to preserve what we have.

—GEORGI MARKOV, The Truth That Killed

CHAPTER TWELVE

"The Warmth of Each Other's Bodies"

"Leaving Bucarest on a dirty little train, you crawl slowly south over the hot plain, passing wretched little villages made of mud and straw, like the habitations of an inferior tribe in Central Africa. . . . You stop at every tiny station, as if the Rumanian Government were contemptuously indifferent of any one going to Bulgaria, and at Giurgiu there is an unnecessarily rigid examination by petty despotic customs officials. . . .

"But across the yellow Danube is another world. . . . Good-natured, clumsy soldiers make a pretense of examining your baggage, and smile you a welcome. . . . It is wonderful to see again the simple, flat, frank faces of mountaineers and free men."

Thus wrote John Reed in 1916. The sensation near the end of the century was the same as that at the beginning. On several occasions in the 1980s, I took the train across the Danube from Romania to Bulgaria. The times I remember best were in winter, at night. There was no heating in the cars and no food to buy on the Romanian leg of the journey. The customs inspection at Giurgiu was unpleasant. But at Ruse, on the Bulgarian side of the Danube, the heating in the train always came on. Food became available. And the friendly customs official was more intent on practicing his English than on inspecting my luggage. The rest of the night was "the cold night of high altitudes." In the morning, I found myself traveling through a rocky gorge, bearded with beeches, firs, pines, and the darkest scrub, with the train running for mile upon mile beside a roaring mountain torrent.

The first time I saw Sofia, in November 1981, snow was falling. White snow. Only after some hours did the polluting lignite fumes turn it brown. But the sweet, deathlike odor of the lignite reminded me of old steam engines and of burning leaves in autumn. And as the lignite mist crept through the web of tram lines and the branches of poplar, black locust, and pollarded horse chestnut trees, along yellow cobblestone streets of such oppressive silence that even the voices of schoolchildren seemed muffled in whispers, it evoked my earliest memories, of visiting my grandparents on Eastern Parkway in Brooklyn in the mid-1950s, a world of doilies and florid upholstery and jam and pickle jars. In the nearing distance, across a great cobblestone expanse, loomed the Grand Hotel Bulgaria, with its marquee and name inscribed in girders on the steep, gabled roof: a hotel peopled with the ghosts of departed newspaper correspondents.

Here Reed had stayed in 1915, and C. L. Sulzberger and Robert St. John at the beginning of World War II. In 1949, the great Australian foreign correspondent and alleged KGB agent Wilfred Burchett was married in the hotel restaurant. In Room 29 of the Grand Hotel Bulgaria, James David Bourchier, the *Times* of London correspondent in the Balkans for a quarter century (who covered both Balkan wars and World War I) died of pneumonia in 1920. Bourchier had become so well known and loved in Bulgaria—he supported Bulgaria's claims to Macedonia—that, on news of his death, crowds gathered outside the hotel. His body then lay in state for several days in the Aleksandar Nevski Memorial Church. Some years after his burial, Bourchier was honored in a way that must have warmed the hearts of many a hard-bitten journalist: a brand of local cigarettes was named after him.

The Grand Hotel Bulgaria was the closest thing to a home that Bourchier, a deaf bachelor who lived out of a suitcase, ever had. He called it the "old familiar hostel." Bourchier, Reed, Sulzberger, and all the other journalists favored the Grand Hotel because it was across the street from the Royal Palace, now a museum: a little mint-green toy of a building with a lead baroque roof—a touching pretense compared to the massive, stone-socketed monuments to royalty in Vienna and Bucharest.

Like Bourchier, I first came to the Grand Hotel Bulgaria (in 1981) only because it was centrally located and cheap, nineteen dollars for a single room. As an untested freelance writer, I couldn't afford anything more expensive. By 1981, however, the hotel's glories were long past. It functioned as a barely heated hostelry for Eastern Bloc tour groups and the occasional down-at-heel businessman from Turkey, India, or elsewhere. The dining room was dark brown with red dados. The rooms lacked heating, and there were many runny noses. The guests huddled in overcoats. The maids wore blue smocks and high white socks over hairy, stockingless legs. Breakfast that first morning consisted of thick, unstrained prune juice, fresh yogurt, goat cheese, salami, apples, and cucumbers, all cold and delicious. There was tea from a samovar but no coffee. I didn't mind. The view from the windows of the park and the former Royal Palace had not changed since World War II. Bourchier, wrote his biographer, Lady Grogan, "felt the charm of Balkan scenery even before he came under the spell of Balkan politics." Regarding Bulgaria, I went through a similar process of falling in love.

I always felt that when, in the following year, 1982, significant numbers of Western journalists began arriving in Sofia for the first time since World War II, to investigate allegations that Bulgaria's Darzhavna Sigurnost ("State Security Police") was responsible for the May 13, 1981, attempted assassination of Pope John Paul II in St. Peter's Square, they missed something crucial by not staying at the Grand Hotel Bulgaria. Most preferred to stay at the historiless, Japanese-designed Vitosha Otani, situated in a drab suburb, because that was where Mehmet Ali Agca (the Sigurnost's hired Turkish assassin) had stayed, before going on his murderous mission to Rome.

Forming a triangle with the old Royal Palace and the Grand

Hotel Bulgaria was the white, neoclassical mausoleum of Georgi Dimitrov, guarded by goose-stepping soldiers in feathered hats and other Ruritanian finery. Dimitrov was the hero of the 1933 Reichstag fire trial, conducting a daring defense of himself and other Communists in a Berlin circus court controlled by Nazi thugs. Later, Dimitrov went to Moscow to head the Comintern (the international organization of Communist parties), before being dispatched home to Bulgaria by Stalin in order to midwife the birth of a Bulgarian Communist state after World War II. Then, considering him to have outlived his usefulness, Stalin had Dimitrov slowly poisoned—a fact deleted from Dimitrov's official biography. According to Bulgarian dissident author Georgi Markov, Dimitrov "was the one who introduced the black limousines and drew their heavy curtains between himself and the ordinary people . . . who allowed his country to be ruthlessly robbed and ruined by those who had sent him to colonize it." After his death in 1949, Dimitrov lay for four decades under glass, preserved in formaldehyde, his mustached face and hands spectrally lit, in a mausoleum modeled exactly on Lenin's tomb in Moscow's Red Square. Bulgaria was a little country, but on my first visit it seemed to me to have big ambitions, and it therefore required a big, impressive facade.

And for questioning this facade—for questioning why the last of Dimitrov's Communist successors, Todor Zhivkov, needed a network of vast estates, each one more luxurious than the little toy palace with the leaky roof where kings Ferdinand and Boris had lived—the dissident author Markov met a macabre end.

Walking over Waterloo Bridge in London on September 7, 1978, Markov, living in exile and working for the BBC's Bulgarian language service, felt a twinge of pain in his leg. Turning around, Markov suddenly noticed a man behind him with an umbrella, who muttered, "I'm sorry." The next morning, Markov became ill. Three days later, he died, slowly and in pain, just like Dimitrov. At the tip of that umbrella had been a minute pellet filled with ricin, a deadly poison—exactly the same weapon that had been used in an attempt to kill another Bulgarian defector in Paris.

But when I arrived for the first time in Sofia on that snowy winter morning near the end of 1981, I knew almost nothing about Bulgaria, and nothing about Markov except the strange facts surrounding his death: facts that, in a vacuum of all other knowledge about his country, were deceiving and prejudicial.

On the unlit and carpeted staircase of the Grand Hotel Bulgaria (the elevator was frequently out of order) during my first evening in Sofia, after a tiring day of trying to arrange interviews through the official Sofia Press agency (I had gotten little sleep on the train from Bucharest the night before), I heard the determined steps of someone following close behind me.

"Excuse me, are you Mr. Robert Kaplan, the distinguished foreign correspondent from America?"

I laughed to myself. For decades, foreign journalists had been so rare in this faraway little country that, when one did show up, it was an event, and he was consequently thought important.

"Yes, how did you know?" I replied, more exhausted than suspicious.

"Well, I represent Sofia Press and was told you were here. My name is Guillermo, Guillermo Angelov. I would like to invite you to dinner at our journalists' club."

I had just eaten and wanted only to sleep. "No thank you. How about tomorrow night?"

"Why?" It was an accusation. "What?" He was now inches behind me, still following me up the stairs. "Do you think that just because I am a Communist I am going to brainwash you? Have you made up your mind already about our country after one day here? It is true, I am a Communist, an internationalist. And I want to take you to dinner in order to listen to what *you* have to say. And you don't want to accept. Are you afraid? Afraid of another point of view, perhaps?"

I turned around. We were now in the hallway, under a lone, dim bulb. Up against my face, breathing heavily, was a man in his late fifties, with long gray-and-white sideburns, gray eyebrows, and a swarthy complexion. His shoulders were hunched forward. At the end of one arm was a battered briefcase. He wore a black beret, a shapeless overcoat, and sneakers. I remember how he sweated around his lips and eyes. He was in late middle age but had the hungry, ambitious look of a young man.

"Come on, I only want to take you to dinner. Did you know that 1981 is our thirteen hundredth anniversary of nationhood?

For thirteen hundred years we have been a people, with roots, an identity. How old is America? *Ah,* you are babies. There is so much you don't know. Please, honor an old man; don't insult me."

Then he took off his beret (he was bald) and placed it over his heart as he bowed gallantly.

How could I say no?

Guillermo gripped me by the arm, his mouth near my ear continuously talking, as he lead me through dark streets to the corner of Alabin and Graf Ignatiev, where two tram lines converged.[1] I remember the oncoming light of a clanging trolley as I shoved Guillermo out of the way. He had become so engrossed in his lecture that he had stopped walking, his arm locked inside mine, in the middle of the tracks. "We are a great nation, my dear. Our wines are the best, better than the French. Our women are the most beautiful—just look at their noble Thracian features, like statues! World civilization has three principal roots: French, Chinese, and Bulgarian. Robby," as though, already, I were his son, "look at what we have lost—Dobruja to Romania, Thrace to the Turks, the Aegean to the Greeks, and worst of all, Macedonia to those Serbs." He said the word "Serbs" with utter contempt. "But I am not a nationalist. . . ." Guillermo was now leading me in circles on the cold, snow-banked street, in front of the journalists' club: he had not finished making his point.

In 1981, there was a bacchanalian feel to the journalists' club. The air reeked of chicken broth, plum and grape brandy, cigarette smoke, and sour perspiration. Mountains of sausage and goat cheese and empty bottles of wine and beer covered stained tablecloths. Men had their arms around the oily backsides of women. There were shouts and laughter, and almost every one of the red velvet chairs was occupied. A massive wall-to-wall mirror reflected the filmy bath of cigarette smoke. I felt an intensity of emotion, a fleshy intimacy, that seemed to be based on confinement and therefore could never be duplicated in the West. While extramarital affairs in the West were mainly a result of middle-class boredom, here I felt they served deeper needs. With politics and

1. Graf Ignatiev refers to the Russian Count ("Graf") who accepted the surrender of Turkish troops at the end of the Russo-Turkish War in 1878. See earlier chapter on Macedonia.

public life so circumscribed, there was a huge well of authentic emotion that even the most ideal of marriages could never consume. And perhaps because you could never escape from the cold, even when indoors, a warm body at night was not enough: you needed one during the day too.

A massive, ruddy-faced, black-tuxedoed waiter with iron-gray hair embraced Guillermo. "This is Lupcho," Guillermo told me. "He reads palms."

"He looks just like Brezhnev," I replied.

Guillermo translated what I had said to Lupcho, who beamed, thaking me for the compliment.

Lupcho led us to a table. *"Slivova* [plum brandy] is bad for the liver," Guillermo advised. So he ordered *grozdova*—grape brandy—for the two of us. A dumpy old woman came up and pressed her cheeks to Guillermo's. "Robby, didn't I tell you how beautiful our women are?" He translated what he had told me into Bulgarian. The woman pulled Guillermo to her bosom. Guillermo smiled at me. His eyes were always so expressive, seeming to change their tone constantly according to his thoughts. Now they said: *why not give the old girl a bit of pleasure?*

Lupcho hovered over us.

"He wants to read your palm," Guillermo said. I put my palm out and Lupcho traced his fingers over it.

"Lupcho says you will meet your true love in the very near future." (As it happened, fifteen months afterward, I met my future wife.)

"I am married for the third time," Guillermo remarked. "Women love us only for our faults, and if we men have enough of them, they'll forgive us anything.

"Look around you, see how happy we are, and all the time, at night, while you in America sleep, we are working, catching up, catching up. Bulgaria is first in the Balkans in robotics," he said, as though confiding a state secret.

Lupcho returned with soups, salads, more grape brandy, and a bottle of dry red wine from the Melnik region, near the Greek border.

"I've already eaten," I told Guillermo.

"Oh, come on, boy," he said, gesturing at the table.

Next, I remember heatedly defending Reagan against the first of Guillermo's many assaults against the American president. "Come on, Robby, don't tell me you're one of those cowboys. One of those Rocky Mountain reactionaries!"

"Cowboys! Better a cowboy than a slave to the Russians! This country is not independent!" I was starting to get drunk. Guillermo interpreted my behavior—the fact that I would shout, and argue, and drink with him—as a compliment. I think this was the moment when our long and ongoing friendship began, and the moment when I really began to understand about Bulgaria.

"Slaves you call us. Yes, there is that silly word you in the West use—a *satellite,* as though we Bulgarians were going around in space. Nonsense. You know nothing about what the Turks did to us, what it was like under the yoke of the sultans. The Russians liberated us from that, but we are proud. We fought the Russians in World War I. Okay, so now we are weak and surrounded by enemies. So we use the Russians as a protector while we *deal"*— Guillermo rubbed his thumb against the back of his fingers— "against the Turks, the Greeks, and the others. The Russians give us great leeway, my dear, in our dealings with the Turks, the Greeks, the Serbs. How can you say we have no freedom? The Russians give us cheap oil and other raw materials. We bleed the Russians. But you Westerners know nothing of what goes on in our corner of the world. Can your cowboys even locate Bulgaria on the map? You care only about the struggle between America and Russia. For us, the struggle of the superpowers is a mere passing phenomenon in our long history. We are the most intelligent of peasants, and thus we know better than you how to survive."

These arguments had their effect on me because I had just come from Romania, which in 1981 had the best reputation in America of any Eastern Bloc state on account of Ceausescu's so-called "independent foreign policy," while Bulgaria had the worst reputation. Yet it was obvious to me that the Bulgarians, as poor as they were, were economically better off than the Romanians, as well as having more personal freedom. Such an easy, drunken discussion would have been unthinkable across the Danube, under the shadow of Ceausescu, whom American policymakers were then rewarding with Most Favored Nation trading status.

"But I am the most pro-American of any Bulgarian," Guillermo went on. "I am a graduate of the last class of the American College of Sofia in 1942. You know I was the first correspondent of the BTA [Bulgarian Telegraphic Agency, the Communist regime's official news service] in China in 1957? How can I put this—our journalists are not like yours. I was sort of the official represent-ative of Bulgaria in China. I was a friend of Mao, of Chou En-lai. And you know how I got that job, my dear: on account of my education at the American College."

"The Nazis closed the college?" I asked.

"No." Guillermo looked a bit embarrassed. "Due to the war, after 1942, the school could not go on, but it was still officially open. It was closed in 1946 . . ."

"By the Communists," I finished the sentence for Guillermo.

Guillermo lifted his eyebrows and shrugged his shoulders, the Oriental way of saying, *yes, what can you do?*

"*Guillermo,* that's not a Bulgarian name?" I asked.

His smile returned. "You see my father, in the first years of the century, went to Alexandria, in Egypt, to make his fortune in the textile trade. His best friend there was a Spaniard, Guillermo. I am named after him. You know that my father served in the Balkan Wars? In World War II, I hid in the forest, so I wouldn't have to serve in the army—Bulgaria was with the fascists, you know? I'll never forget when the Russians came in September 1944. I was safe; I could breathe again."

"Can you still breathe?"

Guillermo smirked playfully and rolled his eyes toward the ceiling. "Oh come on, guy. It is a tragedy what those reactionaries have done to you, Robby. You are so bright, but look how they have twisted your mind."

A man with white hair, who looked quite old and tired, came up and embraced Guillermo. The two held each other for several long seconds.

"Robby, may I introduce the greatest foreign correspondent of the twentieth century: Wilfred Burchett."

Burchett and I shook hands.

"This guy," Guillermo announced, looking at Burchett and holding him tightly by the arm, swelling with pride, "how can I put it, is the greatest, the author of forty books. First into Hiro-shima after Truman—that criminal—dropped the bomb! The only Western journalist to cover the Korean War from the *north*! You know he was first, first down the Ho Chi Minh trail! You see this beret I have. Wilfred bought it for me in Spain, while covering the fall of fascism there in the 1970s."

Guillermo had exaggerated only a little. Burchett had been an eyewitness to practially every war and revolution around the world since World War II, and had published books on just about all of them. He spoke several Asian languages and had been on intimate terms with Mao, Ho Chi Minh, Kim il Sung, and others whom few (if any) Western journalists had access to. Born in rural Australia in 1911, Burchett had been radicalized by his own family's poverty, the worldwide Depression of the 1930s, and the terrors of German and Japanese fascism. He showed up at the 1953 Korean War peace talks as a kind of semi-official spokesman for the North Korean delegation. For years, there had been rumors and circumstantial evidence, never entirely proved but never convincingly refuted either, that Burchett was a paid agent of the KGB. In the 1950s, the Australian government revoked his passport, so Burchett globetrotted with a *laissez passer* provided him by North Vietnam's Communist regime.

If Burchett was on the KGB payroll, he couldn't have been paid much, since he and his family were often close to poverty. Burchett eked out a living as a roving stringer and author of book after book that few people bought. Perpetually broke, multilingual, very emotional, and bubbling with erudite knowledge, Burchett made friends easily. Everybody who met Burchett liked him, including Henry Kissinger. During the 1972 peace talks in Paris, Kissinger used Burchett as a go-between with the North Vietnamese.

Burchett spoke excitedly to me about his latest project. "I'm putting a book together about Bulgaria, with notes that I've been collecting for years." He had, he told me, moved with his Bulgarian-born wife and family to Bulgaria in 1980, around the time of Reagan's election in America, which he said would augur a new cold war and a new attack on the "peoples' democracies." Burchett was to die in Sofia two years after I met him, in 1983.

"Don't be a hack, Robby," Guillermo exclaimed, "like all those rotten guys who call us a satellite! Go deep, deep into history and see for yourself who *we* [the Bulgarians] are!"

Burchett and Guillermo still had their arms around each other.

The three of us poured out into the street. The alcohol, the heated discussion, and the excitement of new acquaintances in a new country had provided me with a second wind. Saying good-bye to Burchett was a long procedure. In the driving snow, Guillermo was providing him with a list of the books he was going to give me to read.

"And Robby," Guillermo whispered. "As I provide you with information, you will provide me with information, too?"

"Such as?"

"There was an issue recently of an American magazine, *Current History,* devoted to China. Can you get it for me? As an old China hand, I like to keep up on developments."

"But you can find that at the American Library in Sofia."

"Robby," holding his hands out. "It's not so easy to just walk in there. Someone in the street, how shall we say, may see me."

"So it's not so free here?"

"Why must you always judge us by *your* standards? You don't know what it was like here during the war." For the first time, Guillermo's eyes seemed out of winning expressions. I wondered about him. What was such a charming man, who spoke perfect English, who as a youth was Bulgaria's first correspondent in Communist China, doing escorting a poor freelancer like me around? By any reckoning, he should by now have been an ambassador, not a flak for the Sofia Press agency. After I promised to meet him the next morning, we parted in the snow.

On that first night in Sofia, I decided to walk around a bit before returning to the hotel. This was a little city of powerful images, I realized. The waves of gilded and leaden green domes of the floodlit Aleksandar Nevski Memorial Church called forth a vision of medieval Byzantium that had an unnerving effect on me, due to the church's proximity to the Communist party head-quarters, with its massive colonnades and archways, and to the Dimitrov mausoleum, with the ghoulishly preserved corpse inside. Here medieval and modern conspiracies, as well as whispers and silences, appeared to intermingle and hang in the air.

"Bulgaria: a small land, easily encompassed by the human heart, but as lavishly endowed as a miniature continent. . . . A handful of heaven possessed by demons," writes Mercia Mac-Dermott in *The Apostle of Freedom,* a biography of Vasil Levsky, the man who led the nineteenth-century Bulgarian guerrilla struggle against the Turks.

The Bulgars, like the Magyars and the Turks who came later to Europe, were a Turkic (or Tartar) tribe from Central Asia. Around A.D. 681 about 250,000 of them, under Khan Asparuh, crossed the Danube into what would later become Bulgaria. The Bulgars interbred with the Slavs, who had arrived on the Balkan peninsula about 150 years earlier. "As is so often the case with mongrel products," writes the historian Nevill Forbes, this new race exhibited considerable "virility, cohesion, and driving-power."

In the early medieval period, Bulgaria was among the most powerful and advanced kingdoms in Europe, a mini-Byzantium that frequently threatened the emperors in Constantinople. In the ninth and tenth centuries, long before the rise of Serbia, the Bulgarian kings, Boris I and Simeon, carved out an empire stretching from Albania in the west to the Black Sea in the east, and from the Carpathian Mountains in the north to the warm waters of the Aegean in the south. In 865, Bulgarians became the first of all the Slav and Slavicized peoples to embrace Orthodox Christianity. From Bulgaria the monks Cyril and Methodius and their disciples spread the Cyrillic alphabet to Russia and elsewhere, making Bulgaria, more than any other land, the birthplace of Slavonic languages and culture. To this day, Bulgarians consider their native tongue the Latin of Slavic languages.

Linguistic pride accounted for a conception of nationality that, by Balkan standards, was quite liberal. Because Bulgarian Jews spoke Bulgarian just as everybody else did, they were not thought of as especially different. Both the pro-Nazi regime of King Boris III and the Bulgarian partisans fighting against him conspired to save the Jews from deportation. As a consequence, Bulgaria, along with Denmark, chalked up the cleanest Holocaust record of any nation in Nazi-occupied Europe—at least within its own borders.[2] Guillermo would often assure me that "the Bulgarians" (Bulgar-

2. Outside their nation's borders, unfortunately, Bulgarian troops were cruel in the extreme: helping the Germans to round up Jews in Macedonia and Greek-speaking Jews everywhere for deportation to death camps.

ian-born Jews) were "the most powerful faction" in Israeli politics, and were always looking after Bulgaria's interests. He found it hard to understand how anyone born in Bulgaria, who spoke Bulgarian as a child, could ever think of himself as anything other than a Bulgarian. He claimed to know an Israeli of Bulgarian origin who understood Bulgarian the moment he arrived back in the country, although this man had never heard the language before. "Our language is carried in the genes," Guillermo claimed.

In the early eleventh century, the Byzantine Emperor, Basil II, defeated King Samuel at Strumnitsa, after which he had 14,000 prisoners blinded—the most horrific moment in Bulgarian history—and Bulgaria fell back under the sway of the Byzantine Empire.[3] But in the twelfth and thirteenth centuries, under kings Kaloyan and Assen II, Bulgaria regained all of its lost territory and rose to even greater cultural and economic heights.

But unlike other countries, whose empires peaked and gradually faded into oblivion, Bulgaria was then cut down in the prime of nationhood by a series of invasions that culminated in a 500-year-long Ottoman Turkish occupation. Because Bulgaria was used by the Turks as their principal military base for further expansion into Europe, Turkish rule was bloodier and more overbearing in Bulgaria than anywhere else. Whole populations were expelled from urban centers; forced labor was prescribed for the conquered peasants; and the relatively advanced feudal system was replaced by a more primitive one. Along with Serbia, Bulgaria was the first Balkan nation to be conquered by the Turks, but it was the very last one to be liberated. "From 1393 until 1877 Bulgaria may truthfully be said to have had no history," writes Forbes. He continues:

> Of all the Balkan peoples the Bulgarians were the most completely crushed and effaced. The Greeks by their ubiquity, their brains, and their money were soon able to make the Turkish storm drive their own windmill; the Rumanians were somewhat sheltered by the Danube and also by their distance from Constantinople; the Serbs also were not so exposed to the full blast of the Turkish

3. Strumnitsa is near the present-day borders of Bulgaria, Greece, and former Yugoslav Macedonia.

wrath, and the inaccessibility of much of their country afforded them some protection. Bulgaria was simply annihilated. . . .

What emerged in the second half of the nineteenth century was a smoldering and dismembered ghost of a nation. "The Turkish slavery is still our biggest national obsession," Guillermo told me.

Significantly, the most solemn day on the Bulgarian calendar was neither a Christian one nor an official Communist one, but the day commemorating the execution of the thirty-six-year-old guerrilla leader Levsky by the Turks in 1873. Beginning at dawn every February 19, throngs of people bearing flowers pass through the streets of Sofia to the square where the Turks hanged Levsky. By full daylight, the memorial obelisk is adorned with a mountain of flowers. Levsky was the Bulgarians' greatest *yunak*—a word indicating a young, fair hero of near-mythical proportions. Originally an Orthodox monk, Levsky built a national resistance network. His lair was the Stara Planina—the "Old Mountain"—a long mountain wall stretching across Bulgaria, more casually known as the Balkan, the Turkish word for "mountain." This range gives the whole Balkan peninsula its name.

Levsky's execution helped spark a nationwide guerrilla uprising in April 1876 that the Turks savagely suppressed. It was an early chapter in what was to be over a quarter century of guerrilla warfare and counterinsurgency operations, during the course of which the Turks burned hundreds of Bulgarian villages, and most of the casualties were civilian. At about this time last century, the Bulgarians' struggle against a decrepit Sultanate occupied the conscience of Western (and Eastern) liberals in the same manner that Vietnam later would. The writers Oscar Wilde, Victor Hugo, and Ivan Turgenev cried out in support of the Bulgarian guerrilla resistance. So did the British statesman William Gladstone, and the hero of Italian unification, Giuseppe Garibaldi. Walt Whitman's passionate lines about liberty in *Leaves of Grass* applied best to Bulgaria in the years when Whitman was revising his epic poem. Bulgaria was the modern world's first "fashionable cause." The West long ago forgot this; the Bulgarians never have.

At this late and critical juncture in Bulgarian history, the Russians arrived. A Russian army swept through Bulgaria in 1877 and 1878, liberating Bulgaria from Ottoman subjugation in order to create a pro-Russian, Bulgarian buffer state against the Turks. Although the 1878 Treaty of Berlin forced newly independent Bulgaria to cede Thrace and Macedonia back to Turkey—triggering a renewed outbreak of guerrilla war—Bulgarian gratitude to the Russians never entirely dissipated. The Russian liberation was one of the few happy moments in Bulgaria's history since the Middle Ages. Construction of the Aleksandar Nevski Memorial Church began in 1882, to honor the 200,000 Russian soldiers who died during that war. But this devotion to "Grandfather Ivan," as Bulgarians sometimes referred to Russia, held nuances that rarely broke through the wall of clichés erected by Western commentators in the period of the Cold War. As Guillermo mentioned, gratitude toward czarist Russia did not prevent Bulgaria from fighting against Russia in World War I.

Territorial irredentism, especially regarding Macedonia, led Bulgaria to defeat in the Second Balkan War of 1913, and into disastrous alliances with Germany in both World War I and World War II. The losses of Macedonia, of an Aegean coastal foothold, and of other areas made Bulgaria a bitter and irrational nation in the first half of the twentieth century. Bulgarians hated everybody: Serbs, Greeks, Romanians, Turks. Between World War I and World War II, Macedonian terrorism made politics in Sofia permanently violent and unstable. Politically, during this interwar period, Bulgaria resembled Syria in the coup-ridden 1950s and 1960s. So when a Russian army arrived for the second time on Bulgarian soil in September 1944, Bulgaria was a spiritually broken nation, harboring an extreme (even by Balkan standards) sense of stolen destiny, which the Soviets were able to exploit.

In terms of military occupation and loss of land, Soviet domination cost the Bulgarians little. Because their country was not contiguous to the Soviet Union, the Soviets had no territorial claims to make—unlike in the cases of Romania, Hungary, Czechoslovakia, and Poland, whom the Soviets forced to give up territory as the Soviet border moved westward after World War II. Located farthest away from the line of confrontation between East and West in Central Europe, Bulgaria was also the least strategically important of all the Warsaw Pact states. Thus, when local Communists consolidated control under the leadership of the Moscow-trained Dimitrov in December 1947, the Soviet army withdrew from Bulgaria, never to return except for yearly maneuvers. Bulgarians bristled at the claim that they were "vassals" of the Soviets, pointing out that while Hungary (which through the 1970s and 1980s enjoyed a high reputation in the West) was hosting 60,000 Soviet soldiers on its soil, Bulgaria had no Soviet soldiers.

Besides no troops, no loss of territory, and positive historical memories, the Russians offered Bulgaria a heady psychological brew: guaranteed protection against Turkey; and numerous opportunities to deal with that hated former colonial master from a position of strength, not weakness. As a Bulgarian diplomat once told me: "It is the bear that protects us from the barking dog."

In September 1982, after my first visit to Sofia, *Reader's Digest* published an article by Claire Sterling, a writer specializing in international terrorism, entitled "The Plot to Kill the Pope." Sterling's thesis was that the Turkish gunman, Mehmet Ali Agca, who shot and wounded Pope John Paul II in 1981, was not an independent lunatic acting alone, as had first been thought. According to Sterling, Agca was being run by the Darzhavna Sigurnost, the Bulgarian "State Security Police." A few weeks after publication of the article, Italian police arrested the Rome station chief of Balkan Airlines (the Bulgarian national carrier), Sergei Ivanov Antonov, charging him with complicity in the attack on the Pope.

The story that began to emerge was this:

In the 1970s, as part of an effort to destabilize the fragile parliamentary system in Turkey—NATO's eastern bastion—the Soviet KGB encouraged the Bulgarians, who shared part of their border with Turkey, to smuggle weapons to just about every Turkish separatist or extremist group, whether right-wing or left-wing. At the same time, the Bulgarians permitted Bekir Celenk, a leading personage in the Turkish underworld, who controlled criminal networks in Turkish immigrant communities throughout Europe, to use Sofia as his base of operations. The Bulgarians, through their state-owned trucking firm, Kintex, were bringing guns into Turkey and helping to smuggle heroin and other drugs out. Agca, a hired assassin for both the neo-Nazi Turkish "Gray Wolves" and the Marxist "Turkish People's Liberation Army," was well known to the talent scouts of both the Turkish underworld and the Sigurnost in Sofia.

In 1978, the Cardinal of Cracow, Karol Wojtyla, became Pope John Paul II. The election of the first Polish Pope helped ignite the anti-Communist Solidarity movement in Poland in 1980. The existence of a Polish Pope was thus undermining the stability of the Kremlin's largest and most populous East European satellite. And who better to handle the contract for the Pope's elimination than the Bulgarians, whose Sigurnost—more than any other East European secret service—was KGB-dominated, and had, courtesy of their Turkish smuggling links, access to a network of obscure "right-wing" assassins who would be nearly impossible to trace back to Moscow?

"From the very beginning, [we were] absolutely convinced that the KGB was behind the plot," a senior Vatican official had told *Newsweek*.[4]

According to Sterling and Italian justice authorities, Agca came to Sofia's Vitosha Otani Hotel in 1980, where he was provided with a forged passport before being introduced to Bekir Celenk, the Turkish underworld boss, who offered Agca $1.7 million to kill the Pope. Agca then spent two months at the luxurious Vitosha Otani: a place wired up and down by the Bulgarian secret police.

Next, Agca, who had grown up in a shantytown in central Turkey, spent $50,000 on a grand tour of Europe, putting as much distance as possible between Italy and Bulgaria, before arriving in Rome, where Antonov and two other Bulgarians arranged Agca's stay, and drove him to St. Peter's Square on the day he shot the Pope. Agca was arrested on the spot, immediately after firing the gun. Police reportedly found five phone numbers on him: two for the Bulgarian Embassy in Rome; one for the Bulgarian Consulate; another for the Balkan Airlines office; and the last—an unlisted number—for the apartment of Todor Ayvazov, a Bulgarian Embassy clerk.

I returned to Sofia in late 1982, again by train from Romania. I carried a copy of Eric Ambler's masterpiece, *The Mask of Dimitrios*, the story of a Balkan underworld type named Dimitrios who

4. *Newsweek:* January 3, 1983, issue.

passed through Bulgaria on his way to Europe and was involved in a murky web of intrigue that mixed drug smuggling with political assassinations. The book was first published in 1939. At the end, Ambler writes: "Special sorts of conditions must exist for the creation of the special sort of criminal that he [Dimitrios] typified . . . while chaos and anarchy masquerade as order and enlightenment, those conditions will obtain."

The Russians give us great leeway in our dealings with the Turks. . . . How can you say we have no freedom? Guillermo had told me the year before. It now occurred to me that, if these allegations were true, the notion of control over the Turkish criminal Agca must have been especially tempting to the Bulgarians. That was the Bulgarians' ultimate revenge: to determine Agca's actions and fate, just as theirs had been determined by Agca's Ottoman Turkish forebears. The object of the exercise, to kill a Catholic Pope, was secondary. The Balkans is a region of narrow visions, and because the Bulgarians had suffered the most under the Turks, their world view was narrower still.

Guillermo met me at the door of the Grand Hotel Bulgaria. I had telexed him ahead of time that I was coming.

"Come on, Robby, we have to go. You have arrived at the perfect time. Unpack later. Are you going to get *news*, my boy! The head of the BTA is holding a press conference at the journalists' club about the West's criminal provocation. What did Wilfred say about a 'new Cold War'?" Guillermo was full of excitement.

It was 11 A.M., December 1, 1982. The journalists' club on Graf Ignatiev was already a wall of cigarette smoke and plum brandy fumes. Standing at the back of the room was a sallow-complected man with receding dark hair, who interrupted his speech now and then to take a pull on a cigarette. Boyan Traikov, the director of the Bulgarian Telegraphic Agency, was the closest thing the hardline Communist regime had to an official spokesman. For the first time since the international media had begun speculating about a "Bulgarian connection" in the shooting of the Pope, a top Bulgarian official was speaking publicly about it. Aside from a few Western diplomats, I was the only foreigner in the room. Guillermo was translating for me.

"Have you got a scoop, my dear! Now you're going to find out what really happened."

Traikov said that Sterling's article and Antonov's arrest by the Italian police were "part of a plot inspired by Western intelligence agencies to kill détente, and to sow anti-Bulgarian feelings in Poland, just as the situation in Poland was returning to normal." By "normal," Traikov had in mind the crushing of Solidarity and the imprisonment of its leader, Lech Walesa, the year before. Although Traikov's appearance was billed as a "press conference," nobody asked questions. Nor did any of the Bulgarian journalists rush out to file stories. After Traikov finished his speech, everyone stayed and continued drinking.

Guillermo then arranged for me to interview Traikov at the latter's nearby office. Traikov told me that Sterling, like every other journalist who wrote disparagingly of Bulgaria, was either a paid CIA agent or a dupe unwittingly manipulated by the CIA. Because the accusations against Bulgaria were, inevitably, a provocation against the Soviet Union and its new leader, Yuri Andropov—who had been the KGB chief when Agca shot the Pope—if this "whole nonsense" about a Bulgarian connection did not stop, détente would collapse. *And is that what the West really wants?* When I tried to talk about specific allegations, such as whether known Turkish underworld figures had been or were still living in Bulgaria, Traikov shifted to another subject. Not once did Traikov come close to offering me real news, or a lead even.

More interesting, though, was Traikov's demeanor, and that of Guillermo in the former's presence. The Bulgarian Telegraphic Agency occupied a massive building on Lenin Boulevard in Sofia. Traikov's office was a long, dark, tobacco-polluted chasm, of immediately intimidating size. Reaching it required passing through a succession of smaller offices occupied by secretaries and guards. The atmosphere there was more appropriate to a police or interior ministry than to a news agency. Traikov had an extremely virile and lecherous grin. His eyes, on the verge of being bloodshot, were devious and devouring. Were I a woman, I would not have felt safe with him. Unlike Guillermo, he wore a Western suit, and offered me a Western filter-tipped cigarette—a luxury in Bulgaria. Guillermo, extremely nervous, was overly lavish in his introduction of Traikov to me, and of me to Traikov, as if to say, *Great One, meet another Great One* (since, were I not important—which by any media standards other than Bulgarian ones, I wasn't—why should Traikov waste his time?). Traikov did not look at Guillermo as much as look through him, the way mob bosses gaze at underlings. When I think back at Guillermo praising Traikov, I think of what the murdered dissident writer Markov said about the glorification of Stalin: "It was the same as spitting on oneself."

After seeing Traikov, Guillermo took me to his apartment in Sofia, in a dilapidated building without heating. His wife, Margarita, had prepared a feast in my honor. The three of us sat close together on an antique chest that doubled as a bench around the kitchen table. "Each is against everyone else and each is with everyone else because this is what the law of survival dictates. In this unbelievably tight proximity we feel the warmth of each other's bodies, our slightest shivers, . . . we can converse for hours without speaking a word," Markov writes.

Guillermo's small living room was filled with the archaeology of his days as a correspondent in China, from 1957 to 1961: vases, statues, silk screens, and dominating a whole wall, the skin of a tiger he said he had killed. He described the hunt for me in detail: the campfires, going to sleep in the forest, and waking up before dawn to stalk the tiger with his Chinese friends. "I had access, I saw things, Robby, in those years that you wouldn't beleve. You know what it was like to go all over China in the 1950s? *Ah,* those were—how do you say—my salad days." Grabbing me by the arm, he said, "A man, Robby, a man is not a man until he is on the open road!"

Guillermo implored, "Write books, Robby! Go deep. Be like Wilfred Burchett. Don't be a hack!

"Have you ever played an instrument, Robby?"

"A guitar. I had no talent."

"I took violin lessons. I hated it. I sold the violin."

A lump formed in my throat. So had my late father, who had taken his violin to a pawnshop.

Deprived of a present, existing in a museum world of shades, Guillermo had only the distant past to fall back on.

"What about Traikov, Guillermo?"

Guillermo twisted his mouth and leaned toward me, as though to whisper: "His wife is a well-known ballet dancer. They are close to Zhivkov. The *nomenklatura,* Robby," he said, tossing his fingers in the air in the cold room and twisting his mouth again. A long moment of silence followed.

The next morning I visited the crypt of the Aleksandar Nevski Memorial Church, which holds one of the most dramatic collections of Byzantine-style icons in the world.

The finest of the icons dated from the late fourteenth century, on the eve of the Turkish invasion. Although 600 years old, these icons had been restored to perfection. The gold leaf, the ruby and pomegranate reds, the ochers, the midnight blues, and even the grays shone after the fashion of precious stones. The eyes of Saint George, the Virgin Mary, John the Theologian, and Saint John of Rila could have been those of the Byzantine emperors, empresses, and courtiers in the medieval era: every emotion was contained in them, but above all, they conveyed the sense of holding back, of guarding a secret. That was the Bulgarian crowd symbol, I realized: the Byzantine icon, a world of surging passion that contained a deep secret.

CHAPTER THIRTEEN

The Price of Friendship

It was now the autumn of 1985, my fifth visit to Sofia. As on previous visits, I had arrived by train from Romania. Guillermo again met me at the door of the Grand Hotel. "We must hurry, Robby. Nikolai Todorov, the Vice President of the Bulgarian Academy of Sciences and the Director of the Institute of Balkan Studies, is waiting for you."

I had returned to Sofia on account of disturbing reports. The Communist authorities were forcing 900,000 people, 10 percent of the country's population, to change their names. The people affected were all ethnic Turks, the human residue of Turkey's 500-year-long subjugation of Bulgaria. Every "Mehmet" was made to become a "Mikhail," and so on.

It usually happened in the middle of the night. The rumble of army half-tracks and the blinding glare of searchlights would disturb the sleep of an ethnic Turkish village. Militiamen would then burst into every home and thrust a photocopied form in front of the man of the house, in which he was to write the new Bulgarian names of every member of his family. Those who refused or hesitated, watched as their wives or daughters were raped by the militiamen. According to Amnesty International and Western diplomats, the militiamen beat up thousands and executed hundreds. Thousands more were imprisoned or driven into internal exile.

I remember Nikolai Todorov only as a gray man in a gray suit in a cold and dark room; I had to sit, with my coat on, by the window in order to see my notebook. Todorov spoke in a monotone. There was no emotion in his voice. Guillermo translated: "The state has to protect the interests of the nation, and in the Balkans a nation means one particular ethnic group. Keeping the peace in this region means that every minority has to be completely assimilated into the majority."

Guillermo then took me to see another Bulgarian official, who was more blunt: "If it weren't for the Turkish invasion in the fourteenth century we would be eighty million now (instead of nine million). They assimilated us; now we will assimilate them. The Turks still have an invoice to pay for killing [Vasil] Levsky.

"When Bayezit rode in here in the fourteenth century, he came with thunder, and thousands of Bulgarians were forced to change *their* names.[1] Where was your Western press then? Our backs are up against the wall; we have no place to retreat," referring to the 2.5 percent yearly birth rate among the Muslim Turks, compared with the zero percent annual increase in birth rate among the Christian Bulgarians.

When I mentioned to Guillermo that I was going to the U.S. Embassy for a briefing on the matter, he looked worried. "What can they possibly tell you there? Come on, boy!" he said, frowning. "Promise me you are not automatically going to believe what those diplomats tell you. Remember, you're a journalist. You're supposed to be skeptical."

What the diplomats told me was that "a very massive violation of human rights had taken place in Bulgaria." But afterward, Guillermo did not ask me about the briefing. He had done his

1. Bayezit, the Turkish Sultan between 1389 and 1403, was called *Yildirim* in Turkish, meaning "the Thunderbolt."

job—trying to convince me not to go to the embassy—and that was that, so far as he seemed to be concerned.

On the street that evening in 1985, I remember it being bitter cold. As Guillermo and I headed toward a Russian restaurant that we often went to, an official motorcade of Chaika limousines came by, delaying us and the rest of the crowd returning from work. Nobody in the crowd waved at the dignitaries, or even seemed curious. People just kept their heads bowed down. Inside the long black limousines, all of the little window curtains remained closed. The gulf between ruler and ruled in Communist Bulgaria appeared awesome.

"We need a change, Robby." Guillermo spoke quickly as we walked.

I looked over at him, startled. There was no expression on Guillermo's face. Never had he been so direct. I felt the time had come: "What happened after you got back from China, Guillermo?"

"My dear, what I am going to tell you I have never told another foreigner, except for Wilfred."

By the time we reached the restaurant, Guillermo had finished his story. Only several hours later, when I returned to my room at the Grand Hotel Bulgaria, a bit drunk, did I have an opportunity to write it down. But Guillermo's words—blazing against my ear in the darkening, cold street lined with chestnut trees—put a spell on me. I know that I remembered them accurately.

"When I got back from China in late 1961, I was made an editor in the BTA's foreign broadcast division. I was thirty-seven, Robby. It was a job where I got to see a lot of sensitive material that was only for circulation within the party. I expected after a few years to get a big posting, maybe as the BTA correspondent in Moscow.

"I had a friend then; he was my very best friend, Boris Temkov. While I was in China, Boris Temkov was at the Bulgarian Embassy in Britain. Temkov was very well-connected in the party. He was a great guy. We were such good friends, you cannot believe!

"Now there was a party official, his name was Ivan Todorov-Garudya. This Garudya, he was accused of being pro-China. Robby, this was just about the time when the problems between

China and the Soviet Union were beginning: you could tell something big was going on. It was in the air. BTA put out a text that Garudya had committed suicide. I gave Temkov the other text—the one that was for circulation only to the party elite, that contained more details about the Garudya case.

"It was late April 1964. Temkov and I had arranged to meet with our wives for dinner at the journalists' club. You see, we had become such good friends that we wanted to introduce our wives to each other."

"Was this your first wife, Guillermo?" I interrupted.

"No, the second. My first wife—our problems began in China, and we split up as soon as we got back to Bulgaria. Oh, China, Robby, I had so many adventures there.

"Boris and I got to the club before our wives did. Then I remembered that I had forgotten a press release at the office. I told Boris to wait and I went back to BTA to fetch it. When I got back to the club after half an hour, Boris was gone. My wife came up to me. She was with Boris' wife—they had introduced themselves. 'Did you see Boris?' I asked them. 'No,' Boris's wife told me. 'He hasn't come yet.' 'Yes, he was here half an hour ago,' I said. We made some calls. Nothing. We waited. Then someone I knew came up to our table and said, 'Boris has been arrested.' 'Why?' I asked. We were so shocked. The man just repeated that Temkov had been arrested. We could find out nothing, not even where they were keeping him.

"Robby, before a trial of a party member, there is always a meeting to expel this person from the party. One night in July 1964, I was at the journalists' club when a man I know from the party came up to me and said that in ninety minutes there was going to be a meeting about Temkov. He said, 'You must be there, Guillermo. You were his closest friend. How will it look if you don't take the lead in denouncing him?'

"It was the worst moment of my life. I'll never forget how I felt. What was I going to do? They had given me no time.

"At the meeting, I saw Temkov for the first time since the night he was arrested. He looked *so* awful, Robby, you cannot believe. One after the other, the members of the Central Committee stood up and started denouncing him. They said *such* things, you would not believe—that Temkov was pro-Chinese and this and that.

They didn't know him. Not one of them had ever said more than a few words to him in the canteen. I sat there, quiet. I was hoping that they would forget about me. Then, all of a sudden, someone said, 'What about you, Guillermo?' It was something worse than a bad dream. When I stood up my eyes saw everything in a cloud. I could not breathe. The air was *so* heavy. It is impossible to describe how I felt. What could I say? I told them that 'Maybe some of what you say is true. I don't know. I know Boris Temkov very well and he never said any of these things to me that the rest of you say he said. I know that to me, Boris Temkov never said anything against the party. I know he always favored Zhivkov.[2] Regarding the problems between China and the Soviet Union, this is unfortunate. But Boris Temkov never said anything to me that was anti-Soviet. If he said any of these things, it wasn't to me. Comrades, I can only tell you what I, Guillermo, know.'

"There was such a silence when I finished to speak. When everyone walked out of the hall, Boris came up to me and clasped my hands. His hands were *so* dry. I could not speak.

"First, they sent him to Belene.[3] Now he is in Pirdop, a town east of Sofia. He has a job there."

"You man he is in internal exile?"

"Yes. After twenty years, he still had no permission to live in Sofia. I used to take his wife to Pirdop in my car. They put pressure on her to divorce him, but she wouldn't. She is such a lovely woman.

"And me. They put me in the refrigerator, Robby. For ten years after the trial, I was, how to say, in the refrigerator, on some desk, pushing papers. I would have been the director of the BTA now. Instead, I had to leave BTA and go to work at Sofia Press. Then, after ten years, someone told me, 'You know, Guillermo, it's okay, you're forgiven.' I started all over again, from the bottom. I was almost fifty years old. I always wanted to be a journalist, Robby, a real correspondent, going all over, roving, like Wilfred Burchett.

"Don't you see, Robby, it all happened on account of China. When I came back from China at the end of 'sixty-one, the split

2. Todor Zhivkov was the hardline Communist boss of Bulgaria from 1954 until 1989.
3. Belene island in the Danube was the site of a notorious prison camp.

with the Soviet Union had already started. I had been the BTA correspondent in Peking, so I was under suspicion. And because I gave Temkov the text about Garudya, they had something to use against him and me."

I didn't follow. I asked Guillermo to explain. But his explanation was murky and I was shivering. Guillermo had me by the arm, leading me in circles outside the Russian restaurant.

Inside, drinking grape brandy under a dim brown canvas of Russian soldiers fighting in the Crimea, Guillermo glowered: "I hate Zhivkov. I hate Traikov. I always believed in social democracy, in internationalism; not in *nomenklatura* or privileges.

"And Robby," he said, leaning across the table, "what is happening now, with the Turks. This is their worst crime, their worst."

Later during the meal, Guillermo told me the truth about the tiger skin. He had not killed the tiger single-handedly. Everyone shot at once. It was difficult to tell whose bullet was responsible. But since Guillermo was the foreign guest, the Chinese decided to let him have the tiger skin. "You see, Robby, your Guillermo is not such a hero."

CHAPTER FOURTEEN

The Bad and the Good

The Sofia I returned to in October 1990, again by train from Romania, was a different city from the one I had previously known. Dimitrov's corpse had been cremated, and the white neo-classical mausoleum across from the Grand Hotel Bulgaria was now defaced with anti-Communist graffiti. Instead of whispering, people laughed and grumbled openly in the street. Icons and other religious art were being sold in the city's parks. In place of one newspaper, *Rabotnichesko Delo* (*Worker's Task*), which nobody read, there were many newspapers that everybody was reading. The Byzantine and neo-Byzantine churches—rather than seem-ing to repose at a fearful, statuesque distance, as in the past—appeared as an organic element of the present, no longer dis-torting public life, but helping to heal it. Even before Zhivkov's November 1989 downfall, these churches had always seen a light trickle of supplicants, mainly old people. But now they stirred with activity. Both old and young lined up to purchase beeswax candles. I recall one pretty dark-haired woman, with purple leotards and matching lipstick, kneeling down on the marble floor in a bath of yellow light from the stained-glass windows, and kissing an icon.

Guillermo found me in the lobby. He wore a tasteful brown suit, with a blue pinstriped shirt and a red tie and matching handkerchief. He was sixty-six, but looked younger than ever.

"My dear, I'm sorry I'm late but I'm *so* busy these days. Robby, I am now a stringer for UPI and, my boy, there is such news in Sofia. We are in a deep economic crisis, Robby. It is worse than the Balkan Wars. At least then we were united against the Serbs and the others. But we Bulgarians are divided. And all they do in Parliament is talk, talk, talk. When will we see some action? Can't they see the population is waiting for new laws? We have too much democracy now in Bulgaria. . . ."

I steered Guillermo across the square to the Viennese Café at the Sheraton Hotel, opened since the last time I had visited Sofia, where Guillermo polished off a cappuccino and strawberry shortcake, with large doses of whipped cream.

Guillermo began pulling papers out of his briefcase. He was unstoppable, insisting on reading me, word for word, the last two stories he had filed for UPI, about the fuel shortages and the power struggle between the Communists, who now called themselves "socialists," and the opposition Union of Democratic Forces (UDF).

"Robby, may I tell you something? These UDF people—do not think that they are such heroes. You think they are former dissidents? Certainly not. Most are the children of the *nomenklatura*. And all of a sudden they have become democrats. They are opportunists. They scream all the time about the crimes of Zhivkov. That's all they can talk about. Robby, you know I have always been in my heart a dissident. But we must stop concentrating on the past. And you know who can help us? The king, Simeon.[1] He lives in Madrid, but maybe he'll come back."

That night we went to the journalists' club. There, too, the atmosphere had changed. The crowd was much younger than I

---

1. Simeon is the son of Boris III, Bulgaria's king who died in 1943.

had remembered it: men in pressed jeans, and attractive women in credible local copies of the latest Italian fashions. Although the table conversations were heated, the feeling of intimacy had vanished. Politics, not personal intrigue, now dominated the discussions. I felt a twinge of nostalgia and of time passing. In a few years or so, I foresaw the club being remodeled: people would smoke less, and the atmosphere would not be altogether different from that of a supper club in Washington, D.C. I also realized what a false and completely selfish perspective this was; for the Bulgarians, such a transformation would, in every respect, be welcomed.

Guillermo mentioned that after forty-five years, he was quitting the Communist—now Socialist—party. The reason: the man the party had just chosen as its new leader, Aleksandar Lilov, was among the Central Committee members who had denounced Boris Temkov that day in 1964, without even knowing him. In the wake of Zhivkov's downfall, Guillermo told me, Temkov had been released from internal exile and for the first time in twenty-six years was free to return to Sofia. At the BTA, the entire staff had demanded, and secured, the ouster of Boyan Traikov as director. "And the most wonderful thing, Robby, is that after forty-four years the American College, my old alma mater, will be reopened."

Although it was only October, the weather was freezing and overcast. Rain clouds smudged the sky like candle smoke on an icon. The café where I met Guillermo the next morning, like all the interiors in downtown Sofia apart from the Sheraton Hotel, was unheated. The night before, I had slept curled up under many blankets in the Grand Hotel Bulgaria, able to see my breath in the dark. I was still cold: not the pleasant, temporary cold of the West, where you get warm as soon as going indoors; but the grinding, continuous cold of Eastern Europe, where your stomach and ribs ache from clenching your muscles for hours on end, bent over, trying to keep warm. This was the cold that Bulgarians were gearing up for, as they faced the economic aftershocks of the Gulf crisis—which had begun the previous August when Saddam Hussein invaded Kuwait—and the collapse of Communism. Here, as elsewhere in the Balkans, you had to suffer with the others in order to understand.

"This is the most exciting time in our history, but also the most difficult time," Guillermo told me. "The state security files may not be opened, at least while most of us are alive. Yes, people want to know about the murder of Markov, about the Pope, but there is more to it than that. For forty-five years, Robby, we were under this system. Everybody has a file. All of us at one time or another said this, or that. Robby, believe me, you must believe, I was not like others. I never worked for the DZ [state security]. But maybe, if the files were opened, it will be written that, at such and such a time, your friend Guillermo said such and such a thing that was used against such and such a person." Guillermo was raising his eyebrows and pulling up his shoulders under his overcoat in an expression of infinite possibilities and levels of interpretation.

"Do you want to set neighbor against neighbor? Nobody wants to open those files. And if they open them, what will they find? Okay, maybe something about the Markov murder, but also something about how this or that bigshot in the UDF was once an informer for the *DZ*. We will see. But Robby, one thing you must know"—he gripped my arm—"I, Guillermo Angelov, was always a social democrat, an internationalist. I never worked for the DZ." Guillermo looked worried, paranoid that I might suspect him of something.

The wind rattled the windowpanes of the café. I looked out at the leaden sky and the waves of gilded church domes that defined Sofia's skyline. I knew that whatever it was that Guillermo might have done, if he had done anything at all, I had long ago forgiven him for it.

In the blackening twilight, I walked up Boulevard General Zaimov. The globular street lamps had come on only a few minutes before. Now they went out again: another blackout. Due to the fuel shortage, one hour in three there was no electricity. I pushed open a creaky iron door and entered a dark hallway whose gray walls bore graffiti. I walked up the steps and knocked at the door on the second floor. The door opened. In a candle's flickering shadow was a short woman with straight gray hair and a face that was at once lively and intelligent. A candle in her hand, she led me into the living room, whose windows faced the ghostly horse chestnut trees of a park across the street.

"I'm Vessa. This is my daughter, Anna, and my granddaughter, Vanessa."

I shook hands with a pretty, dark-haired woman and admired an eighteen-month-old baby that was raising havoc. The room was cold. The partial darkness revealed a few Oriental carpets, some book-lined shelves, and Asian (particularly, Chinese) artifacts. For an author of forty books, Wilfred Burchett hadn't collected all that much. I thought of the massive libraries I had seen of people who had not accomplished a fraction of Burchett's literary activity. Like Reed and Bourchier, Burchett had led a gypsy life, living out of a suitcase, collecting friends, not things. Unlike Reed, whose books sold well in his lifetime, and Bourchier, who received a staff salary and pension benefits from *The Times* (of London) near the end of his life, Burchett really went out on a limb: withdrawing to Communist Bulgaria at age sixty-nine, in order to write a book and work as a freelancer for Bulgarian journals.

Burchett died in 1983, two years after my first visit to Bulgaria. Vessa met her husband during Burchett's first trip to Bulgaria in 1949, to cover the purge proceedings against Traicho Kostov, a Communist wartime Resistance hero who was executed that year as a "Titoist" spy, only to be posthumously rehabilitated. "I was working at BTA then and was assigned to be Wilfred's Bulgarian translator. We fell in love. I was expelled from the party for having married a foreign journalist. It was difficult to convince people in the party that Wilfred was not hostile like the other Westerners, but sympathetic to us."

"How do you think your husband would have reacted to the revolution in Eastern Europe?"

"He would have been fascinated. It's not true that Wilfred was a Communist. He was not a spy. Deep in his heart, Wilfred was a *perestroika* man before his time. He once said to me, 'Vessa, we must admit that the people's democracies do not work.'"

"Tell me," Anna broke in, "how is Guillermo, is he still a Communist?" Her tone was mocking.

"I don't think Guillermo is a Communist," I said.

"Good, so he has learned." Anna said that the problem in Bulgaria was that the Communists were still trying to retain power, and what the country needed was capitalism and the return of exiled King Simeon.

The mother shot the daughter a harsh look. "Royalty is the

new fad," Vessa said. In her opinion, the opposition, by refusing
to cooperate with the ruling Communists, was responsible for the
instability in the country. Burchett's family was little different
from any other: the children had rebelled against the political
values of the parents.

The lights went back on as I was preparing to leave. "My father
was not a Communist," Anna said to me in a pleading tone.

"Was his book on Bulgaria ever published?"

"Only in Portuguese, by a Brazilian publisher."

On that last trip to Bulgaria in 1990, I set out from Sofia with
my backpack to tour some of the country. Unlike in Romania,
hitchhiking was impossible here; there were simply too few cars
on the road due to the fuel shortage. I took buses instead.

In Kurdzhali, a town not far from the border with Turkey,
in a region of Bulgaria that was 80 percent ethnic Turkish, a
statue of Georgi Dimitrov, the father of postwar Communist
Bulgaria, dominated the park. Dimitrov, haggard and bent over,
coat draped over his shoulder, was depicted as an avuncular
servant of the people. Behind Dimitrov, as part of the same
sculptural unit, stood a series of massive black granite blocks—
one on top of the other—meant to signify the modern industrial
state that emerged from Dimitrov's labors. But what these un-
gainly blocks actually revealed was utter and profane contempt,
as if to say: "We can crush you, and there is nothing you can do
about it."

The difference between Burchett and Dimitrov was this, I
realized:

Burchett was a man with a rich and profound soul, but he was
so driven in his search for heaven that he wound up serving hell,
however innocently. Whatever bad there was in Burchett—or in
Guillermo, for that matter—was bad only by accident. But with
Dimitrov (and with Stalin, too, of course), what was good was good
only by accident. Dimitrov's defense of Communism at the Reichstag fire trial was moral to the extent that what the Nazis were
offering was much worse.[2] But for the rest of his life, especially
as regards the subjugation of Bulgaria, Dimitrov served Stalin's

2. In February 1933, a fire destroyed the German Reichstag (Parliament) in Berlin. Dimitrov and other Communists were falsely accused by the Nazis of setting the fire and
were put on trial. Dimitrov's stirring defense helped force the trial to end in disarray.

every wish and whim. Had Hitler not broken his nonaggression pact with Stalin, then Stalin (and his lieutenants such as Dimitrov) would just as readily have divided up Europe with Hitler as with the Western allies.

"I was going to school in Varna at the time," a Bulgarian woman I met on that visit to Kurdzhali began telling me.[3] "In late 1984, I arrived back in Kurdzhali for my Christmas holiday. Nobody had told me anything. The whole train station was filled with soldiers and militia, in groups of four. Everywhere there were soldiers. The Turkish area of town was completely sealed off. We imagined that terrible things were happening there. We kept quiet. We were afraid. It was the Turks' problem. It was terrible what happened. But except for changing their names—which now can be changed back—what bad did we Bulgarians do?"

"What about the murders and rapes?" I asked her.

"Yes, there were murders and rapes. That was terrible. But now the Turks have more rights than we Bulgarians have. All you foreigners care about is the Turks. That is the only reason you come here. Now we fear that Turkey will take us over. They are larger than us and have a stronger economy."

She was right. Turkey, with fifty-five million people, is over six times as populous as Bulgaria. By Western standards, Turkey has a weak economy, with a high inflation rate, and produces low-quality goods. But unlike Bulgaria, Turkey has had a free-market economy for decades. Considering what Bulgarian consumers have been used to under Communism, and what they can now afford, Turkish products—waiting just over the border—may do very well. At the beginning of the last decade of the twentieth century, Turkish businessmen were poised to overrun Bulgaria, and the Turkish economy was poised to engulf the smaller and weaker Bulgarian one. Turkish domination, which the Communists tried so brutally to prevent, was now coming to pass directly as a result of Communism. For decades, Bulgarian Communists played on the hatreds and obsessions of the past, hatching the most outlandish plots and conspiracies, for the sake of avoiding the very fate that they themselves unconsciously had prepared.

3. Varna is a city on Bulgaria's Black Sea coast.

*   *   *

That October of 1990 I traveled through a mountainous land of willows, poplars, cypresses, Balkan firs, and apple trees. I saw scene after rustic scene of intimate tawny beauty. Bulgaria's particular attraction was that it hovered between the cold and dark climate of Europe and the warmer Mediterranean one of Greece. Its flora was a luxurious combination of both.

I came to Batak: a name that once echoed around the world as My Lai later did. I had long ago promised Guillermo that I would go to Batak. But it wasn't until late 1990, on my seventh visit to Bulgaria, that I went there.

Batak sat nestled in fog, amid pine, spruce, beech, and fir trees, a collection of houses with red-tiled roofs, high in the alpine grasslands of the Rhodopes, in southern Bulgaria not far from Greece. In April 1876, the Turks decided to set an example here. They unleashed the Bashibazouks—murderous bands of Bulgarians converted to Islam—who burned and hacked to death 5,000 Orthodox Christians, nearly the whole population of Batak. Much of the slaughter occurred inside St. Nedelya's Church, where J. A. MacGahan of the London *Daily News,* one of the first observers on the scene, found naked and bloodstained corpses piled three feet deep.

In the museum at Batak, I noticed a clipping from an English newspaper. Because of the way the page was torn, it was impossible to discern either the paper's, or the writer's, identity. Dated August 30, 1876, the article attacked the British Prime Minister, Benjamin Disraeli, for stating that reports of Turkish atrocities in Bulgaria had been "grossly exaggerated." Adopting a cynical tone, the writer says that, in Disraeli's view, it was no great crime "to kill many thousands," but it was a greater crime for a newspaper correspondent to say "thirty thousand were killed when in fact it was only twenty-five thousand, or to say that a sackful of human heads was carried and then rolled down the streets of Phillipopoulis (Plovdiv), when in fact the heads were rolled in front of the door of the Italian Consul at Burgas." I sighed, thinking of countless similar arguments thrown back and forth over the decades across editorial pages, about killings and human rights violations in the Middle East and in other parts of the Third World. To think that, in modern times, it all began here.

I followed the silent, steady stream of visitors into the cold and wintry light of St. Nedelya's, with its sunken roof and smoke-charred white walls, from which the blood stains of 114 years ago had never been washed away. Under glass, in a marble crypt, with stage lights shining in, lay a vast mountain of skulls and bones. The crowd kept coming: Bulgarians of all ages and walks of life; peasant women wearing kerchiefs, and city people in fancy clothes. No one said a word.

My last stop in Bulgaria was at the Rila Monastery.[4] From the grave site of the late British journalist J. D. Bourchier, the monastery appeared as the archetypal vision of Shangri-la: a rhapsody of warm and sensuous colors, topped by domes, roofs, and a medieval tower, clashing perfectly with the austere, sylvan tones of the landscape. The sunlight shone through dark and towering pine trees as Nadia led me up the hillside. Bands of mist, which made me think of high ideals, floated between the peaks. Everywhere I heard the scream of mountain torrents.

It was Nadia who first made me aware of Bourchier. I met her at the Rila Monastery. She was a scholar of Bulgarian medieval history, living and doing research at the monastery while acting as a guide. "I am not religious," she told me. "For me, Christ, Mohammed, it makes no difference. But I came here in search of some higher moral authority—a vision—that Communism never offered us in Bulgaria."

Bourchier's tomb, an impressive granite slab all alone in a clearing, overlooked the main entrance to the monastery. "I come here every day," said Nadia. "It is the most beautiful and peaceful place in the area. On a visit here with King Ferdinand, Bourchier fell in love with this spot. He mentioned that this was where he would like to be buried. When Bourchier died [in 1920], King Boris, who was the new king, granted Bourchier his wish. It is called Vallee Bourchier." The flowers on the tomb were Nadia's.

Sensing my interest, Nadia led me to her room in the monastery compound, where she had a book about Bourchier's life.

She took me up steep wooden stairs and down a long gallery, the floorboards creaking beneath me. Then she turned over a

4. John of Rila, a Bulgarian saint, founded the Rila Monastery. See the Prologue.

large key that opened onto a cold and whitewashed cell: here, I thought, I could blissfully live out my old age, and die.

Sunlight poured through the dusty window onto a wooden table holding an old Cyrillic typewriter. On the floor was a striped Oriental carpet. A colorful peasant cloth covered Nadia's bed. The room's two rows of shelves included a handful of illustrated books about iconography and the Orthodox Church. Nadia's two-month-old kitten crouched inside the bar of sunlight.

It was late autumn at an altitude of 5,000 feet. The room was freezing. Nadia brought me a steaming cup of herbal tea and placed a book with a handsome black binding on my lap. The inside cover bore a stamp that read PROPERTY OF THE AMERICAN COLLEGE OF SOFIA. I looked at the due dates. The last time someone had checked out the book was June 10, 1941. Nadia explained that, when the Communists closed the American College in 1946, many of the books from the college library were brought to the monastery for the monks to protect.

The book was *The Life of J. D. Bourchier* by Lady Grogan, published in London in 1932. "Bourchier [Nadia pronounced it BOW-cher] was a great friend of Bulgaria. He loved our country as a second home. I can't believe you don't know about him." Nadia smiled and left the big, heavy key on the wooden table. "I must go back to the courtyard now, in case there are any tourists. You can stay here as long as you like to read."

She closed the door behind her. I glanced out through the window at the lines of spruce and holm oak trees on the steep mountainside. Then I began to read.

James David Bourchier was born in 1850 of an Anglo-Norman-Irish background. He was educated, and later taught, at Eton, where he was plagued by shyness and a realization that he was going deaf. His deafness, noted the biographer, is what saved Bourchier from a life of mediocrity as an unsuccessful schoolmaster. At the age of thirty-eight, unmarried and with few friends, he left for Europe with the notion of becoming a writer. A series of coincidences saw him go to Bucharest in 1888 to write a report for *The Times* on a peasant rebellion threatening the rule of King Carol I. Bourchier then became *The Times*'s stringer in the Balkans. At this point his whole personality seems to have undergone a transformation. In new and exotic surroundings. where nobody

knew him as Bourchier the shy schoolmaster, and with a new job
that forced him into contact with important and interesting people, Bourchier's shyness was turned inside out: he developed an
intense sociability and an empathy for the various ethnic groups
he had to report on. "He identified himself in turn with the Cre-
tans or with the Bulgars of Macedonia, or with Greeks or Rumanian peasants," writes Lady Grogan. The Greek Prime
Minister, Eleftherios Venizelos, would later refer to Bourchier as
"the friend of Greece," while King Ferdinand would call him "the
friend of Bulgaria." In 1892, *The Times* made Bourchier its staff
correspondent for the Balkans, a job he held for more than two
decades, covering the two Balkan wars and World War I. During
that time, Bourchier also wrote the sections on Greece, Bulgaria,
and Romania for several editions of the *Encyclopedia Britannica*.
At the end of World War I, Bourchier showed up at various peace
conferences as the British champion of Bulgaria's claim to Macedonia—the same role that Lawrence of Arabia was then performing for the Arabs, but a hopeless task because Bulgaria had
sided with the Germans, who had lost the war.

As someone who has always considered himself a late bloomer,
I warmed to Bourchier's recollections of his first journeys through
the Balkans, when he was nearly forty: "Ah! the freshness of
youth!" he wrote. Bourchier also liked staying at Balkan monasteries, as I did. In Athens, where Bourchier was once the dean
of the press corps, I was sure that none of the current journalists
had ever heard of him. It had all happened so long ago: the
Macedonian guerrilla struggle, the Balkan wars. Yet here in this
forest, an attractive, intelligent woman, who could have been
doing other things, was keeping alive Bourchier's flame. If there
is such a thing as being in communion with the dead, I felt something akin to it then, after closing the last page of Bourchier's life
story. If anyone could ever have appreciated my feelings toward
this lovely little country, I was sure it was he.

PART IV

Greece: Western Mistress, Eastern Bride

*Following the tradition of reason and empirical inquiry, the West bounds forward
to conquer the world; the East, prodded by frightening subconscious forces,
likewise darts forward to conquer the world. Greece is placed in the middle; it
is the world's geographical and spiritual crossroads.*

—NIKOS KAZANTZAKIS, Report to Greco

CHAPTER FIFTEEN

Farewell to Salonika

In October 1990, I left the Rila Monastery for Bulgaria's southern border, from where it was only another fifty miles to the harbor of Greece's second largest city, Salonika. In Salonika, I sat down at a café table facing the warm Aegean water. On either side of me, stretching for miles along the sweeping, sickle-shaped bay, were dun masses of poured-concrete apartment buildings with rusted balconies, and plastic neon signs advertising fast-food restaurants and video-game parlors. The blue-and-white Greek flag snapped in the dusk from the White Tower, built in the fifteenth century, the only remnant of the decades and centuries before World War II within my line of vision. For the woman who took the chair opposite me at the table, that flag flying over this city represented not the liberating purity of marble ruins on a blue seaboard, but the grim and uncompromising reality of the East.

Greeks are a flamboyant people of gesture: the delicious snap, crackle, and pop of Greek syllables are meant to be punctuated with upward-thrusting jaws and outward-thrusting arms. Greeks spend much of each day talking at café tables. "We Greeks are the most talented of peoples: it is an art to take four hours to finish a small cup of coffee," a writer friend once exclaimed to me in mock-seriousness. But the woman before me now was notably economical in her movements, and, as she coldly pointed out, had only the next forty-five minutes free. She had dark hair and eyes, and a harsh, wounding stare. "Take out your notebook," she said.

Salonika—Thessaloniki in Greek—was named after Salonike, Alexander the Great's half-sister. John Reed, when he arrived here in the spring of 1915, sketched its history:

> Here Alexander launched his fleets. She [Salonika] has been ... a Byzantine metropolis second only to Constantinople, and the last stronghold of that romantic Latin Kingdom, where the broken wreck of the Crusaders clung desperately to the Levant they had won and lost. Saracens and Franks ... Greeks, Albanians, Romans, Normans, Lombards, Venetians, Phoenicians, and Turks succeeded each other as her rulers, and St. Paul bored her with visits and epistles. Austria almost won Salonika in the middle of the Second Balkan War, Serbia and Greece broke the Balkan Alliance to keep her, and Bulgaria plunged into a disastrous war to gain her. Salonika is a city of no nations and of all nations.

Then Reed added: "But all the centre of the city is a great community of Spanish Jews expelled from Spain by Ferdinand and Isabella."

According to the British Balkan specialist Nevill Forbes, also writing from the vantage point of 1915: "the city of Salonika was and is almost purely Jewish, while in the country districts Turkish, Albanian, Greek, Bulgar, and Serb villages were inextricably confused." J. D. Bourchier thought the "ideal solution" for the city's future "would be a Jewish republic and a free port under the protection of the Great Powers." Jews themselves, for centuries, referred to Salonika as "the Mother of Israel."

*   *   *

Rena Molho, the woman seated opposite me, was a Spanish Jew, one of 850 Jews left in this city of a million Greeks; the Bulgarian, Serbian, and Turkish communities numbered even less. She was here to speak about a city that no longer existed: the same way that Greeks from Alexandria spoke mournfully of their own multi-ethnic Mediterranean city, also with a sweeping sickle-shaped harbor, that for centuries has been dominated by Greeks, but now was completely Arab. Facts rushed forth from Rena.

The first Jews came to Salonika in 140 B.C. In A.D. 53, St. Paul—Rabbi Saul of Tarsus, that is—preached at the Etz Haim ("Tree of Life") Synagogue on three successive Sabbaths. Jews from Hungary and Germany arrived in 1376. Following the conquest of Salonika by the Ottoman Turks, 20,000 Jews from Spain received permission to settle there in 1492, radically transforming the city's culture and demographic character. In 1493, came the Jews from Sicily. From 1495 to 1497, after the Inquisition had spread from Spain to Portugal, the Jews from Portugal arrived. "In 1913," Rena lectured, "the population of Salonika was 157,000: made up of 80,000 Jews, 35,000 Turks; of whom 10,000 to 15,000 were *Domnes* (Jews who had been converted to Islam in the course of Ottoman rule), 30,000 to 35,000 Greeks, and 7,000 to 12,000 Bulgarians, Serbs, and Albanians."

Rena fired off the titles of books—complete with names of authors and publishers, and dates of publication—to back up her statistics and to say, in effect: *Look at everyone gesturing at the other tables. There you get style, I give you substance. I dare you to dispute any of my facts!*

One book Rena mentioned was *Farewell to Salonica*, by Leon Sciaky, the story of a boy growing up at the close of the Ottoman era in a sleepy city of gardens, minarets, whitewashed walls, green shutters, and red-tiled roofs. I later tracked down a copy of this long-out-of-print book at the British Council library in Salonika. Sciaky refers to the Salonika of that time as the "preponderantly Jewish capital" of Macedonia. In his school class of fifteen, only one student was Greek. The author calls this a "fair cross-section" of the city. It is a memoir laden with historical expectation: "The century was drawing to a close. Stealthily, the West was creeping in, trying to lure the East with her wonders."

At the turn of the century here in Greek Macedonia, the reactionary tyranny of the Turkish sultans was finally collapsing. But fear and uncertainty loomed: in a region of great ethnic diversity, the Jews had carved out a niche. The intolerant—perhaps because it was so long repressed—nationalism of the Bulgarians, who occupied the hinterland around Salonika, and of the Greeks, who occupied all the territory to the south, represented a much more threatening tyranny than that of the imperial Turks. "You have to understand the climate," said Rena. "In 1913, Greeks broke into four hundred Jewish shops on account of a rumor that the Jews had poisoned the wells." In *Report to Greco,* Nikos Kazantzakis gives his own account of anti-Semitism in Greece during this period:

> I wanted to learn Hebrew in order to read the Old Testament in the original . . . my father called the Rabbi, and they agreed that I should go to him three times a week to receive lessons. . . . The moment our friends and relatives heard, their hair stood on end and they ran to my father. "What are you doing!" they shrieked. "Have you no feelings for your son? Don't you know that on Good Friday those crucifiers put Christian children in a spike-lined trough and drink their blood?"

In 1916, Greek troops occupied Salonika. In 1917, a great fire destroyed the entire Jewish section of the city, along with thirty-four synagogues. The homeless numbered 73,448, of whom 53,737 were Jews. Still, noted Rena, Salonika was "a Jewish city. The lingua franca, and the language of the street kids, was Judeo-Spanish (Ladino). The port closed on *shabbat* [the Jewish Sabbath] until 1923, when Greek law forced it open." In that year, 100,000 Greek refugees from Asia Minor—recently overrun by the Turkish army under a new nationalist leader, Mustafa Kemal "Ataturk"—were resettled in Salonika. "The Jews allowed their schools to be used as refugee shelters. For a time after, Jewish children could not attend school," said Rena, anger rising in her voice.

When the Nazis captured Salonika in April 1941, the Jews were the second largest community after the Greeks. Although the size of the community had diminished, Salonika was still the world cultural capital of Sephardic ("Spanish") Jewry. "It took the Nazis two years, working every day, to loot Jewish Salonika of its artistic treasures," said Rena. "And it took fifteen trainloads over a period of five months to empty Salonika of its Jews. A whole city was moved to a concentration camp. The 500,000 graves in the cemetery, maybe the largest Jewish cemetery in the world, were all destroyed." I was shown a photo of a swimming pool the Germans had built, lined with Jewish tombstones.

Of all the cities in Nazi-occupied Europe, Salonika ranked first in the number of Jewish victims: out of a Jewish population of 56,000, 54,050—96.5 percent—were exterminated at Auschwitz, Birkenau, and Bergen-Belsen. The successful roundup and deportation of the Jews of Salonika helped make Adolf Eichmann infamous. In the early 1990s, the world's most wanted, still-surviving Nazi war criminal, Alois Brunner (an Austrian, like Eichmann), was being sought from his Syrian hideout specifically for his crimes in Salonika.

When the Nazis occupied Salonika, Rena's mother escaped to central Greece, then under Italian occupation. With false identity papers, Rena's father escaped to Athens, where he sold cigarette paper. "The day Athens was liberated was the greatest day in my father's life, he told me, greater than the day that any of his children or grandchildren were born."

Now Rena came to the heart of her message: "The Jews owned twelve thousand houses in Salonika before the German invasion. After the war, they made only six hundred claims. The Greek authorities acted on thirty of them. Today, at the university in Salonika, there is not a department, not a course, nothing about the Jews—or about the Turks or other communities either. There is nothing in the historical institutes. Nothing in the city's museums. Hardly a book in the Greek bookstores. Nothing. As if we were never here.

"You know the fairgrounds, where every year there is a trade fair and the Prime Minister gives a speech? It is built over the Jewish cemetery. There is not a plaque. Nothing."

Rena got up to leave. She had another appointment.

Rena had not been exaggerating. After forty-five years, the Municipality of Salonika had yet to act on a request to name one street in the city—any street—"the Street of Jewish Martyrs." The effacement of the city's multi-ethnic past had been so total as to be unconscious. The speeches about Salonika throughout the post-war era by Greek politicians, from all shades of the political spectrum, rarely (if ever) contained a reference or a tribute to the non-Greek side of the city's past. In Greek eyes, Salonika and the rest of Macedonia were, are, and always will be purely Greek.

Molho's bookshop, owned by Rena's father-in-law, Saul— opened by his forebears in 1870, and the oldest bookstore in the city, located at 10 Tsimiski Street—is the lone thriving remnant of Jewish Salonika. At the eastern edge of town, past miles of concrete blocks and tacky storefronts, stands the Villa Mozdah, an architectural landmark, named after a prominent family of Spanish Jews whose home it was. The blue-and-white Greek flag flew over its onion-bulb roof and white neoclassical columns and pilasters. There was no plaque outside, no mention of any kind in any local guidebook of the building's non-Greek past.

I unburdened myself on the whole issue of Jewish Salonika to a Greek-American friend, Aristide D. Caratzas. Caratzas, a specialist in Byzantine history, is both an active member of the Greek lobby and an academic publisher of books on Greek-related subjects, modern and ancient. Caratzas's firm was soon to publish a book about the Jews of Salonika.

This is what he said: "From classical antiquity through the beginning of the fifteenth century, Salonika was a Greek city. The Greeks were expelled by the Ottoman Turks, who then welcomed the Jews. It's true, for five hundred years, the Jews dominated Salonika; and in historical terms, they preserved the city for the Greeks, who only reclaimed it in the twentieth century—partly due to another Turkish expulsion, this time from Asia Minor *to* Salonika. But in Greek political mythology, Salonika can only be Greek. There can be no mention of the Jews. The building of a national consciousness in this part of the world sometimes means that what everybody knows privately is what also can never be openly stated or admitted." Caratzas then quoted a sixth-century Greek philosopher, Stephen of Byzantium: "Mythology is what never was, but always is."

In other words, there was little unusual about this story. Just as Serbia, Albania, Romania, and Bulgaria brutally smashed through the undergrowth of Ottoman tyranny and diversity to erect ethnically uniform states, so did Greece. And as the memory of the Albanians was erased by the Serbs, as the memory of Greek Northern Epirus was erased by the Albanians, that of the Hungarians by the Romanians, and that of the Turks by the Bulgarians, so too was the memory of Salonika's Jews and other ethnic groups erased by the Greeks. Greece is part of the Balkan pattern, particularly in this city, the former capital of Ottoman-era Macedonia.

And thus I finally come to the matter itself: Greece, the southern dagger point of the Balkan Peninsula, considered the birthplace of our Western culture and value system—what Greece is, has been, and never was.

I lived in Greece for seven years, and have visited it often before and since. I speak and read Greek, albeit badly. I met my wife in Greece, got married in Greece, and had a son born in Greece. I love Greece. But the Greece I love is a real country, warts and cruelties and all; not the make-believe land of the university classicists or of the travel posters.

Because I did not have a "travel experience" in Greece so much as I had a "living experience," my attitude toward Greece is more obsessive than my attitude concerning the rest of the Balkans. My living experience revealed Greece to me as a Balkan country. What made Greece particularly Balkan in the 1980s, when I lived there, was the politics. This is why I will dwell at length on Greece's modern political atmosphere: a subject about which little has been written, compared with all the books on Greek travel.

Before the end of the Cold War, when the existence of the Warsaw Pact enforced an artificial separation between Greece and its northern neighbors, only Westerners like me, living in Greece, realized how Balkan Greece was. Those on the outside were determined to see Greece as a Mediterranean and Western country only: the facts be damned. As I began work on this book in 1989— when Macedonia was known only as the birthplace of Alexander the Great, and not as the geopolitical problem it currently is— people advised me to leave Greece out of the story, since it "was not really part of the Balkans." I resisted. Events have borne me out. As the 1990s began, Greece was increasingly making the news in connection with border disputes in Macedonia and southern Albania. And Greece's political behavior in the region, despite a democratic tradition going back to antiquity, appeared no more reasonable than that of its neighbors to its north, whose democratic tradition was generally nonexistent.

The first time I arrived in Greece was by train from Yugoslavia. The second time was from Bulgaria, also by train. A third time was by bus from Albania. Each time, upon crossing the border into Greece, I became immediately conscious of a continuity: mountain ranges, folk costumes, musical rhythms, races, and religions, all of which were deeply interwoven with those of the lands I had just come from. And just as everywhere else in the Balkans, where races and cultures collided and where the settlement pattern of national groups did not always conform with national boundaries, this intermingling was hotly denied.

"No Turks live in Greece," Greece's former Deputy Foreign Minister, Ioannis Kapsis, once told me: "There are only some Greeks who happen to be Muslim and happen to speak Turkish to each other. Nor are there any Macedonians . . . " Kapsis railed. He was unstoppable. In all the years I lived in Greece, from 1982 through 1989, I never once heard a Greek—outside of a few well-known politicians—bring up the question of the Parthenon (Elgin) Marbles and the British Museum's refusal to return them. And if that issue—which received so much publicity in the West—was brought up by a foreigner, I never heard native Greeks speak long or passionately about it. But hours of my life have been spent sitting quietly at a Greek table, hearing out paroxysms of rage on issues such as the Turks and Constantinople, the Serbs and Macedonia, and the persecuted Greek minority in Albania. When I arrived in Greece in 1990 from Macedonia and Bulgaria, I tried to explain the position of the Slavic Macedonians to a group of Greek friends. They fumed, practically in unison: "Just because those dirty Gypsies in Skopje filled your head with lies doesn't make it true!" To these Greeks, all Slavs who called themselves "Macedonian" were "dirty Gypsies."

That is why, when I arrived in Greece from Bulgaria in 1990, I did not think of myself as having left the Balkans, but as having entered the place that best summed up and explained the Balkans. The icon was a Greek invention. The Greek Orthodox Church was the mother of all Eastern Orthodox churches. The Byzantine Empire was essentially a Greek empire. The Ottoman Turks ruled through Greeks—from the wealthy, Phanar ("Lighthouse") district of Constantinople—who were often the diplomats and local governors throughout the European part of the Turkish empire. *Constantinople* was a Greek word for an historically Greek city. Even the Turkish word for the place, Istanbul, was a corruption of the Greek phrase *is tin poli* ("to the city"). The elite corps of Ottoman soldiery, the Janissaries, included many Greeks, who had been taken from their parents as young children and raised in the sultan's barracks. The Cyrillic alphabet, used in Bulgaria, Serbia, Macedonia, and Russia, emerged from the Greek alphabet when two monks, Cyril and Methodius, left Salonika in the ninth century A.D. to proselytize among the Slavs. The modern Greek race has been a compound of Greeks, Turks, Albanians, Romanians, assorted Slavs, and others, all of whom migrated south into the warm-water terminus of the Balkan Peninsula. The fact that few distinguishable minorities have survived in Greece is testimony to the assimilative drawing power of Greek culture. The peasants of Suli in western Greece, for example, and the Aegean islanders of Spetsai and Hydra, were originally of pure Albanian stock. "The Greece of the classical heritage and of the romantic philhellene has gone, and anyhow has always been irrelevant to the Greek situation," writes Philip Sherrard, a translator of modern Greek poetry. "Greece . . . never had any Middle Ages, as we understand them, or any Renaissance, as we understand it, or an Age of Enlightenment. That elevation of the reason over the rest of life had not taken place."

Greece is Europe's last port of call, where the Balkans begin to be dissolved completely by the East. As such, approaching from the opposite direction, Greece is also where the oxygen of the West begins to diffuse the crushing and abstract logic of the Mesopotamian and Egyptian deserts. This, after all, was the ultimate achievement of Periclean Athens (and by extension, of the West): to breathe humanism—compassion for the individual—into the inhumanity of the East, which was at that time emblemized by the tyrannies of ancient Egypt, Persia, and Babylonia. At the National Archaeological Museum in Athens, I saw this process at work, as the fierce and impersonal statues of the Early and Middle Bronze Ages, bearing the heavy influence of Pharaonic Egypt, gradually, feature by rounded feature, metamorphosed over two millennia into the uplifting beauty and idealism of classical Greek sculpture.

Classical Greece of the First Millennium B.C. invented the West by humanizing the East. Greece accomplished this by concentrating its artistic and philosophical energies on the release of the human spirit, on the individual's struggle to find meaning in the world. Meanwhile, in Persia, for example, art existed to glorify an omnipotent ruler. But Greece was always part of the East, albeit on its western fringe. To see Greece in its true Oriental light is to recognize the magnitude of the ancient Greeks' achievement.

Moreover, understanding Greece's historic role as the ideological battleground between East and West lends a deeper insight into the process by which Western democracy and values, in our era, can influence the political systems of the Third World. Greece is the eternal sieve, through which the assaults of the East on the West, and of the West on the East, must pass and immediately deposit their residue.

"Welcome back to the Orient," said Sotiris Papapoulitis, a leading member of Greece's conservative New Democracy Party, as he treated me to an expensive seafood lunch at a restaurant in the port city of Piraeus, adjacent to Athens. I had just arrived by bus from Salonika. "But in the Orient," Papapoulitis cautioned me, "you must never confuse an open heart with an open mind."

Papapoulitis was referring to hmself. In the fall of 1990, he was engaged in an ultimately unsuccessful bid to be elected mayor of Piraeus. He was flamboyant, sophisticated, naive, and narrow-minded all at once. He was the kind of fellow who could quote from Descartes and believe a conspiracy theory, while wearing a tight shirt open to his navel. Papapoulitis knew this and relished the fact that his very personality, like the scene around us—yachts, blue sea, sunshine, mountains of seafood, inefficiency, and chaos—constituted the perfect synthesis of the Balkans, the Mediterranean, the European West, and the Levantine East.

"I hate the term *Greek*. It is a corruption of a Turkish word for dog or slave," Papapoulitis exclaimed for all the customers to hear. "Call me a *Hellene*. Call me a *Romios* even. But don't call me a Greek."

Hellene was what the ancient Greek called himself, and it has come to symbolize a Greek (or that part of the Greek psyche) whose roots are in the West. *Romios* literally means Roman, and refers to a Greek of the Eastern Roman Empire (often referred to as Byzantium), whose roots are in the East. Patrick Leigh Fermor, a British travel writer with an unrivaled knowledge of the Greek language and culture, identified more than sixty characteristics and symbols that distinguish the Hellene mentality from the Romios mentality. Whereas the Hellene relies on principle and logic, the *Romios* relies on instinct; whereas the Hellene sees Greece as being part of Europe, the Romios sees Greece as lying outside Europe; whereas the Hellene is a man of enlightened disbelief, the Romios believes in the miracle-working properties of icons; whereas the Hellene follows a Western code of honor, the Romios evinces a lack of scruples for achieving personal ends; and so on . . . Obviously, as was the case with Papapoulitis and so many other Greeks I knew, both the Hellene and Romios aspects of the Greek personality could exist side by side within the same person.

Fermor, like many philhellenes ("foreign lovers of Greece"), was keenly aware of Greece's Oriental aspect. A case in point: Lord Byron, the nineteenth-century Romantic poet and volunteer in the Greek War of Independence, destested scholars of classical Greece, whom he called "emasculated fogies" full of "antiquarian twaddle." Byron's philhellenic commitment was based on a true vision of the country, not on a myth. As for the squabbling Greek guerrilla fighters he encountered in the mosquito-infested swamps of western Greece in the 1820s, the English poet observed: "Their life is a struggle against truth; they are vicious in their defense." Kazantzakis, who was not a foreigner, also had no doubts about the true soul of Greece: "The modern Greek . . . when he begins to sing . . . breaks the crust of Greek logic; all at once the East, all darkness and mystery, rises up from deep within him."

To Greeks, the East—the realm of this darkness, mystery, sadness, and irrationality—includes specific memories and events that are central to the Byzantine and Ottoman legacy.

For Western tourists and admirers of Greece, the country's crowd symbol would have to be the Parthenon, erected by Pericles in the fifth century B.C.—the golden age of Athenian democracy, the period of Greek history with which all of us in the West are

familiar. In school, we learned about how the Minoan and Mycenaean civilizations developed over several centuries into the
Greek city-states, among them Athens and Sparta, which fought
wars against each other and against the Persians, a people who
at the time represented the "barbarous East." We learned how
Greek culture survived and was spread through the conquests of
a Greek Macedonian, Alexander the Great. And we are generally
aware of the scope and grandeur of ancient Greek history: how
the world of Homer's *Iliad* and *Odyssey,* associated with Mycenaean
culture of the Second Millennium B.C., is separated by nearly a
thousand years from the world of Socrates, Plato, and Aristotle.
Greek history, as we in the West have been taught it, is a long
and inspiring saga. Unfortunately, this great saga was just one
element in Greece's past, and the past did not end when the Dark
Ages began. For what admirers of ancient Greece consider the
Dark Ages was, in truth, the beginning of another period of Greek
grandeur, that of Byzantium.

Thus, for the Greeks themselves, another building, far from
the Parthenon—indeed, standing outside the borders of present-
day Greece altogether—elicits far deeper surges of emotion and
nostalgia.

The Greeks, like other Orthodox Christian peoples, are fixated
on their churches, which are not only places of worship but trea-
sure houses of their material culture that survived the awful centuries of Ottoman rule. C. P. Cavafy, the greatest modern Greek
poet, described this feeling in his poem "In Church":

> . . . *when I enter a Greek church,*
> *the fragrance of its incenses,*
> *the voices of the liturgy and harmonies of sound,*
> *the orderly appearance of the priests,*
> *each moving to most solemn rhythm,*
> *all garbed in vestments most magnificent,*
> *recall to mind the glories of our race,*
> *the greatness of our old Byzantine days.*[1]

And among Greek churches, one above all stands out: the
Church of Hagia Sophia, or "Divine Wisdom," built in the middle

1. Translation by Memas Kolaitis. See bibliography.

of the sixth century A.D. by the Byzantine Emperor Justinian and rising majestically—a flat, wide dome mounting a chorus of semi-domes and flaring buttresses, as though in an act of levitation—over the scummy waters of Seraglio Point in Constantinople (Istanbul). Even today, stripped of its gold and silver, with its frescoes faded and begrimed, there is arguably no building in all the world whose interior conjures up such a sense of boundless wealth and mystical power. I visited Hagia Sophia several times in the 1980s. Each time, I instinctively knew that the political passions of modern Greece might be explained here—much more than at the Parthenon. Passing through the imperial door toward the main dome, I always felt as though I were inside a great indoor city of marble walls, galleries, and colonnades, and of mosaics, with vast, ambiguous spaces lurking in the peripheries. Hagia Sophia became the prototype for all Orthodox cathedrals, for St. Mark's Church in Venice, and for mosques throughout Turkey.

But Hagia Sophia is no longer a church. It is the Turkish "Museum of Aya Sofya." In place of bells, incense, and priests are massive round, green plaques hung above the wall corners, that bear Arabic inscriptions, saying "Allah is Great." Although Greek tourists travel to Turkey to visit the "Museum of Aya Sofya," many come home unsettled by the experience, and the overwhelming majority of Greeks cannot bring themselves even to go. "The idea of going to our church in what for us was the greatest of Greek cities and seeing those Muslim signs, I cannot tell you how it would make me feel. It is something terrible," an Athenian friend once told me. Istanbul will forever be Constantinoupoli in Greek eyes, even if "Constantine's city" no longer exists. Greeks cannot bring themselves to say the word *Istanbul.* Upon hearing it on the lips of a foreigner, they wince much as Israelis wince at the word *Palestine,* or many Arabs wince at the word *Israel.* His Holiness, Bartholomew, the Patriarch of the Greek Orthodox Church, sits not in Athens, but in Constantinoupoli, in a woodframed building amid narrow, dirty lanes. This is all that remains of Byzantium, a civilization and an empire created in A.D. 324, as the successor to Rome, and destroyed more than 1,100 years later by an invading army of Ottoman Turks in 1453. During those eleven centuries, the Byzantine Empire was a Greek empire, and Greece then was much more than the classical Mediterranean culture with which the West is familiar: it was a northerly cultural realm of unimaginable depth and texture, whose influence spread to medieval Muscovy.

But the Turks smashed it all. That is why Hagia Sophia expresses in stone and marble what Greeks cry out silently in their hearts: *We have lost so much, not one inch more, not Macedonia, not anything more will we lose!*

The pain of this loss was sharpened by the modern experience of war and exile. George Seferis, the Nobel Prize–winning Greek poet, writes in "The House Near the Sea":

> *The houses I had they took away from me. The times*
> *happened to be unpropitious: war, destruction, exile;*[2]

The cause of Seferis's suffering was the Greek-Turkish War of 1922—the final event in the series of Balkan military struggles (beginning with the 1877 Russo-Turkish War in Bulgaria) that dominated news headlines from the last quarter of the nineteenth century through the first quarter of the twentieth, and set the boundaries of the Balkans more or less as they were in 1990, on the eve of the Yugoslav civil war.

Although the Ottoman Turks had ejected the Byzantine Greeks from Constantinople in the fifteenth century, large Greek communities survived in Istanbul and along the western shore of Asia Minor—particularly in the city of Smyrna—through the end of World War I. The dismemberment of the Ottoman Empire in the wake of World War I provided the Greeks (who had sided with the victorious Allies) an opportunity to regain this lost territory, where over a million ethnic Greeks still lived. But the Greeks wanted even more. For years, the British Prime Minister and romantic philhellene, Lloyd George, had encouraged them to believe that, whatever Greece did, the Western Allies would certainly support a Christian nation and the heir to ancient Greece against the Muslim Turks. This naive trust, fortified by spreading anarchy in Turkey following the collapse of the Sultanate, caused the Greeks to embark upon their Megali Idea, the "Great Idea": the return of every inch of historic Greece to the motherland. Again,

2. Translation by Edmund Keeley and Philip Sherrard. See bibliography.

there was the same old Balkan revanchist syndrome: each nation claiming as its natural territory all the lands that it held at the time of its great historical expansion.

In 1921, the Greek army, against all military logic, advanced beyond the Greek-populated western coast of Asia Minor, and deep into the mountainous Anatolian interior, only 150 miles from Ankara. This move made the army's supply lines so weak and disorganized as to be nonexistent. A reporter for the *Toronto Daily Star,* Ernest Hemingway, writes that the Greek officers "did not know a god-damned thing," while the Greek troops came to battle in the ceremonial, nineteenth-century uniform of "white ballet skirts and upturned shoes with pompoms on them."

At that point, in August 1922, the ruthless and charismatic young Turkish general Kemal Ataturk, who was in the midst of whipping together a new Turkish republic out of the anarchic morass of the Ottoman Empire, unleashed his forces. Hemingway writes that the Turks advanced "steadily and lumpily." In only ten days, Ataturk drove the Greek army back to the Aegean coast, where Greek troops deserted to offshore ships, leaving the Greek population of Smyrna exposed to fire and the Turkish soldiery. The Greek dead numbered 30,000. In the massive population exchange that followed, 400,000 Turks from Greek Thrace marched into Turkey, and 1,250,000 Greeks from Asia Minor went into exile in Greece—homeless, ill-clothed, and starving—increasing the population of Greece by 20 percent. The refugees overwhelmed Salonika and more than tripled the size of Athens.

Concurrently, 3,000 years of Greek civilization in Asia Minor came to an end. Smyrna became a Turkish city and was renamed Izmir. Greece was again small, insecure, reeling with poverty, utterly humiliated, and seething with hate. The dictatorial regimes of the 1920s and 1930s in Athens provided no stabilizing outlet for such emotions. Then came the horrors of the Nazi invasion and occupation, which left 8 percent of the population dead, a million homeless, and the countryside destroyed. Greek resistance against the Nazis was widespread, but the guerrilla movement it spawned was as divided as it was heroic. All of these divisions boiled over in the 1946–1949 Greek Civil War, which saw even more casualties and destruction in Greece than had the war against the Nazis.

The United States backed the royalist Greek government in Athens, while the Soviet Union and its allies backed the Communist insurgents in the countryside. It was the first and last Cold War counterinsurgency that the American-backed side won outright. However, the civil war in Greece was about much more than capitalism versus Communism.

Capitalism had never really existed in Greece, which in the mid-twentieth century was a poor Oriental society of refugees in which a small number of rapacious landowners and shipowners exploited everyone else, and where a middle class barely existed. The American-backed Greek government was characterized by corruption and pointless intrigue. Its supporters had only a vague notion of democracy and a free press, and they numbered more than a few former Nazi sympathizers. They were Western only in the sense that they aspired to be Western. The Greek Communists, meanwhile, had a completely different historical orientation—seeing Russia and the Kremlin not only as beacons of an ideology they supported, but as a second motherland that, since the fall of Byzantium in 1453, had served as the protector of the Eastern Orthodox nations against the Turks. It may be no accident that the first proxy battle of the Cold War, the archetypal East-West struggle, occurred on Greek soil.

In the learning centers of the West, however, the most recent 2,000 years of Greek history were virtually ignored in favor of an idealized version of ancient Greece, a civilization that had already died before Jesus' birth. The West would not accept that Greece was more a child of Byzantium and Turkish despotism than of Periclean Athens. As a result, few Westerners could understand what began happening in Greece in the 1980s, an era when Greece's former Prime Minister and President, Constantine Karamanlis, described the country as a "vast lunatic asylum."

But before addressing that most recent period in Greek history, we must explore another romantic myth about Greece, built on top of the Western classicist one: a myth that took firm root in America, before being so tragically decapitated in the 1980s.

CHAPTER SIXTEEN

"Teach Me, Zorba. Teach Me to Dance!"

In this age of packaged truth, many lands, particularly those of the Mediterranean, have tourist myths associated with them: a calculated blend of images, involving history and landscape, that form a slick vision of romance under exotic circumstances. But unlike the other tourist myths, the Greek myth was born out of a movement in twentieth-century literature that was eventually crystallized by one of history's most memorable films.

The year 1935 is as good as any to mark the beginning of this process. That summer, twenty-three-year-old aspiring novelist and poet Lawrence Durrell, his wife, his mother, two brothers, a sister, and a dog named Roger traveled from England to the Greek island of Corfu to take up residence. The Anglo-Irish Durrells had lived in India, where Lawrence's late father had worked as an engineer. Upon the father's death, the family moved to England, where they never quite struck firm roots. This led to the somewhat eccentric and off-the-cuff decision to try Corfu.

"Our life on this promontory has become like some flawless Euclidean statement," writes Durrell in *Prospero's Cell*, a diary-cum-memoir of his four-year stay on Corfu. *Prospero's Cell* was a fresh kind of travel book: a travel-in-residence guide to the "landscape and manners" of an island, that openly combines real and imagined events in a magical setting—magical because Greece was somehow different from other places in the Mediterranean. What this difference was Durrell could describe, but he could not as yet define it, because he had never been this far east since leaving India at age ten.

Durrell wrote enthusiastically about Greece to his friend in Paris, Henry Miller, who paid Durrell a visit in 1939. A writer of unmatched exuberance and ego but little restraint, Miller, like Durrell, went through a kind of spiritual rebirth in Greece. *The Colossus of Maroussi* may be the least flawed of Miller's handful of great but flawed books. A work of uncanny power and inspiration, it reads like a nonstop series of aphorisms that have become clichés, only because Miller's phrases have been the grist for two generations of copy writers in the Greek tourist industry: "Greece had made me free and whole. . . . Greece is of the utmost importance to every man who is seeking to find himself. . . . It [Greece] stands, as it stood from birth, naked and fully revealed. . . . It breathes, it beckons, it answers."

But Miller also noticed "confusion, chaos . . . The dust, the heat, the poverty, the bareness," all of which he realized were necessary ingredients for this atmospheric magic act that he, too, could describe but not quite define. There was a missionary zeal to Durrell's and Miller's books about Greece that was absent in other travel books, and it was linked to an enjoyment of the physical senses that bordered on annihilation. Here is Durrell, entering the water in Corfu:

> I feel the play of the Ionian, rising and falling about an inch upon the back of my neck. It is like the heartbeat of the world. . . . It is no longer a region or an ambience where the conscious or the subconscious mind can play its incessant games with itself; but penetrating to a lower level still, the sun numbs the source of ideas itself. . . .

Durrell and Miller were selling Greece in almost the same way that the hippie movement would later sell California and India: as a place to escape from the world and get in touch with your inner self. But in the 1930s, as fascism spread across the map of Europe—and during the war that followed—the world had no use for such self-indulgence. Only after the dehumanizing horrors of World War II did the hedonistic message of these authors suddenly acquire an urgency. Due to the Greek Civil War, however, Greece remained a devastated country that was not ready for tourism.

In the mid-1950s, Durrell began writing a series of novels, to be known as The Alexandria Quartet. At the same time, a New York City filmmaker, Jules Dassin, went to live in Greece with his new wife, a Greek actress, Melina Mercouri. Dassin, in a conversation with me at his home in Athens in 1989, explained what happened next: "Melina's mother had just returned from the movies and was talking about this film she had seen. We got into some argument—I can't remember it exactly—that made me realize what I was: just some American telling everyone here in Greece how to live their lives. My original concept was a film about a busybody. But because Greece at the time, as an actual place, was practically unknown in America, the movie became something else."

Never on Sunday was a low-budget, ninety-four-minute, black-and-white film in Greek, with English subtitles. "We spent as much on a publicity party at Cannes in 1960 [where *Never on Sunday* won the Grand Prize] as on the film itself."

The movie begins in the port of Piraeus, where a group of boorish sailors accept a dare from a prostitute, Illia (played by Melina Mercouri), to join her in a swim in the harbor. At that moment, a cruise ship appears. Seeing the prostitute in the water, a Greek on board yells: "Where is the American, the intellectual, he should see this." A tourist wearing a baseball cap is brought on deck. His name is Homer, and he is played by Dassin himself. Eyeing the nude woman swimming in the sea surrounded by men, this amateur philosopher is overwhelmed with inspiration and jots in his diary: "There is the purity that was Greece!" As the camera moves in on the diary page, the rousing *bouzouki* music strikes up and the film's title flashes across the screen.

Rather than Periclean perfection, what Homer quickly finds is a sleazy world of seaside bars, where rude waiters serve thick, syrupy coffee and an aniseed-flavored spirit, ouzo; where men stub unfiltered cigarettes out on the floor and dance and smash plates to the sounds of *bouzouki* music (written especially for the film by the since-famous Greek composer Manos Hadjidakis). Homer, an expert on Greek classical drama, realizes he knows nothing about the strange country he finds himself in. He laments to Illia, the prostitute, whom against his better instincts he has fallen in love with: "I don't understand it, Greece was once the greatest country in the whole world." And she, sensuously beckoning and stretching her arms out on a bed, replies: "It still is."

What Homer found of course was not classical Greece, but something better, or at least more fun, and certainly much more unexpected. He found the Orient and the Balkans, with their harshest edges softened ever so slightly by the Mediterranean.

The success of *Never on Sunday* came during the same year, 1960, when Durrell published the last volume of the Alexandria Quartet, whose complex plot, sensuous prose, and overt sexual themes made it a bestseller.[1] Although the Quartet is ostensibly about the Egyptian Mediterranean port of Alexandria, it is also about Greece. The narrator lives in peaceful reflection on an unnamed Greek island in the Cyclades. The Alexandria that Durrell remembers is a Greek city, whose most memorable characters are Greek or Greek-influenced. A recurrent theme in the four books is humanity's need for a pagan counterpart (which Durrell associates with Greece) to the ethical rigors of Judeo-Christian morality.

The popularity of the Quartet chain-reacted with *Never on Sunday*. "There are probably no statistics, but someone told me that, in one year, tourism to Greece shot up eight hundred percent," Dassin told me. In the early 1960s, Miller's *The Colossus of Maroussi* and Durrell's *Prospero's Cell* were rediscovered and went into one reprint after another. The high point came in 1964, with the release of *Zorba the Greek*, Michael Cacoyannis's film of the Kazantzakis novel.

Zorba the Greek portrays Greece in the same stark, black-and-white realism as *Never on Sunday*, only more so. The film also

1. The books of the Quartet are *Justine, Balthazar, Mountolive,* and *Clea.*

begins in Piraeus, but in this case it is winter and there is a rainstorm. The hero, Zorba, played by Anthony Quinn, sings Klephtic tunes from Macedonia and confesses to raping and looting "because they were Turks or Bulgarians." Zorba's companion is a shy Englishman of Greek origin, played by Alan Bates, shocked by what he sees and hears after he and Zorba arrive on the island of Crete.

There, villagers loot a house before the occupant, an old Frenchwoman, has even finished dying. A widow is stoned and then has her throat slit outside an Orthodox church, for the sin of enticing a younger man. In the background, always, are the vindictive stares of peasants, and men unloading their bilious hatred of women in miserable coffee shops. In place of Hadjidakis's bright, explosive *bouzouki* tunes from *Never on Sunday, Zorba the Greek* introduced the world to another Greek composer, Mikis Theodorakis, who worked with a darker and more mysterious strain in Greek music. While Mercouri fluttered across the dance floor in a wildly exhibitionist *syrtaki* step, Quinn danced a slow-motion, meditative *zeimbekiko* to the drumroll of a Theodorakis melody. When Quinn wheeled his body around on one foot, ever so slowly, his eyes fixed toward the sky, it was like the earth turning on its axis.

After watching the peasants ransack the Frenchwoman's house, after watching the widow have her throat cut, for the first time in the life of Zorba's introverted and Westernized companion, a well of emotion breaks down his protective cerebral wall. "Teach me, Zorba," he begs, suddenly overtaken by a fit of comprehending madness. "Teach me to dance!"

What these books and movies said was essentially the same: there was a certain something about Greece that Spain, Italy, and other poor, sun-drenched lands lacked: something unique and inspiring precisely because it was so harsh and unforgiving; something beautiful because it was so ugly; something happy because it was so sad; something unique yet simultaneously familiar.

Greece was where you came to lose your inhibitions. The sea and the sun-scorched stone performed as your guru. Nothing more was needed. The islands—petrified gray forms lifting magnificently out of an inky-blue sea, and sleekly graced by the blindingly white walls of cubist villages—became a terrain of lust and passion and hallucination. The Greek tourist boom of the early 1960s was a precursor of the drug cult and the sexual revolution. Leonard Cohen was a little-known Canadian poet and songwriter when he first came to Greece and settled on the island of Hydra, where he composed many of the songs for his second album, *Songs from a Room,* including "Bird on a Wire," that helped make him an icon for introverted hippies.

The early and mid-1960s constituted the golden age of Myconos, after that island had been discovered by *Vogue* magazine and an "in" group of performing artists—Jean Seberg, Yul Brenner, and Yehudi Menuhin (a friend of Durrell's)—had acquired houses there. Elizabeth Herring, a columnist for *The Athenian* magazine in Athens, telescoped Mykonos's history for me: "When I first sailed into the island, in 1961, at the age of ten, I recall extreme poverty. There were skinny, naked kids, and you couldn't even buy pasteurized milk. By the late 1970s, the streets were filled with gold jewelry shops and on the beach I had to step over a couple making love."

The certain something that Greece had that other countries lacked—that was unique yet so familiar—was a faultlessly proportioned, atmospheric mix of East and West. The ululating quarter tones of *bouzouki* music, the raw material for Hadjidakis's theme song for *Never on Sunday,* are, in fact, siblings of Bulgarian and Serbian rhythms, and are close cousins of the Arab and Turkish music that, heard in its pure form, gives most Western listeners a headache. Yet run through a Mediterranean musical filter, these monotonous and orgasmic sounds of the Orient appeal perfectly to Western ears, especially when they are heard in the setting of a Cycladic island like Mykonos. The abstract grace of Cycladic island sculpture and architecture in the Third Millennium B.C. was the seminal force behind the artistic values that, 2,000 years later, created the Parthenon. Architecturally, what we label as "Western" first appeared in the Cyclades. This was principally why Western tourists felt so comfortable on the Greek islands while listening to that strange music whose roots they could never identify. The fact that this music was often very sad—because for the Greeks it is meant to evoke memories of the loss of Byzantium, Hagia Sofia, and Smyrna—made it no less beautiful.

The Greek tourist myth depended on this fragile yet subtle

recipe: of Greece being a summation of the Balkans, yet also being something apart; of Greece being only ninety minutes by plane from the tiresome and dangerous hatreds of the Middle East, yet also being millions of miles away.

The dictatorship of the Greek colonels, who came to power in 1967, let some of the helium out of the Greek tourist balloon, but only some. The coup d'état of April 21 in Athens was not completely unexpected. The conservative leader Karamanlis remarked afterwards: "One can say that democracy in Greece was murdered by a free regime. The colonels simply inflicted a mercy killing." After all, Greece had had so many coups and constitutional crises since achieving independence from the Ottoman Turks in 1829 that they were clearly beyond counting.

The three years of parliamentary democracy preceding the coup had been a carnival of vendetta and irresponsibility. The center-left Prime Minister, George Papandreou, had come to power in 1964 with a sweeping majority, intent on punishing the conservative establishment led by Karamanlis. Papandreou replaced Karamanlis's tight fiscal strategy with increased social services and subsidies. By themselves, these measures were responsible, given the abysmal lack of a social safety net. But Papandreou chose an awkward time for his largess: not long after the last of the $10 billion in American economic aid from the Truman Doctrine had run out. Moreover, Papandreou increased the restrictions on foreign investment. As inflation surged, Papandreou criticized NATO, put his armed forces on alert against Turkey, and further stirred the waters of the already bubbling Cyprus dispute, calling for *enosis* ("union") between Greece and that formerly British-administered island in the Eastern Mediterranean. Cyprus had a Greek majority but a sizable Turkish minority. When the Turks launched a military action against the Greek Cypriots in the summer of 1964, Papandreou's forces did nothing, causing the Greek Cypriot leader, Archbishop Makarios, to become even more cynical about the value of Papandreou's support. Subsequently, Makarios signed a treaty with the Soviet Union for an arms supply, dumped the idea of *enosis,* and talked instead of "complete independence" for the island.

Papandreou clearly had enough on his hands without the activities of his forty-five-year-old son, Andreas, a deputy cabinet minister. Born in 1919 on the island of Chios, near the Turkish coast, where his father was then the prefect, Andreas had the coldest of relationships with his well-known father. In 1939, Andreas left Greece for the United States to continue his education. By 1944, he had obtained a doctorate in economics from Harvard and had become a United States citizen. He also married twice, the second time to a Minnesota woman, Margaret Chant, with whom he would have four children. The younger Papandreou remained in America until 1959—escaping the whole of World War II and the civil war in Greece—instead serving in the U.S. Navy and later teaching at several American universities, including the University of California at Berkeley, where he eventually became chairman of the economics department.

Andreas, in the way of so many youthful immigrants, completely reinvented himself in America. After divorcing his first wife, a Greek-American psychiatrist, he had few (if any) Greek friends; and for years he evinced no interest in the Greek-American community. Had it not been for the confluence of three events, he might never have returned to Greece at all.

Just as his academic career in California reached its peak, an interesting offer came from the conservative leader, Karamanlis, for Andreas to set up an American-style economics research center in Athens. Meanwhile, Andreas saw that his father's political fortunes were suddenly rising, making George Papandreou a likely prospect to succeed Karamanlis as the prime minister. In Greece's nepotic political culture, this unleashed opportunities for the eldest son. Andreas read the stars: he made up with his father and, securing Fulbright and Guggenheim Foundation grants, took his American wife and their children to live in Greece.

Remaking himself as an American while in his twenties was not strange: it was something that many immigrants have done. But remaking himself into a Greek while in his forties, as Andreas now undertook to do, was not natural and must have exacted a psychological price.

In 1964, Andreas formally gave up his American citizenship in order to be elected to the Greek parliament. As a deputy minister in charge of economics in his father's newly elected government, Andreas soon began speaking on a wide range of subjects.

In an October 1964 interview with the Paris daily, *Le Monde,* Andreas called Greece a "satellite" of NATO, while calling the Soviet Union's support of the Greek Cypriots "a positive contribution to the maintenance of world peace"—even as Moscow was in the midst of switching sides on the Cyprus issue; from being pro-Greek to being pro-Turkish. These remarks further undermined the stability of his father's government and forced Andreas to resign his cabinet post.

Following twenty productive and apparently happy years in America, Andreas's anti-Americanism appeared difficult to explain. Conspiracy-mongers on the Greek right decided it could not be explained: the younger Papandreou was obviously a "CIA agent" who had been sent back to his Greek homeland to sow political instability. Another theory held that, as the pampered son of a famous Greek politician, Andreas resented having to work his way up the ladder in America's egalitarian society. Thus, although he ranted against America's foreign policy, deep down inside, he could not abide America's classless nature. American liberals, meanwhile, along with the Greek left, saw Andreas's remarks as a natural reaction to the heavy-handed American domination of Greek affairs that had followed the Greek Civil War. This would explain Andreas's criticism of U.S. policy toward Greece, but not the emotional frenzy that went with it. Yet another theory was that Andreas's United States had always been the make-believe world of university campuses, where during the 1940s and 1950s certain American intellectuals retained a romantic fascination with Stalin and Communism. In other words, according to this view Andreas had not remade himself into a Greek at all. Instead, he was behaving the way any left-wing American intellectual would: slaying his own government for failing to live up to its professed principles abroad. This view seemed credible through the 1970s, when Andreas suddenly began acting in a manner far removed from that of any American left-wing intellectual.

In July 1965, King Constantine dismissed George Papandreou as Prime Minister—a move that Papandreou's supporters saw as a subversion of the Greek Constitution. From there it was all downhill. In Athens, the politicians, the journalists, the royal family, and the army generals kept scheming and accusing each other, until the colonels—a group of grudge-bearing bumpkins from remote villages, led by one George Papadopoulos—toppled the lot of them.

In the West, people knew only that a group of uncouth middle-level officers had, without reason or explanation, snuffed out democracy in the land of its birth—the land, moreover, of *Never on Sunday* and *Zorba the Greek*.[2]

The colonels were Romios in the worst sense. They were not educated or well-spoken. Besides advocating a return to the most puritanical teachings of the Orthodox Church, they had no vision. They knew nothing about finance or economy, except how to take and reward bribes. And they were physically cruel in a typical Balkan way. The demon of torture returned to the police stations. Prison camps rose on barren islands.

The colonels arrested Andreas, holding him in prison until American intervention won his release. Andreas then went into exile in the West, along with other members of the Athenian political and cultural establishment, including the conservative former prime minister Karamanlis; the actress Mercouri; and the composer Theodorakis. Almost all of these celebrities, on account of their education and high birth—Mercouri, for instance, was the daughter of a former mayor of Athens—epitomized the most sophisticated Hellene aspect of the Greek personality, and in their campaign against the dictatorship, they succeeded in portraying the colonels as un-Greek usurpers.

So in the West, while the colonels were hated, the Greeks were still loved, even more so because they were oppressed. Greece, in addition to being a myth, became a cause, and this heightened its appeal.

In spite of pleas from Mercouri and her friends to boycott Greece, tourists kept coming. Only the most politically astute of them noticed and were troubled by the sullen mutterings common to populations living in repressive states. After all, there was no instability, no terrorism, not even the breathless fear so palpable under more extreme dictatorships in the Middle East. The Greek tourist myth wobbled a bit, but it held.

---

2. The West's bad image of the Greek colonels, incidentally, also came from a film, Z, by Costa-Gavras.

Even after 1974, when the colonels abdicated and a whiff of open anti-Americanism followed that included a bombing at the American Express office in Athens, Greece's image in the West was unaffected. These were isolated incidents, and Karamanlis's new conservative government kept a lid on what was at the time still building. Only in the 1980s would the world begin to find out just how close to the Balkans and to the Middle East Greece really was.

▓▓ CHAPTER SEVENTEEN

The Secret History

"The misdeeds of Justinian were so many that eternity itself would not suffice for the telling of them. It will be enough for me to pick out from the long list and set down a few examples by which his whole character will be made crystal clear to men yet unborn," writes Procopius in *The Secret History,* an uncensored report of the rule of Justinian and his ex-prostitute wife, Theodora, in sixth-century Constantinople.

"Either they must rule over us like gods, or they refuse to govern at all," writes Michael Psellus in the *Chronographia,* a first-hand account of fourteen Byzantine emperors in the tenth and eleventh centuries, considered the outstanding memoir of the Middle Ages.

Complex yet forgettable sagas of greed, lust, personal cruelty, and ambition in medieval Byzantium, these stories are the only useful historical mirror for understanding Greek politics in the

1980s. As in that earlier epoch of decline, complexity merged with superficiality, lending an absurd pointlessness to the proceedings.

In the seven years I lived in Greece, few things irked me more than to see foreign correspondents explain the local political turmoil with such phrases as "After all, the Greeks invented theater" and "Not only is *democracy* a Greek word, but so is *anarchy*." Then there were the cute references to "Greek tragedy" and "Greek comedy." I, too, in a lazy period, once fell back on ancient Greek "theater" and "masks" to explain modern Greek politics. Editors and readers in America and England had studied Greek drama at school and could therefore relate to the reference. But what did any of them know of Byzantium or of medieval Greek writers like Psellus and Procopius? The media reports, rather than explaining modern Greece, merely illuminated the West's ignorance of the longest and most important stretches of Greek history.

"More than anything, our politics show how Oriental and Byzantine we are," said Panayote Dimitras, one of Athens's leading pollsters. We were talking in 1990, on my arrival in Greece from Bulgaria; it was a time when Greece was beginning to reel from the chaos of the 1980s. "In our politics, I would say we are completely Oriental. We look at the West like Middle Easterners. Like the Arabs, we [as Orthodox Christians] were also victims of the Crusaders. . . . Greeks are married to the East. The West is our mistress only. Like any mistress, the West excites and fascinates us, but our relationship with it is episodic and superficial."

In addition to the aspects of Levantine suspicion and intrigue, something else about Greek political life was wonderfully captured in the medieval tales of Psellus and Procopius: politics in Greece is erotic. It is probably no accident that so many of the Greek words dealing with political power are feminine: *kyvernisi* ("government"), *eklogi* ("election"), *ideologia* ("ideology"), *poreia* ("protest march"), *eksoussia* ("authority"), *tromokratia* ("terrorism").

Significantly, the gutter press in Greece, unlike its counterpart in America, is not concerned with the personal lives of celebrity entertainers, or even with the personal lives of politicians. Greeks are not puritanical, and nothing—almost nothing, that is—shocks them. The Greek gutter press writes about politics, pure and simple. Politics in Greece is not the domain of think tanks and serious books and newspapers. It is too much rude fun for that: take the career of Andreas Papandreou.

My sojourn in Athens from 1982 through 1989 corresponded closely with the rule of Andreas Papandreou as Prime Minister. Because Greece is a small, relatively poor country bordered by historical enemies, its politics is much more intense than the politics of Western countries. And because Greek politics during Andreas's rule was overtly anti-American, my own personal experience of Greece was, to a large degree, shaped by Andreas. The legacy of his rule explains Greece in the 1990s, just as the Communist legacy helps explain the other Balkan countries. Chronicling the Papandreou era is, in my view, the one essential exercise for grasping today's Greece.

After America intervened with junta leader George Papadopoulos to spring Andreas from jail ("You tell Papa-what's-his-name to release the other Papa-what's-his-name," President Lyndon Johnson reportedly advised the Greek Ambassador), Andreas went into exile in Sweden and Canada, where he organized what was later to become the Pan-Hellenic Socialist Movement, whose Greek acronym was PASOK. From those six years of exile, 1968–1974, one image and one fact were to retain their relevance into the 1990s: in several of the photographs, Andreas had on a black leather jacket; and while married with four children, he fathered an illegitimate daughter with a Swedish woman.

In 1978, Aristide Caratzas, the Greek-American publisher, went to PASOK's Athens headquarters to talk to Andreas. Caratzas will never forget the experience: "The entrance was filled with tough-looking young men wearing black leather jackets with bulges. When I told them I was there to see Mr. Papandreou, they responded aggressively: 'So, you have an appointment with the *archegos* [leader]?' They made it clear that he was to be called 'the leader,' as though it were an insult to say his name. It made me think of what Mussolini's headquarters must have been like prior to the 1922 fascist coup in Italy."

PASOK, from its inception, was never a *komma*, a "party," like the other political groupings in post-junta Greece. As its name specifically advertised, it was a *kinesis*, a "movement": the Pan-Hellenic Socialist Movement. In other words, it was supposed to be revolutionary and dynamic. Stated Papandreou in 1977: "Are

we Marxists, yes or no? . . . we must say yes. And that is why we
are in complete opposition to optimistic liberal thought."

PASOK was certainly undemocratic, with no constitution or
bylaws. For years, there was not even the pretense of elections for
party leader. It was not necessary. PASOK *was* Papandreou—a
name that in post-junta Greece meant Andreas and not his father,
George, who had died in 1968 at the age of eighty. The worship
of political chieftains, something bordering on a personality cult,
had been common to twentieth-century Greece. George Papandreou once headed a political party called the "George Papandreou party." Greeks of the center and the left migrated toward
PASOK because they saw it as the natural inheritor of George
Papandreou's political legacy. But Andreas Papandreou was not
George Papandreou, nor was PASOK the George Papandreou
party.

George Papandreou was more a man of the center than of the
left. Foolishness, more than ideology or wounded pride, motivated
his actions in the mid-1960s. His party was himself because of the
paternalistic, coffeehouse nature of Greek politics at the time.
Groups naturally coalesced around strong personalities, without
much attention to detail or organization. George Papandreou's
formative years were spent entirely in Greece. His impulses, like
those of his conservative rival, Constantine Karamanlis, were normal and uncomplicated. But Andreas Papandreou, who spent
thirty months in the U. S. Navy but never wore a Greek uniform,
was very complicated. In his study, prominently displayed, were
photographs of Fidel Castro and Marshal Tito. Papandreou
(henceforth used to mean Andreas) saw nonaligned Communist
Yugoslavia as the ideal model for Greece.

PASOK forged early links with the Syrian Baath party "based
on our common ideological-political positions," explained Papandreou in 1975. In February 1977, eight months after the hijacking
of an Air France planeload of Israelis from Tel Aviv to Entebbe,
Uganda, Papandreou praised Ugandan leader Idi Amin: "He is
a fighter of the metropolitan centers of the West and he himself
is their target. This by itself places him on the global chessboard
in the area of the anti-imperialist forces."[1] Later in 1977, Papandreou traveled to Muammar Qaddafi's Libya, whose regime Pa-

1. *Ta Nea* ("The News"), February 28, 1977. Interview with Papandreou.

pandreou declared was "not a military dictatorship. The contrary is true. It is governed on the model of the *demos* of the ancient Athenians." Consistent reports, in both the Greek and foreign press, alleged that Qaddafi helped fund PASOK's successful 1981 campaign, in which Papandreou was elected Prime Minister. In 1984, publicly addressing Papandreou in Athens, Qaddafi's second-in-command, Major Abdel Salam Jalloud, said, "Brother Papandreou, we have examined you carefully, we have tested you and we trust you. We are determined to do everything we can to strengthen your position because it is in our interests that you remain in power."

PASOK's inner workings demonstrated a totalitarian style that was unprecedented in Greece, outside the Communist guerrilla movement. After a few years in Greece, I realized that PASOK's supporters included three basic types of persons.

The first group—the urbane and culturally sophisticated left, the "beautiful people," so to speak—would have been irrelevant, were it not for the fame of Melina Mercouri. Made the Minister of Culture and Science when Papandreou was elected Prime Minister in October 1981, Mercouri was the only one of Papandreou's ministers to be reappointed after each of his fifteen cabinet reshuffles during eight years in power. Unquestionably loyal to Papandreou, she was not in his inner circle and was not tainted by the later scandals and prison sentences that destroyed his government. Her status as a Greek cultural symbol, on account of *Never on Sunday,* provided Papandreou with a veil of legitimacy, particularly abroad. In Greece, she was popular among Communists and PASOK supporters but despised by the 40 percent or so of the Greek population that voted with the right. The insult I got tired of hearing about her was: "Melina did not have to act in *Never on Sunday*; she really behaves like that. What is it you foreigners see in her?"

The second group were the young intellectuals, educated abroad, who returned to Greece after the fall of the junta. Some were highly qualified technocrats, who, given the stark choice between an old-fashioned right and a revolutionary left, preferred the latter because the right had been discredited by the junta. Costas Simitis, PASOK's Minister of National Economy, later sacked and publicly humiliated by Papandreou, and Andonis Tritsis, PASOK's first Minister of the Environment, also sacked, fell into this category. Tritsis's sin was to apply environmental protection laws equally to businesspeople of both the right and the left.

Many of the young intellectuals, however, were not technocrats. From humble backgrounds, they went to America or some other Western country, where they received a smattering of a liberal arts education—enough to give them an air of sophistication and false hubris when they returned home. V. S. Naipaul had a phrase for such half-formed people. Referring to the band of American-educated Marxist idealists who ruled the Caribbean island of Grenada (before they had a falling out and began killing each other), Naipaul called them "little men" whose heads were stuffed with "big" vague ideas that they had but a faulty notion of how to apply. PASOK had many such "little men," oppressed by hatreds and too many chips on their shoulders. They filled the ranks of the Green Guards: ideological enforcers dispatched by Papandreou to Greek embassies abroad, to watch over career diplomats. In 1988, when a Howard University scholar, Nikolaos Stavrou, published a book critical of Papandreou, a Green Guardist at the Greek embassy in Washington was quoted thus in the *New York Times*: "Mr. Stavrou—he cannot write books, he can only teach niggers at a most mediocre university."[2]

But the third group—and the most important people in PASOK—I noticed, had no experience abroad and rarely spoke a language other than Greek. They were people from the villages or from working-class neighborhoods in the city, who fingered worry beads, used language suffused with curse words like *malaka* ("asshole"), and in other circumstances might as easily have worked with the junta as against it. This third group worshipped Papandreou. Unlike the other foreign-educated intellectuals in PASOK, Papandreou was at home in their smoke-filled coffeehouses and was devious to the core. Papandreou had a virile and demagogic speaking style, which the urban poor and the inhabitants of the Greek countryside responded to. His was a political style reminiscent of Argentina's Juan Peron, or Israel's Menachem

2. "Book on Greek Leader Stirs Diplomatic Dispute," by Edwin McDowell, *New York Times*, July 1, 1988.

Begin: another Western-educated, dynamic orator whose base of support was situated among the poorest and most Oriental part of the population, which he had prodded into ascendancy over the European half.

Thus the Romiots, not the Hellenes, surrounded Papandreou, formed his inner circle, and ran PASOK for him. Their loyalty to him was tribal and not affected by issues. They were men such as Agamemnon Koutsogiorgas—the second most powerful man in Greece throughout the 1980s—who, in 1990, found himself behind bars, in the same Piraeus prison as the junta leader, Papadopoulos.

Papandreou kept one of these men permanently on staff in the Foreign Ministry. This particular fellow actually straddled the border between tough axman and would-be intellectual. Unlike the others, he spoke English and once gave a long speech in support of the "Third World Information Order," in which he justified the censorship imposed by various African governments on grounds that imperialism was also a form of censorship. In his office in 1987, I asked him whether Greece was moving too close politically to Africa and the Third World. He leaned over his desk and said to me, in a knowing manner: "Greece is less close to Africa than America. Do you ever see a Greek holding hands with a nigger in the street like Americans do? Don't worry, we know how to deal with Africa and the Third World . . . we tell those Pakistanis that if they recognize Turkish Cyprus, we'll throw their damn Pakistani seamen working on Greek ships into the sea."[3]

Papandreou's blood-brother relationship with such men, of whom this particular fellow was among the most sophisticated, has always fascinated me. It lies at the core of Papandreou's undeniable appeal to Greek women—despite a paunch and a bald, gray fringed head—and by extension, of his charisma.

Here was a man who had spent the years from 1940 to 1959 on American university campuses. No one seemed more at home in the rarified world of Berkeley dinner parties, year after year, than Andy Papandreou, with his pipe, sport jacket, and turtleneck sweater. Yet in another incarnation, he was wearing a leather jacket and developing deep, lifelong friendships with a Balkan blue-collar element, bordering at times on the criminal, whose

---

3. Pakistan has traditionally been among the most pro-Turkish of all Muslin countries.

political fortunes he took total command of. How many university professors, even those who like to wear hiking boots and consider themselves at ease with the common folk, could do that? In Greece, it was the foreign-educated types in PASOK—those like Papandreou himself—that Papandreou kept at a certain distance.

Papandreou demanded adulation, and in a sense he earned it, through a rare ability to move through, to dominate, and to manipulate starkly different social worlds.

One of the three times I met Papandreou was during the summer of 1986 at the luxurious Astir Palace Hotel, in the seaside Athenian suburb of Vouliagmeni. Papandreou, in a bathing suit and wearing a towel around his neck, entered the sun-drenched pool area flanked by one of his sons, also named Andreas, and two bodyguards wearing tight-fitting black bell-bottom trousers and white shirts open to the navel. One bodyguard, I recall, had an assault rifle dangling from his shoulder which he laid down on a deck chair. My two-year-old son crossed Papandreou's path. Papandreou, good-naturedly, walked around him and, I think, patted him once on the head. I went up and introduced myself to Papandreou. "Who do you write for?" he asked. I mentioned *The Atlantic*. "Ah," he said, nodding, "fine old Boston magazine. I used to read it at Harvard." His accent and the wide-open look in his eyes were still—twenty-seven years after leaving U.S. shores—almost American. Then Papandreou shot a glance at one of the bodyguards, lifting his bushy gray eyebrows in Levantine shorthand, and the guard quickly darted off on some errand. Because of what was going on in Greece at the time, which I must now relate, the experience of greeting Papandreou was akin to shaking hands with an underworld celebrity at the ballpark.

After Papandreou was elected Prime Minister in 1981, he won praise for recognizing the Communist resistance movement against the Nazis; for allowing Communist veterans of the Greek Civil War—in exile for decades in the Eastern Bloc—to return home; for reforming the divorce laws to be more favorable to women; and for legalizing civil marriages. (I was married in Greece in a civil ceremony: *Thank you, Andreas.*) These measures were expected and overdue. But in the critical area of Greek democracy, unsettling things began happening.

In 1982, Papandreou virtually stopped attending sessions of

parliament. He fired several dissenting cabinet ministers, and added eighty advisers to his personal staff. This reduced his dependence both on the government and on the grass roots of PASOK. He could now rule through his inner circle, with an iron fist.

In the years preceding his election, Papandreou had purged hundreds of PASOK members from the movement on grounds of "deviationism." Anyone who questioned his judgment on anything was thrown out. When Papandreou was first elected, many PASOK members thought that PASOK would evolve into a democratically run party. That did not happen. When Aristides Bouloukos, a PASOK parliamentary deputy, disagreed with Papandreou on an electoral reform bill, Bouloukos was expelled from PASOK. When Stathis Panagoulis, the Undersecretary of Interior, criticized Papandreou for not living up to some of his election promises, he too was formally expelled from the movement. Papandreou then publicly accused Panagoulis of "treason" and "conspiracy." State-run television and radio repeatedly broadcast Papandreou's charges, while ignoring Panagoulis's replies.

Papandreou referred to criticism of some of his individual policies by PASOK members as "apostasy"—a word that in its original Greek form, *apostassia,* carries a strong theological undertone from the days of Byzantium, when emperors, ruling by Divine Right, were judged "infallible," thus making their critics "heretics" or "apostates."

The expulsions continued throughout the years of Papandreou's rule. The pattern rarely altered. After the member was purged by a PASOK disciplinary council, the PASOK-controlled media launched a campaign of character assassination against him. The method was also used to settle personal vendettas and to ease the state's plundering of private companies. At the end of 1982, for instance, a rumor campaign was orchestrated against the head of a local state-supported news agency, accusing the man of being a transvestite. He was forced to resign his post and leave Greece temporarily.[4] In 1983, the official media accused George Tsatsos, the managing director of Heracles General Cement Company, one of Greece's most successful exporters, of "fraud" and "cur-

4. Sometime later he was reinstated in his old job.

rency violations." Using the media reports as a pretext, the state then took over Heracles Cement. Over the next three years, the company lost $$52 million, compared with profits of $25 million for the three years preceding the takeover. The courts soon dismissed all charges against Tsatsos: there had never been any evidence to substantiate them.

Greek state television and radio, by 1982, had become carbon copies of the party-controlled media in the Communist countries to the north. Greek television and radio had never been free, but under the conservative leader Karamanlis, the practical control amounted to keeping the left-wing opposition off the air; the broadcasts lacked any aggressive, ideological tone. Papandreou, moreover, campaigned for *allaghi* ("change"), including a pledge to liberalize the media. Under him, however, the evening television news became a parade of Papandreou speeches and ribbon-cutting appearances. Nothing was neutral. Every group mentioned—Palestinian guerrillas, Nicaraguan *contras*—were either "freedom fighters" or "fascists," whatever the PASOK world view demanded. When an American naval officer was assassinated by terrorists in Athens, PASOK newspapers labeled the murder "a CIA conspiracy," explaining that the Central Intelligence Agency had its own man murdered "in a deliberately timed effort to create anti-Greek sentiments in the United States."[5] Papandreou told his audiences at televised rallies that America was "the metropolis of imperialism." The American military bases in Greece were, this veteran of the U.S. Navy maintained, "the bases of death." Papandreou was then traveling to the Eastern Bloc more often than any other NATO leader. During a visit to Poland, still under martial law, Papandreou derided Solidarity as "negative, dangerously negative." Papandreou still lived with his American wife and four children, all of whom were U.S. citizens.

Writing of Romanus III, the Emperor of Byzantium from 1028 to 1034, Psellus said, "this particular emperor aspired to a reputation for piety . . . this led to extravagance in discussions about problems of divinity." For Papandreou, piety implied "peace." In Papandreou's name, Culture Minister Mercouri organized

---

5. Captain George Tsantes, Jr., was killed on November 15, 1983.

"human peace chains" around the Acropolis, even as Greek state companies were selling arms to both sides in the Iran-Iraq war, and to the two warring African states of Rwanda and Burundi. One or another peace symposium always seemed to be taking place in Athens, I remember. Papandreou conferred back and forth with the Romanian President, Nicolae Ceausescu, on a joint peace plan for Europe.

Like the Eastern Bloc leaders, Papandreou refused almost every interview request from Western media. He would not even make the yearly appearance at the Athens Foreign Press Association, where, in an orchestrated setting, he could have selected in advance which questions to answer. Journalists like me could fly to Turkey anytime and interview its Prime Minister, Turgut Ozal. But Papandreou would never see us, even though we lived in Greece. Among the handful of interviews he granted in eight years was one with former CBS "60 Minutes" correspondent Diane Sawyer, who asked him if he felt any gratitude toward America for keeping Greece out of the Eastern Bloc in the 1940s. Papandreou replied:

"I'm grateful to no one about anything."

Like the leather jacket and the affair with the Swedish woman, that statement was a portent of things to come.

When Papandreou came to office, he disbanded a police unit investigating the "November 17" terrorist group. November 17 was to remain through the early 1990s the most enigmatic and impossible-to-penetrate terror squad in Europe or the Middle East.

On November 17, 1973, the junta dispatched tanks to massacre student protesters at the Athens Polytechnic University, a crime that in Greek left-wing mythology came to be blamed on the Americans. On Christmas Eve of 1975, Richard Welch, later identified as the CIA station chief in Greece, was assassinated. November 17 claimed credit, explicitly stating that it aimed to punish the Americans for their imperialistic attitude toward Greece. Welch's murder set the pattern for others. Two men on a motorcycle would pull up alongside the victim's car during the morning or evening rush hour. The man riding on the back of the motorcycle would fire at the victim through the vehicle's window; then the motorcycle would speed off between the lines of crawling cars. In a city of constant traffic jams and daredevil motorcycle drivers, it was a method perfectly suited to the environment. And the pre-attack intelligence—the identification of Welch's role at the U.S. Embassy, his car, and his route to work—was flawless. The next big November 17 attack was the November 1983 murder of the U.S. naval officer, timed to coincide with the tenth anniversary of the Athens Polytechnic uprising.

Four months later, in March 1984, a gunman identified as an "Arab" murdered a British Embassy officer, Kenneth Whitty, and his Greek assistant on a busy Athens street in broad daylight. In May, a self-declared Libyan "suicide squad," dedicated to "chase traitors and stray dogs wherever they are and to liquidate them physically," marched through downtown Athens with a Greek police escort. A string of assassinations of anti-Qaddafi Libyan dissidents followed, occasionally written off by Greek police as a "settlement of personal differences." Papandreou permitted the number of "diplomats" accredited to the Libyan People's Bureau in Athens to rise to fifty. By this time, the Syrians had begun regularly carrying out assassinations of PLO members on Greek soil. And the Abu Nidal terrorist group had set up the Al Noor import-export company on Solonos Street in the Greek capital, as a front for organizing operations and moving weapons through-out the Mediterranean.[6]

None of these incidents led to any arrests. When in 1983 American and British intelligence agents identified an Arab, living in a working-class Athens suburb, as the man responsible for smuggling liquid explosives into Israel on Olympic Airways, the American agent involved in the investigation was expelled from Greece, while the man occused of terrorism was not even arrested.[7] Papandreou said that "acts of national liberation" could not be considered terrorism. Both the Reagan Administration and the International Air Transport Association (IATA) spent a year of quiet diplomacy trying to get the Greek Prime Minister to toughen security at Athens Airport. Papandreou responded by pressuring

6. U.S. Ambassador to Greece Robert Keeley delivered a confidential protest to the Greek Foreign Ministry over the Abu Nidal presence.
7. Fuad Hussein Shara, a Jordanian passport holder, was later required to leave Greece and go to a country "of his choice."

the airlines to abolish their own second line of electronic screening at the airport.

The Greek tourist myth burst all at once: in June 1985, when two Shiite terrorists hijacked a TWA jetliner from Athens Airport to Beirut. The men had spent the entire previous night in the transit lounge, presumably armed with their pistols and grenades. The day after the hijacking, I flew into Athens from Sudan, where I had been covering the African famine. There was still no airport surveillance. Not one customs official was present as passengers collected their baggage and walked out into the street. A few days after that, the Reagan Administration issued a "travel advisory" warning Americans to avoid Greece. Although the PASOK media cried "provocation," within hours of Reagan's announcement, the airport was full of security police for the first time since Papandreou had taken office.

Now, however, it was too late. Tourist cancellations reached into the tens of thousands. Greece lost hundreds of millions of dollars. Between 1985 and 1986, the number of American visitors to Greece plummeted by 80 percent. The era that had begun a quarter-century earlier with *Never on Sunday* appeared to have come to an end.

The situation then got further out of control. Four months after the TWA hijacking, Arab gunmen hijacked an Egypt Air jet from Athens Airport and diverted it to Malta: sixty people died when Egyptian commandos stormed the plane. In 1986, at least twenty bombings occurred in Athens, four claimed by November 17, which had begun assassinating not just Americans, but Greek politicians and business figures. Cars belonging to American military personnel and offices associated with developing Greek private enterprise were among the targets. November 17 was now supplemented by other Greek terrorist groups that went by such names as "Wild Geese of the City," "Anarchist Group of Iconoclasts-Nihilists," and "Anti-Power Revolutionary Struggle," the last taking responsibility for an explosion at a Greek army base in 1987.

On June 28, 1988, a car bomb detonated outside his home killed the U.S. Defense Attaché, William Nordeen. Thirteen days later, Arab terrorists killed nine tourists and wounded eighty others in an attack on the Greek ferry boat *City of Poros*. Papandreou's spokesman, Sotiris Kostopoulos, charged that the *City of Poros* attack was part of an American plot to pressure Greece into signing a "soft" agreement for the continued leasing of military bases.

The same year, the Greek government released a jailed terrorist, Ozama Al Zomar. Zomar was suspected by Italian police in the 1982 machine gun and grenade attack on a Rome synagogue that killed a two-year-old boy and wounded thirty-seven others. Papandreou's Justice Minister, Vassilis Rotis, defended Zomar's release, explaining that the synagogue attack "falls within his struggle to regain the independence of his homeland and consequently suggests action for freedom."

Western observers by now detected a definite "synergy" between hard-left elements within PASOK and the terrorist groups. Because Papandreou was a figure of such endless fascination, mere political or ideological motives were hardly considered by the Greeks in attempting to explain his behavior. They talked about Papandreou only in the most subjective psychological terms.

"Andreas is like Oedipus," Papapoulitis, the conservative politician, explained to me at the luncheon table in Piraeus. "As a boy he was very close to his mother. His revolt against his father continued well into manhood. Revolt against the father often means a general revolt against authority. In my opinion, Andreas was emotionally attracted to radical liberation struggles because of the anarchy they unleashed."

September 13, 1987, was the first anniversary of an earthquake in the southern Greek town of Kalamata that left twenty people dead and over 300 injured. Papandreou, pleading a heavy workload, said he had no time to attend the memorial ceremonies. The sixty-eight-year-old Prime Minister was, it turned out, embarked on a three-day cruise with an Olympic airline hostess, Dimitra Liani. Liani was an attractive brunette, less than half Papandreou's age, who was married at the time to a senior official in Greece's "Maoist Revolutionary Communist Party."

In continental Europe, and in Greece especially, the fact that a political leader has a young mistress is generally a matter of little significance. But Papandreou had committed two unpardonable sins. He had been observed bathing and dancing with Liani on, what for the Greek nation, was a day of mourning. And by appearing regularly with Liani in public, he was disgracing his wife and family. Papandreou provided Liani with her own television talk show. He publicly berated Margaret, his wife of thirty-seven years and the mother of four of his children, saying "she had never even cooked me an egg." He chose the day of their wedding anniversary to announce his intention to marry Liani, who was herself in the process of getting a divorce. When Papandreou and his new fiancée returned from England, where Papandreou had been recovering from triple-bypass heart surgery, PASOK staged a massive "spontaneous outburst of affection" from "the simple people." Greek state television showed flowers thrown by the PASOK rent-a-crowd, crushed beneath the wheels of the Prime Minister's car.

Thereafter, some PASOK newspapers began referring to Liani as "the official mistress." A cult of personality began forming around her, as this former stewardess formerly married to a Maoist began to emerge as the Prime Minister's intellectual companion. There were suggestions that Liani, following in the tradition of Eva Peron, could emerge as PASOK's next leader.

But besides in Argentina, something like this had happened before, in eleventh-century Constantinople. The Byzantine Emperor Constantine IX had forced his wife, Zoe, and the Senate to officially ratify the power of his mistress, Sclerena. Psellus writes that "despite their embarrassment, the senators still praised the agreement as if it were a document sent down from heaven." Psellus might have been writing about PASOK. For example, Papandreou's top aide, Dimitris Maroudas, declared that any criticism of the Prime Minister's extramarital affair was "unholy" and "profane." Maroudas told the nation that Papandreou's actions demonstrated "*levantia* [manliness]," something about which the Greek people should be proud. Cynical Greeks called Maroudas "Minister to the Bedchamber."

After the Liani affair came the "Koskotas scandal" in the late summer of 1988. George Koskotas was a multimillionaire banker who claimed to have helped Papandreou siphon more than $200 million from state-owned corporations into a PASOK slush fund. The money was reportedly used to buy Greek newspapers that were critical of Papandreou; to tie up world rights to an offensive book manuscript about Papandreou that had been written by his first wife, a Greek-American psychiatrist, Christina Rasia; to provide Papandreou with money for a divorce settlement with his second wife, Margaret; and to make cash payments to various government officials. The scandal was related to others. For instance, allegations were made that the Greek intelligence service was tapping the phones of Papandreou's political enemies, and that top government officials had received hundreds of millions of dollars in illegal commissions, paid into Swiss bank accounts, for Greece's purchase of forty French Mirage jets and American F-16s. Several top government officials were convicted of criminal charges, and Papandreou was indicted for complicity. In a trial marked by pro-Papandreou demonstrations (organized by PASOK) and Papandreou's own refusal to testify in court, the Prime Minister was found not guilty. Papandreou called the charges against him a plot by "dark forces of reaction" and "foreign circles" to "destabilize" Greece.

A story started to circulate in Athens—apocryphal, I strongly suspected, but nevertheless full of symbolism. A Greek general supposedly came to see the Prime Minister, carrying a shopping bag full of $10,000 worth of Greek drachmas. The general said that the money was his way of showing devotion to the *archegos* ("leader"). Papandreou kept the general standing, while ordering him to leave the shopping bag at the foot of his desk. Afterward, Papandreou fired the general. It was the way of the Oriental potentate: *How dare this man insult me by offering me a part of what is already mine by right.*

"Greece's only successful fascist regime probably was Andreas Papandreou's," explained the Greek-American scholar and publisher Aristide Caratzas in 1990. "Both the military regime of John Metaxas, from 1936 to 1941, and the junta from 1967 to 1974, never achieved a broad level of popular response to their message, which was seen as artificial, even ridiculous. By contrast, Papandreou's posturings and habits reassured a people who harbored a mistrust and envy of the West that their way of life was legitimate. Much like Mussolini, Papandreou succeeded as the embodiment of a nationalist-populist resentment. He was the ideal Greek everyman. He threatened America and backed up these threats by embracing America's enemies—Qaddafi and the terrorists. Papandreou danced the traditional Greek dances in public. He distributed the wealth to his partisans as a reward for their loyalty. Even with the Liani affair, in a male-oriented society like Greece's there was a certain resonance. Papandreou projected the Mussoliniesque image of the nation's *first lover*. His divorce and humiliation of Margaret Chant not only reinforced his (and Greece's) break with America, but also with another threatening demon of the Greek male, feminism."

The pollster Dimitras buttressed that analysis. The fact that close to 40 percent of the electorate still supported Papandreou, he said, even after Papandreou was indicted for embezzlement and wire-tapping, "shows the Third World–Latin American–style populism of Greek politics. It is tribal, xenophobic. . . ."

An anti-American backlash in Greece in the 1980s had been expected. Although the United States had kept Greece out of the Communist orbit, and American taxpayers in the 1950s had forked over billions of dollars in economic aid to rescue Greece from East European–type poverty, many Greeks interpreted this aid only in terms of domination. In the late 1960s and early 1970s, Greeks saw the Nixon administration provide critical backing to the repressive junta. And in 1974, Secretary of State Henry Kissinger appeared to encourage the brutal Turkish invasion of Cyprus. But Papandreou cynically manipulated this disappointment with the United States, which in any case did not warrant the vile demagoguery about "plots" and "conspiracies," or the support for international terrorism.

Soon after Papandreou's 1981 election, Nicholas Gage, a former *New York Times* investigative reporter, as well as the author of *Hellas: A Portrait of Greece* and *Eleni*—a bestseller about the Greek Civil War—related a story about Papandreou's youth.

The young Andreas and his wealthy friends were dining at a well-known seafood restaurant in the Athens suburb of Glyfada. When the tray of fish was served, Papandreou, without asking, took the biggest one. His friends protested. So Papandreou put the fish back on the tray, but only after spitting on it. Gage then put the question: if Papandreou ever had to relinquish his hold on Greece, would he do so willingly, or would he spit on the country first?

Papandreou provided the answer a few weeks before the national elections in 1989. Despite PASOK's continued appeal, the polls indicated that the New Democracy Party, its conservative rival led by Constantine Mitsotakis, was headed for victory. Papandreou, therefore, rammed a new electoral law through Parliament. Unlike the old law, which encouraged political stability by awarding extra seats to the party that got the most votes, the new law followed the Israeli example of pure proportional representation, thus making it next to impossible for any one party to form a noncoalition government. As in Israel, there would now have to be at least one small-party kingmaker: the still-Stalinist Greek Communist Party.

Greece then suffered the agony of three general elections in one year. In the first two elections, the conservatives won by the same point spread as had PASOK four years previously; but due to the new law it could not form a government. The conservative leader, Mitsotakis, was forced to strike coalition deals with hardline Communists at a time when Communism was collapsing all over Eastern Europe. Papandreou gloated, while instructing his ministers not to cooperate in the handover of power. Official documents, treaties of state with other nations, and official cars went missing. In the third general election, in April 1990, the conservatives won by one of the largest pluralities in Europe, but were only able to form a government with a bare one-seat majority. PASOK, helped by the Communist Party, encouraged a series of general strikes to try to bring down the new government.

Terrorism continued. The economy was collapsing. To increase subsidies and create jobs for the PASOK faithful in the state bureaucracy, Papandreou had borrowed during the 1980s in the same way that Eastern European leaders had borrowed during the 1970s. Greece's external debt was $21.5 billion in 1989, $6.5 billion more than that of Communist Hungary, whose population was slightly smaller than Greece's.

When I returned to my former home in 1990, Athens had become an urban disaster zone. Greek newspapers compared it to Cairo. The phone service was the worst in Western Europe. In the mid-1980s, Papandreou had rejected bids from several Western firms to rebuild the Greek phone grid. Persistent and credible reports indicated that he had awarded the contract to a friend, who had upgraded the system piecemeal, using equipment imported from East Germany.

Meanwhile, the vote by the International Olympic Committee (IOC) to decide the host city for the centennial 1996 Olympic Games was fast approaching. Because the Olympics were born in ancient Greece, and because the modern Games were reborn in Athens in 1896, Greece had for years been the odds-on favorite to win the vote. In the 1980s, when I lived in Athens, it was automatically assumed by everyone that Athens would host the "Golden Olympics." But terrorism, political instability, and a crumbling urban infrastructure had shocked the visiting IOC delegates. The decision was now in doubt.

Mitsotakis's weak conservative government pleaded with PASOK and the Communist party to postpone another wave of strikes until after the IOC's September 18, 1990, vote in Tokyo. Papandreou answered with a speech on September 17, whose words made their way to Tokyo. To a square filled with striking workers, the ex-Prime Minister shouted: "Down with the Mitsotakis junta!"

When the decision to award the Games to Atlanta was announced, Papandreou called it "an American theft." And Melina Mercouri, PASOK's candidate in the 1990 mayoral elections in Athens, complained: "The IOC wanted to know what the pollution level in Athens was going to be in 1996. How can anyone know what things will be like in six years? How dare they ask us such a question. Anyone who asks such a question is out of his mind!" Her words reminded me of what Homer, played by Jules Dassin, said to Illia, played by Mercouri, in *Never on Sunday:* I wish I could put "reason in place of fantasy" into her mind.

"We Greeks are the worst people and the Olympic decision proves that God wants to destroy us," a former neighbor of mine exclaimed to me. Even Papandreou's enemies, who had comprehended what was happening to Greece in the 1980s, were devastated by the IOC decision. After the cruel misfortunes of civil war and military dictatorship that had followed World War II, the "Golden Olympics" were finally going to establish Greece's modern identity, by linking it with the glories of the ancient past.

These Olympics were going to be a benchmark historical and mythic occasion in Greek history. As in ancient times, poetry and music competitions—promoted by the composers Theodorakis and Hadjidakis—were to be held side by side with the athletic events. By returning the Olympics to Greece, the Greeks had hoped to restore intimacy, magic, and romance to the Games, which in recent decades had been undermined by the warlords of big business, commercialization, and high-performance drugs. If Athens was currently in an abysmal state, we all knew that Greeks possessed *philotimo,* an untranslatable word implying self-honor, that would ensure the city's preparedness for the Olympics—even if everything was built at the last minute. Mercouri bitterly summed up the local attitude. Referring to Atlanta as America's soft-drink capital, she said that the IOC "chose Coca-Cola over the Parthenon."

But the IOC itself was aware of this. For reasons of powerful historical sentiment, Athens had always been the delegates' first choice, until a study revealed that, in terms of security and infrastructure, Athens was the least fit of the competing cities—behind even Belgrade, the Yugoslav capital threatened by a looming civil war. Atlanta did not win the Games; Athens clearly lost them.

Moments after the IOC decision was announced, I took a walk through the National Garden in the center of Athens to the old Olympic Stadium, a small and poignant white marble edifice where the 1896 Games had been held. Peeking inside, I could almost imagine the small gathering of athletes, cheered on by women in straw hats and the wealthy and aristocratic philhellenes from Europe who were responsible for reviving the Games. Athens was then a picturesque village, with a sleepy Ottoman ambience. I looked at the sharp curve at the far end of the Stadium, which runners had had to manage without turning their ankles. *Glory is fleeting* was the phrase that entered my mind.

I turned around. Cars belched heavily leaded exhaust fumes into the air. Mountains of black plastic garbage bags rose starkly off the gray concrete, uncollected for days due to a strike. The apartments opposite were lit by candlelight, as striking electricity workers had shut off the power. The workers had legitimate complaints, but their strikes were part of a larger scene of chaos and societal strife that were the undeniable refuse of Papandreou's rule. The twentieth century had been a disappointing one for Greece, held back by innumerable dictatorships, by Nazi invasion, by civil war, by another dictatorship, and finally by the eight-year rule of a man who had destroyed the country's economy, brought the anarchy of the Middle East to the country's doorstep, and played fast-and-loose with the principles of democracy itself.

In the autumn of 1990, Greece was as much a part of the Balkans as it had been during the days of direct Ottoman rule in the early nineteenth century. It had become just another Eastern European country: its population emerging, completely bewildered, into an unsentimental world where efficiency and hard work, rather than notions of past glory and *philotimo*, were all that mattered.

Papandreou was the most original of Balkan ghosts, a man of our own times who moved in the depths of the darkest past: more baffling than Cardinal Stepinac, Gotse Delchev, or King Carol. I will always remember Papandreou on the platform before frenzied supporters, his arms held straight out, Christlike, and his eyes glaring upward toward the sky: the eternal victim of Turkish and American persecution. Like Enver Hoxha, Albania's charismatic tyrant, Papandreou was the prodigal son of a well-off family sent abroad for his education (Hoxha went to France), only to return home smoldering and shedding his Western cloak. Papandreou was never physically cruel—unlike Hoxha, a mass-murderer. Nor did Papandreou become a dictator, although he flouted constitutional safeguards. Greece's harshest edges are softened by the Mediterranean; there, close up, I could explore the beginnings of processes that matured elsewhere in the Balkans, and in the Middle East, too.

But in 1992, as if to punctuate Greece's true Balkan soul, came the Macedonian crisis. Actually, it had been building for years. As an issue, Macedonia had come late in Greece's modern history, and therefore it evoked a particularly potent dynamic. As Evangelos Kofos, the Greek scholar noted, Greece had been content with its northeastern border, recognizing that the people in Yugoslavia were Slavs and not oppressed ethnic Greeks, as in Albania. Therefore, Kofos suggested, Greece (unlike Bulgaria) long imagined that it had solved its Macedonian dilemma. But when it became apparent that the Tito-instigated "Macedonian" nationalism—encouraged to separate Slavic Macedonia psychologically from Bulgaria—had taken on a life of its own, Greece felt threatened. Greeks didn't mind that there were "Slavs" or "south Serbians" on its frontier, but "Yugoslav Macedonians" made them uneasy because Macedonia was the name of Greece's own northern province, associated with Alexander the Great. When in late 1991, Yugoslav Macedonia declared its independence as "Macedonia," Greece went wild. Hundreds of thousands of people demonstrated in the streets of Salonika, and the Greek army went on border "maneuvers." Because the Mitsotakis government had such a weak parliamentary majority, and was under constant attack from PASOK, Mitsotakis could not easily back down on this issue.

Nevertheless, Greece was not without hope. PASOK was undergoing long overdue reform. And in the conservative New Democracy Party, Mitsotakis was clearly going to be the last of the Karamanlis-style "oligarchs." The *paleo-politiki* ("old politics") was ending. *Perestroika* was finally coming to Greece. Pollster Dimitras saw evidence of an "apolitical, yuppie business mentality" taking root among the young.

There was no other way forward. Athens, Piraeus, and Salonika had become ugly and despoiled cities, badly in need of modernization. The drowsy and empty streets of Piraeus, plodded by trolleys, existed only in the black-and-white celluloid of *Never on Sunday*. The little house beside a plane tree and a Turkish cemetery, where Lawrence Durrell had once lived on the island of Rhodes, was now down the street from a virus of neon-advertised discos and fast-food joints, far uglier than any McDonald's arch. The miles of unspoiled beach on the Greek archipelago were shrinking each year. Had the 1980s brought decent and determined administration rather than Oriental plunder, the myths might have been preserved longer. "The century was drawing to a close," writes Leon Sciaky about the Salonika of a hundred years ago. "Stealthily the West was creeping in, trying to lure the East with her wonders."

This time, I felt, she might succeed.

EPILOGUE:
THE ROAD TO ADRIANOPLE

"All afternoon we crawled southeast through a blasted land. The low, hot air was heavy, as if with the breath of unnumbered generations of dead," observed John Reed, while crossing the plain of Thrace.

From Athens in late 1990, I returned to Salonika. From there I headed east. My bus moved through sleepy, tobacco-brown fields, fringed with poplars and dying oleanders blowing in the dust. To the left were the rosy, bouldered humps of the Rhodopes, stubbled with lichen, on the other side of which lay Bulgaria. To the right was the Aegean Sea, a milky and drowsy blue. The narrow plain between had heard the drumroll of untold armies, advancing and retreating. The Greek soldiers on the bus wore large, gold Byzantine crosses around their necks. The radio roared out a rhythm from Asia Minor. Drama, Philippi, Kavalla, Xanthi, Komotini, Alexandropoulis: sad inflammations of concrete squares and neon; burdened, as though against their will, with historical greatness—places where, in the last decade of the twentieth century, the children still learned by rote.

In Komotini, black-veiled Turkish women swept past my window. I saw tumbled-down mosques, jailed-in on three sides by tall apartment blocks, across from an immaculately lawned Greek Orthodox cemetery that was protected by cypress tress. *"Exo Tourkos* [Out with the Turks]!"* read the Greek graffiti, spray-painted on a cinder-block wall.

At Alexandropoulis, the bus headed north, along the Greek-Turkish border of the Evros River. More towns whose beautiful old names robbed them of a present: Soufli, Orestias. Then, visible for miles across fields of ripening sunflowers from the Greek side of the frontier, I saw a nest of minarets and bubble domes: the first in a chain of great Islamic cities stretching all the way to India—Adrianople. I had arrived at Europe's forgotten rear door.

At the border post, under a violent red standard of the Crescent, hung a discolored photograph of the Gazi ("Leader"), Mustafa Kemal Ataturk, the founder of the Turkish Republic. He resembled an Aryan Dracula; attired in a black dinner jacket, peering down on me with heavy eyebrows, a widow's peak of blond hair indicating a mixed Macedonian birth.

"The Ottoman Empire has disappeared into history. A new Turkey has now been born," Ataturk declared in 1922. "The countries may differ but civilization is one and the same. . . . The decline of the Ottoman Empire started on the day when, very proud of its triumphs over the West, it cut its ties with the European nations. This was a mistake which we will not repeat." Ataturk assured his people that Turkish civilization was now on "a steady course . . . marching from the East to the West." This march had stalled for long periods, and many miles remained to be traversed. I crossed a wide, slow-moving river. In the middle of the bridge was a marble Ottoman pavilion with Arabic inscriptions, under which an armed soldier in khaki, with a white helmet, stood motionless. The expression on the soldier's face was proud and obedient: he looked capable of great cruelty.

The warren of Adrianople's streets began, pulverized by heat and dust in the summer, and by mud and driving rain in the winter. I was already too far inland to be affected by the moderating winds of the Aegean. I considered the road signs:

BULGARISTAN, 18 KILOMETERS.
YUNANISTAN (GREECE), 5 KILOMETERS.
ISTANBUL, 235 KILOMETERS.

Founded by the Roman Emperor Hadrian in A.D. 125, at the strategic crossroads of Europe and Asia, Adrianople was always at center stage: repeatedly put under siege by the Crusaders, later the first capital of the Ottoman Empire. From here, Mehmet the Conqueror marched on the Byzantine Greek capital of Constantinople, which the Turks have held ever since. During the first three decades of the twentieth century, there were few better datelines for a journalist than "Adrianople." In the First Balkan War of 1912, Bulgarian and Serbian troops captured Adrianople from the Ottoman Turks; then the Turks took Adrianople back in the Second Balkan War of 1913, only to lose the town to an invading Greek army in 1920. In 1922, prior to Adrianople's final recapture by the forces of Ataturk, Ernest Hemingway spent one of the worst nights of his life here, ill with malaria on a bed practically crawling with lice. The entire agony of the Greek-Turkish conflict was encapsulated in his description of Greek refugees "walking blindly along in the rain."

Today, Hemingway's refugees were back, only this time they were Turkish. In the early summer of 1989, Bulgaria's hardline Communist regime, in its last and greatest criminal act, forcibly expelled more than 100,000 ethnic Turks across the border into Turkey. "They were hitting us with the guns and letting the dogs attack us," one refugee had reported, displaying bite marks on her arms and legs.[1]

I went to the refugee camp at the railway station. The Turkish government had provided prefabricated housing, schooling, and new clothes for the refugees. Three schoolboys in black ties and white shirts, and a young girl in a black dress and a white lace

1. See "Turkey: A Nameless Death at Edirne" by Edward McFadden, *Wall Street Journal Europe,* August 3, 1989.

collar, gathered before my camera. They all had the darkest hair and eyes. Halted frieght cars formed the background between their makeshift homes. Like statues these refugee children posed for me—so patient, so expressionless, as though able to wait forever.

Adrianople no longer lay on any strategic crossroads. The town appears on international maps under the Turkish name of Edirne, a word that holds no charm for the ears of English-speakers. Thus, it has simply vanished as one of the great place-names of history: a sepia-toned photograph lost in an attic; the ultimate backwater.

But the dead-end location had advantages. Because modern development had passed it by architecturally, Adrianople remained relatively pure: a toy town of cobbled alleys, covered bazaars, tiled roofs, and some of the finest mosques in Turkey. Dominating the skyline was the massive Selimiye Cami, Sultan Selim's Mosque, designed in 1568 by the Sultan's architect, Sinan, who built several of the shrines surrounding the Hagia Sophia church in Istanbul. The minarets stood like proud generals over silent, empty courtyards. At dusk, when the domed prayer halls filled with worshippers, and the hypnotic chant of Koranic verses echoed through the bazaars, for the first time on my journey the dynamism of Islam became palpable. The peppery anger of the Serbs, the Romanians, the Bulgarians, and the Greeks was here a memory. Everyone was quiet and polite, adopting a complacent, dignified air that I realized was the luxury of the conqueror. The Turks had no chips on their shoulders, because they had done the oppressing.

"Isn't my native realm an Ottoman Empire now?" asked the Russian-born writer and Nobel Prize winner Joseph Brodsky, wondering whether the fate of Ottoman Turkey might presage something similar for Russia. For Brodsky, Turkey had become a land "plundered" by the past, existing only in a "third-rate present" ever since the scepter of Eastern despotism had traveled north to the Kremlin after World War I. Although Brodsky did not carry the comparison further, the parallels between the decline of the Ottoman Empire and the decline of the Soviet Empire were indeed striking. Abdul Hamid, the Turkish Sultan from 1876 to 1909, was, at the outset of his rule, a cautious reformer like Nikita

Khruschchev. But like Leonid Brezhnev, he quickly withdrew the sultanate behind the old wall of terror for yet another (and as it turned out, crucial) generation. And Abdul Hamid's own elite, like Brezhnev's, secretly plotted the societal transition that would have to follow. Enver Pasha and the Young Turks, like Mikhail Gorbachev and his allies, dictated reform from the top down, hoping to preserve the empire, in looser form, through dramatic liberalization. But the plan was overpowered by centrifugal forces that drove the subject populations to demand full independence; and by fears of the people in the streets, who wanted to retreat backward into the past rather than to advance forward into the future. The Young Turk Revolution eventually made the Young Turks themselves irrelevant. A new man had to come forward: Ataturk.

Ataturk had a vision—described by his biographer, Lord Kinross—"of a new (and modern) Turkish nation, surgically freed from the canker of its outlying limbs to regenerate itself as a compact healthy body rooted in the good earth of its forbears."

Whoever was to lead Russia out of chaos must be an Ataturk: a product of the reactionary system, who, nevertheless, realized that the core nation had used up so much of its resources keeping together the empire that an entire epoch, perhaps a century, would have to be spent on the humdrum task of catching up with the rest of the world.

Until 1918, when the Ottoman Empire collapsed, Turkish was an important foreign language for diplomats and journalists. Then, in a breathtakingly short period of time, it became just another obscure tongue. As the world moved into an age in which politics was becoming submerged beneath economics and trade competition, would Russian join Turkish in obscurity?

Had the poison of eastern despotism and decline, seeping from Byzantium, to the Sultan's Palace, to the Kremlin, finally expended itself?

I felt it had. Here, at world's end, at a place whose very collapse gave the twentieth century its horrifying direction, there was still not much optimism among the people I had met along the way; that would have to come later. As I observed the violent disintegration of Yugoslavia and the turmoil that was sure to continue in other Balkan states, I was reminded of a line from Shakespeare's

Life and Death of King John: "So foul a sky clears not without a storm." Conflicting ethnic histories, inflamed by the living death of Communism, had made the Balkan sky so foul that now, sadly, a storm was required to clear it.

But clear it it would.

I sensed an overwhelming exhaustion: of not wanting to pursue any dreams except the most personal and materialistic ones. Although people had always been motivated by the prospect of a better life for themselves and their children, never before did they seem so determined—and so politically able—to accept nothing less. The Enlightenment was, at last, breaching the gates of these downtrodden nations. A better age would have to follow.

▓ ▓ SELECTED BIBLIOGRAPHY

Aksan, Akil. *Quotations from Mustafa Kemal Ataturk*. Ankara, Turkey: Ministry of Foreign Affairs, 1982.

Alexander, Stella. *The Triple Myth: A Life of Archbishop Alojzije Stepinac*. Boulder, Colorado, and New York: East European Monographs and Columbia University Press, 1987.

Ambler, Eric. *Judgement on Deltchev*. London: Hodder & Stoughton, 1951.

———. *The Mask of Dimitrios*. London: Hodder & Stoughton, 1939.

Andrews, Kevin. *The Flight of Ikaros: Travels in Greece During a Civil War*. Boston: Houghton Mifflin, 1959.

Antoljak, Stjepan. *Samuel and His State*. Skopje, Yugoslavia: Macedonian Review Editions, 1985.

Attwater, Donald. *The Penguin Dictionary of Saints*. Harmondsworth, England: Penguin Books, 1965.

Averoff-Tossizza, Evangelos. *By Fire and Axe: The Communist Party and the Civil War in Greece, 1944–49.* New Rochelle, New York: Caratzas Brothers, 1978.

Bassett, Richard. *The Austrians: Strange Tales from the Vienna Woods.* London: Faber & Faber, 1988.

———. *A Guide to Central Europe.* New York: Viking Penguin, 1987.

———. "Siebenburgen Besieged." *Spectator,* September 8, 1984.

Belgrade Cultural Centre. (Special edition to mark the fortieth anniversary of the city's liberation.) Belgrade, Yugoslavia, 1984.

Bellow, Saul. *The Dean's December.* New York: Harper & Row, 1982.

Bischof, Henrik. *Wirtschafts—Und Systemkrise in Rumanien.* Bonn: Friedrich Ebert Stifftung, 1987.

Brodsky, Joseph. "Flight from Byzantium." *New Yorker,* October 28, 1985.

Burchett, Wilfred. *At the Barricades.* New York: Times Books, 1981.

Byron, Robert. *The Byzantine Achievement.* London: Routledge & Sons, 1929.

———. *The Station: Athos, Treasures and Men.* New York: Alfred A. Knopf, 1949 (first published in 1926).

Canetti, Elias. *Crowds and Power.* (Translated from the German by Carol Stewart.) London: Victor Gollancz, 1962.

Cavarnos, Constantine. *Orthodox Iconography.* Belmont, Massachusetts: Institute for Byzantine and Modern Greek Studies, 1977.

Clogg, Richard. *A Short History of Modern Greece.* Cambridge, England: Cambridge University Press, 1979.

Conrad, Joseph. *Under Western Eyes.* New York: Harper & Brothers, 1911.

Corneanu, Nicolae. *The Romanian Church in Northwestern Romania Under the Horthy Scourge.* Bucharest: The Bible and Mission Institute of the Romanian Orthodox Church, 1986.

Craig, Gordon A. *Germany: 1866–1945.* Oxford, England: Oxford University Press, 1981.

Cullen, Robert. "Report from Romania: Down with the Tyrant." *New Yorker,* April 2, 1990.

Djilas, Milovan. *Conversations with Stalin.* New York: Harcourt, Brace & World, 1962.

———. *Rise and Fall.* New York: Harcourt Brace Jovanovich, 1985.

Doder, Dusko. "Albania Opens the Door." *National Geographic,* Washington, July 1992.

Dragut, Vasile. *La Peinture Murale de La Moldavie.* Bucharest: Editions Meridiane, 1983.

Dryansky, G. Y. "Goodbye Romania." *Conde Nast Traveler,* April 1989.

Dumitriu, Petru. *The Prodigals.* (Translated by Norman Denny.) London: Collins, 1962.

Dunford, Martin, and Holland, Jack, with McGhie, John. *The Rough Guide to Yugoslavia.* London: Harrap Columbus, 1989.

Durrell, Gerald. *My Family and Other Animals.* London: Rupert Hart-Davis, 1956.

Durrell, Lawrence. *The Alexandria Quartet: Justine; Balthazar; Mountolive; Clea.* London: Faber & Faber, 1957, 1958, and 1960.

———. *Prospero's Cell: A Guide to the Landscape and Manners of the Island of Corfu.* London: Faber & Faber, 1945.

———. *Reflections on a Marine Venus.* London: Faber & Faber, 1953.

———. *Spirit of Place.* (Edited by Alan G. Thomas.) New York: E. P. Dutton, 1971.

Eminescu, Mihai. *Poems.* (Translated by Corneliu M. Popescu.) Bucharest: Editura Cartea Romaneasca, 1989.

Feldner, Josef. *Grenzland Karnten.* Klagenfurt, Austria: Verlag Johannes Heyn, 1982.

Fermor, Patrick Leigh. *Between the Woods and the Water.* London: John Murray, 1986.

———. *Roumeli: Travels in Northern Greece.* London: John Murray, 1966.

Forbes, Nevill; Toynbee, Arnold J.; Mitrany, D.; and Hogarth, D. G. *The Balkans: A History of Bulgaria, Serbia, Greece, Rumania, Turkey.* Oxford, England: Oxford University Press, 1915.

Fussell, Paul. *Abroad: British Literary Traveling Between the Wars.* New York: Oxford University Press, 1980.

Gage, Nicholas. *Eleni.* New York: Random House, 1983.

———. *Hellas: A Portrait of Greece.* Athens: P. Efstathiadis & Sons, 1987.

Glendinning, Victoria. *Rebecca West: A Life.* London: Weidenfeld & Nicolson, 1987.

Goltz, Thomas. "Anyone Who Resists Will Be Killed Like a Dog." *Reader's Digest,* 1987.

Grogan, Lady. *The Life of J. D. Bourchier.* London: Hurst & Blackett, 1932.

Hanak, Peter. *One Thousand Years: A Concise History of Hungary.* Budapest: Corvina, 1988.

Hemingway, Ernest. *The Snows of Kilimanjaro.* New York: Charles Scribner's Sons, 1961.

Hilberg, Raul. *The Destruction of the European Jews.* New York: Quadrangle Books, 1961.

Hitler, Adolf. *Mein Kampf.* (Translated by Ralph Manheim.) Boston: Houghton Mifflin, 1943. (Originally published in 1927.)

Holden, David. *Greece Without Columns: The Making of the Modern Greeks.* London: Faber & Faber, 1972.

Holy Bible (Authorized King James Version). Philadelphia: National Bible Press, 1970.

Hoppe, E. O. *In Gipsy Camp and Royal Palace: Wanderings in Rumania* (with a preface by the Queen of Rumania). London: Methuen, 1924.

Ilievski, Done. *The Macedonian Orthodox Church.* Skopje, Yugoslavia: Macedonian Review Editions, 1973.

Internal Macedonian Revolutionary Organization. *The Memoar.* Sofia, Bulgaria: 1904.

Ivandija, Antun. *The Cathedral of Zagreb.* Zagreb, Yugoslavia: Glas Koncila, 1983.

Kampus, Ivan, and Karaman, Igor. *Zagreb Through a Thousand Years.* Zagreb, Yugoslavia: Skolska Knjiga, 1978.

Kann, Robert A. *A History of the Habsburg Empire 1526–1918.* Berkeley: University of California Press, 1974.

Kazantzakis, Nikos. *Report to Greco.* (Translated by P. A. Bien.) New York: Simon & Schuster, 1965.

———. *Zorba the Greek.* (Translated by Carl Wildman.) London: Faber & Faber, 1961.

Keeley, Edmund, and Sherrard, Philip. *C. P. Cavafy: Collected Poems.* Princeton, New Jersey: Princeton University Press, 1967.

———. *George Seferis: Collected Poems (1924–1955).* Princeton, New Jersey: Princeton University Press, 1967.

Keresztes, Peter. "Reconsidering Transylvania's Fate." *Wall Street Journal* (European Edition), May 4, 1987.

Kinross, Lord. *Ataturk: The Rebirth of a Nation.* London: Weidenfeld & Nicolson, 1964.

———. *The Ottoman Centuries.* New York: William Morrow, 1977.

Kissinger, Henry A. *A World Restored: Metternich, Castlereagh and the Problems of Peace 1812–1822.* Boston: Houghton Mifflin (no date).

Koeva, Margarita. *Rila Monastery.* Sofia, Bulgaria: Sofia Press, 1989.

Kofos, Evangelos. "National Heritage and National Identity in Nineteenth- and Twentieth-Century Macedonia." In *Modern Greece: Nationalism and Nationality.* Athens: ELLIAMEP, 1990.

Kolaitis, Memas. *The Greek Poems of C. P. Cavafy. Volume I: The Canon.* New Rochelle, New York: Aristide D. Caratzas, 1989.

Koneski, Blazhe. *Blazhe Koneski: Poetry.* (Edited by Georgi Stardelov.) Skopje, Yugoslavia: Macedonian P.E.N. Centre, 1983.

Korobar, Pero, and Ivanoski, Orde. *The Historical Truth: The Progressive Social Circles in Bulgaria and Pirin Macedonia on the Ma-*

cedonian National Question 1896–1956. Skopje, Yugoslavia: Kultura, 1983.

Kostich, Dragos D. *The Land and Peoples of the Balkans.* Philadelphia: J. B. Lippincott, 1962, 1973.

Lawrence, T. E. *Seven Pillars of Wisdom.* New York: Doubleday, 1926.

Logoreci, Anton. *The Albanians: Europe's Forgotten Survivors.* London: Victor Gollancz, 1977.

Lukacs, John. *Budapest 1900: A Historical Portrait of a City and Its Culture.* New York: Weidenfeld & Nicolson, 1988.

———. "In Darkest Transylvania." *New Republic,* February 3, 1982.

MacDermott, Mercia. *The Apostle of Freedom: A Portrait of Vasil Levsky Against a Background of Nineteenth Century Bulgaria.* Sofia, Bulgaria: Sofia Press, 1979.

———. *Freedom or Death: The Life of Gotse Delchev.* London and West Nyack, New York: Journeyman Press, 1978.

Macedonia: Documents and Material. Sofia, Bulgaria: Bulgarian Academy of Sciences, 1978.

Mahapatra, S., and Boskovski, J. T. *Longing for the South: Contemporary Macedonian Poetry.* New Delhi: Prachi Prakashan, 1981.

Mainstone, Rowland J. *Hagia Sophia: Architecture, Structure and Liturgy of Justinian's Great Church.* London: Thames & Hudson, 1988.

Mann, Golo. *The History of Germany Since 1789.* London: Chatto & Windus, 1968.

Manning, Olivia. *The Balkan Trilogy: The Great Fortune; The Spoilt City; Friends and Heroes.* London: William Heinemann, 1960, 1962, 1965.

Markov, Georgi. *The Truth That Killed.* (Translated by Liliana Brisby.) New York: Ticknor & Fields, 1984.

Matkovski, Alexandar. *A History of the Jews in Macedonia.* Skopje, Yugoslavia: Macedonian Review Editions, 1982.

McCarthy, Mary. *The Stones of Florence.* London: Willliam Heinemann, 1959.

Miller, Henry. *The Colossus of Maroussi.* London: Secker & Warburg, 1942.

Milosevic, Desanka. *Gracanica Monastery.* Belgrade: Institute for the Protection of Cultural Monuments of the Socialist Republic of Serbia, 1989.

Mortimer, Edward. *Faith and Power: The Politics of Islam.* London: Faber & Faber, 1982.

Newby, Eric. *On the Shores of the Mediterranean.* London: Harvill Press and Pan Books, 1984, 1985.

Njegos, P. P. *The Mountain Wreath.* (Translated and edited by Vasa

D. Mihailovich.) Irvine, California: Charles Schlacks, Jr., 1986.

Osers, Edward. *Mateja Matevski: Footprints of the Wind.* Boston and London: Forest Books, 1988.

Ostrogorsky, George. *History of Byzantine State.* (Translated from the German by Joan Hussey.) Oxford, England: Basil Blackwell, 1956.

Pacepa, Ion Mihai. *Red Horizons: Chronicles of a Communist Spy Chief.* Washington, D.C.: Regnery Gateway, 1987.

Pakula, Hannah. *The Last Romantic: A Biography of Queen Marie of Roumania.* New York: Simon & Schuster, 1984.

Petkovic, Sreten. *The Patriarchate of Pec.* Belgrade: Serbian Patriarchate, 1987.

Pfaff, William. "Beginning of the End for the Conducator." *International Herald Tribune,* December 21, 1989.

———. "The Fascists in Romania May Be the Men in Power." *International Herald Tribune,* June 21, 1990.

Poljanski, Hristo Andonov. *Goce Delcev: His Life and Times.* Skopje, Yugoslavia: Misla, 1973.

Procopius. *The Secret History.* (Translated by G. A. Williamson.) Harmondsworth, England: Penguin Books, 1966.

Psellus, Michael. *Fourteen Byzantine Rulers.* (Translated from the *Chronographia* by E. R. A. Sewter.) New Haven, Connecticut: Yale University Press, 1953.

Radice, Betty. *Who's Who in the Ancient World.* Harmondsworth, England: Penguin Books, 1973.

Ravitch, Norman. "The Armenian Catastrophe: Of History, Murder & Sin." *Encounter,* 1983.

Reed, John. *Ten Days That Shook the World.* New York: Boni & Liveright, 1919.

———. *The War in Eastern Europe.* New York: Charles Scribner's Sons, 1916.

Richardson, Dan, and Denton, Jill. *The Rough Guide to Eastern Europe: Hungary, Romania and Bulgaria.* London: Harrap-Columbus, 1988.

Roth, Joseph. *Hotel Savoy.* (Translated from the German by John Hoare.) London: Chatto & Windus, 1986. (First published in 1924.)

———. *The Radetzky March.* Berlin and Harmondsworth, England: Gustav Kiepenheuer Verlag and Penguin Books, 1932, 1974.

Sakellariou, M. B. *Macedonia: 4,000 Years of Greek History and Civilization.* Athens: Ekdotike Athenon, 1982.

Schorske, Carl E. *Fin-de-Siècle Vienna: Politics and Culture.* New York: Alfred A. Knopf, 1980.

Sciaky, Leon. *Farewell to Salonica: Portrait of an Era.* London: W. H. Allen, 1946.

Seton-Watson, Hugh. *The "Sick Heart" of Modern Europe: The Problem of the Danubian Lands.* Seattle and London: University of Washington Press, 1975.

Sevastianos, Metropolitan of Dhriinoupolis. *Behind Albania's Iron Curtain.* Athens: Pan-Hellenic Association of Northern Epirots, 1990.

———. *Northern Epirus Crucified.* Athens: Pan-Hellenic Association of Northern Epirots, 1989.

Sherrard, Philip. *The Wound of Greece: Studies in Neo-Hellenism.* London: Rex Collings, 1978.

Shirer, William L. *Midcentury Journey: The Western World Through Its Years of Conflict.* New York: Farrar, Straus and Young, 1952.

Sitwell, Sacheverell. *Roumanian Journey.* London: Batsford, 1938.

Skilling, H. Gordon. *The Governments of Communist East Europe.* New York: Thomas Y. Crowell, 1966.

St. John, Robert. *Foreign Correspondent.* London: Hutchinson, 1960.

———. *From the Land of Silent People.* New York: Doubleday Doran, 1942.

Starkie, Walter. *Raggle-Taggle: Adventures with a Fiddle in Hungary and Roumania.* London: John Murray, 1933.

Stavroulakis, Nicholas. *The Jews of Greece: An Essay.* Athens: Talos Press, 1990.

Sterling, Claire. "The Plot to Kill the Pope." *Reader's Digest,* September 1982.

Stoicescu, Nicolae. *Vlad Tepes: Prince of Wallachia.* Bucharest: Editura Academiei, 1978.

Stoker, Bram. *Dracula.* Harmondsworth, England: Penguin Books, 1979 (first published in 1897).

Sulzberger, C. L. *A Long Row of Candles.* Toronto: Macmillan, 1969.

Thomas, Hugh. *Armed Truce: The Beginnings of the Cold War 1945–1946.* New York: Atheneum, 1987.

Thursby, J. M. "Cyril and Methodius: Bridging East and West." *The Athenian,* August 1985.

Tifft, Susan. "A Bitter Battle for Names." *Time,* March 4, 1985.

Tismaneanu, Vladimir. "Homage to Golania." *New Republic,* July 30 and August 6, 1990.

Todorovski, Gane. *Gane Todorovski: Poems.* (Translated by Graham W. Reid and Ljubica Tdorova-Janeslieva.) Bradford, England: University of Bradford, 1976.

Toynbee, Arnold J. *The Western Question in Greece and Turkey.* London: Constable, 1922.

Tsigakou, Fani-Maria. *The Rediscovery of Greece*. London: Thames & Hudson, 1987.

Vacalopoulos, Apostolos E. *A History of Thessalonika*. Salonika, Greece: Institute for Balkan Studies, 1963.

Waldeck, R. G. *Athene Palace Bucharest: Hitler's "New Order" Comes to Rumania*. London: Constable, 1943. (Originally published in 1942 in Garden City, New York, by Blue Ribbon Books, under the title *Athene Palace*.)

Ward, Philip. *Albania*. New York: Oleander Press, 1983.

Ware, Timothy. *The Orthodox Church*. Harmondsworth, England: Penguin Books, 1963.

Watson, Russell. "The Plot to Kill Pope John Paul II." *Newsweek*, January 3, 1983.

West, Rebecca. *Black Lamb and Grey Falcon*. New York: Viking Press, 1941.

West, Richard. "The Agincourt of Yugoslavia." *Spectator*, December 19/26, 1987.

Weyr, Teddie. Unpublished papers on Austria's Slovene minority. Vienna 1988.

White, William. *By-Line: Ernest Hemingway*. New York: Charles Scribner's Sons, 1967.

✾✾INDEX